RAILROADS
ACROSS
NORTH AMERICA

AN ILLUSTRATED HISTORY

CLAUDE WIATROWSKI

DEDICATION

This book is dedicated to my father-in-law, Evan Ammeson. Evan never got to meet my father, who died so young. It was my great fortune to marry Margaret and gain a superb new father—and one who was a railroad buff as well! This book is also dedicated to my wife Margaret and children, Kevin and Karen. Their support was vital not only to writing this book, but in pursuing railroad history and photography for most of my life.

This edition published in 2012 by
CRESTLINE
a division of BOOK SALES, INC.
276 Fifth Avenue Suite 206
New York, New York 10001
USA

This edition published by arrangement with Voyageur Press.

First published in 2007 by Voyageur Press, an imprint of MBI Publishing Company, 400 First Avenue North, Suite 300, Minneapolis, MN 55401 USA

Editor: Dennis Pernu
Designer: LeAnn Kuhlmann

Library of Congress Cataloging-in-Publication Data

Wiatrowski, Claude A.
  Railroads across North America : an illustrated history / by Claude Wiatrowski.
    p. cm.
  Includes bibliographical references and index.

ISBN-13: 978-0-7858-2967-6
1. Railroads—United State—History. 2. Railroads—Canada—History. 3. Railroad engineering—History.I.Title.
TF22.W53 2007
385.0973—dc22

                        2007007649

Front cover: At the west end of the North Platte River's Wendover Canyon at Cassa, Wyoming, a westward empty BNSF coal train waits for a meet with eastbound loads under an ominous June 2000 sky. *Hal Reiser photograph*
Inset: The New York Central's signature locomotive was the Henry Dreyfuss–designed *Hudson*, with a 4-6-4 wheel arrangement. Streamlined locomotive No. 5450 celebrates Independence Day on July 4, 1941. *www.cabincreekcds.com*

Frontis: Detail from a 1945 Pennsylvania Railroad advertisement. *Voyageur Press collection*

Title pages: The Chicago & North Western's Proviso roundhouse, 1942. *Jack Delano, LC-USW361-583, Library of Congress, Prints and Photographs Division*

These pages: Two locomotives head a huge passenger train, including 4 baggage cars and at least 10 visible passenger cars. The odd, squarish shape of the boiler top near the cab of each locomotive was called a Belpaire firebox. Invented in 1860, it was more common in Europe than in America and was standard on modern Pennsylvania Railroad locomotives. *Voyageur Press collection*

Printed in China

Reprinted in 2013

CONTENTS

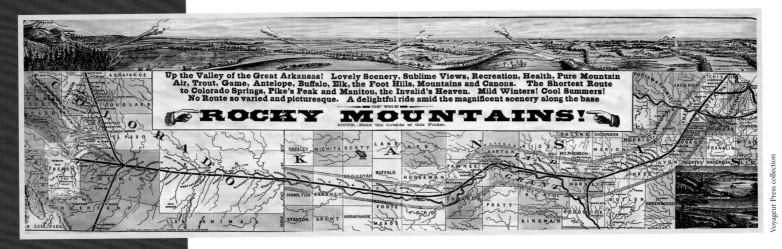

Voyageur Press collection

ACKNOWLEDGMENTS

No project with as broad a scope as this book could be completed without the help of many expert individuals and relevant organizations. I especially thank my son, Kevin, for all his help with ideas and reviews of copy and images. His help made this a much better book. I also thank the following individuals for their assistance:

Charles Albi, Evan Ammeson, Lindsey Ashby, Don Barnes, Bob Bartizek, Mark Bassett, Brittany Bower, Ed Boyle, Richard Braden, Bob Brown, Jerry Carson, John Coker, Paul Conn, David Conrad, Steve Crise, Kyle Davis, Richard Davis, Holly Delants, Doug Doane, Karen Dougherty, Michael Dregni, Stephen Drew, Greg Gardenour, Amy Getz, Bob Goldsack, Jack Gurner, Marc Horovitz, Tom Janaky, Cody Jennings, Dwight Johnson, Doniele Kane, Doug Kaniuk, George Lawrence, Josh Leventhal, Bill Lock, Paul Loyd, Dan Markoff, Kara Marshall, Bill McBride, Scott McCandless, Mel McFarland, Joe Minnich, Linn Moedinger, Gordon Osmundson, Tom Palmer, Bob Parker, Tom Parker, Wendy Pifher, Ken Postma, Larry Powell, Teresa Propeck, Kathy Przybylski, Dan Ranger, Phil Raynes, Alan Reff, Dave Reynolds, Ellen Roberts, Susan Robinson, Dave Schackelford, Steve Schroeder, Rene Schweitzer, Paul Scoles, Mike Shea, Sara Sheldon, Patrick Sirois, Brooke Smith, David Tanis, Wilma Taylor, Karen Wiatrowski, Kevin Wiatrowski, Margaret Wiatrowski, Jay Wimer, John Winfield, and W. Spencer Wren.

The following organizations also provided assistance for which I am grateful:

7+ RAILROADER magazine; American Short Line and Regional Railroad Association; Archives of Advertising; Association of American Railroads; Baltimore & Ohio Railroad Museum; Belton, Grandview and Kansas City Railroad Company; Bionik-Media Photo Lab; California State Railroad Museum; Colorado Railcar; Colorado Railroad Museum; Durango & Silverton Narrow Gauge Railroad; Friends of the Cumbres & Toltec Scenic Railroad; *Garden Railways* magazine; Genessee & Wyoming Incorporated; Image Archives; Iowa Interstate Railroad; Kansas City Southern; Leanin' Tree Museum of Western Art and Sculpture Garden; Manitou & Pikes Peak Railway; *Narrow Gauge & Shortline Gazette*; Nevada Northern Railway; Norfolk Southern Corporation; *O Gauge Railroading* magazine; OmniTRAX, Incorporated; Railroad Development Corporation; Royal Gorge Route; Shortlines of Chicago Historical Society; Strasburg Rail Road; *The Grand Scales Quarterly* magazine; Tourist Railway Association Incorporated; Ute Pass Historical Society; Valley Railroad; Verde Canyon Railroad; Water Valley Railroad Museum; White Pass & Yukon Route; World Museum of Mining; and Yakutat & Southern Railroad Restoration Incorporated.

Omitted are hundreds of friends with an interest in railroads who have contributed indirectly to the creation of this book.

Top: This 1876 Santa Fe brochure appealed to tourists, settlers, and freight shippers. It included a rather sparse passenger timetable with only two eastbound and two westbound trains daily between Atchison, Kansas, and Colorado Springs, Colorado.

What is it that quickens the pulse when a train passes? If you have ever stood near a high-speed train (but not too close!), you know of the roar of engines, the blurring of colors, the shaking of the ground. The experience is all the more moving if a steam locomotive is pulling the train. The smells of coal smoke and hot oil. The shriek of the whistle. The clanking of the rods. The rapid-fire sound of the exhaust. It is no wonder that a large community of fans follows these steel monsters.

Magazines are printed. Books are published. Videos, computer games, and simulations are produced. Miniature railroad empires grow in basements! I understand that fans exist for all modes of transportation. But airplanes are too high to see en route. Neither trucks nor buses have the size and majesty of a train. Ships spend most of their time on the high seas. Perhaps antique automobiles come closest to trains in inspiring aficionados.

It's not just the railfan who has an interest. Almost everyone follows the trials and tribulations of the U.S. railroad passenger service. Though they may not ride trains, they are sorry to see them decline, because they know they are such an important part of U.S. history. They also have a vague, and quite correct, feeling that passenger trains *should* be making their travels easier if only they *worked*. Anyone who has traveled the European railroad systems knows that U.S. policy toward rail transport is seriously lacking.

I know that you are interested in trains or you wouldn't be holding this book in your hands. The basic thread of the text, presented in five chapters, is a short history of U.S. railroads from their very beginnings to the present. Scattered among those chapters are dozens upon dozens of sidebars covering everything from Circus and Carnival Trains to Snow Plows. If you are not up to reading every word, you might

Clyde Osmer DeLand, LC-USZ62-109364, Library of Congress, Prints and Photographs Division

The Delaware & Hudson had the distinction of operating the first steam locomotive on a commercial American railroad. Its 3-mile run so damaged the track—not designed for heavy 7-ton locomotives—that neither it nor its three sister locomotives were ever used.

page through the book and chose sidebars of interest to you. You might enjoy topics of general interest such as Streamliners or Steam Locomotives. Or, consider reading the captions of photos you find compelling. Many tell short, interesting stories about the image they describe.

The history of U.S. and Canadian railroads would fill volumes. This short volume is an abbreviated look at U.S. and Canadian railroads. I hope you find the time to visit a preserved railway or railroad museum—some are listed in Appendix B—and experience how railroads once impacted the daily life of Americans. Many such railroads and museums have gift shops that feature a variety of additional books and videos on railroad subjects. Model railroad hobby shops and bookstores (physical or Web-based) are additional resources. Buy a few railroad magazines just to scan the advertisements. You'll find tour companies ready to send you riding trains in Colorado or China!

Wave at a train. The engineer will almost surely wave back. There is a long tradition of friendly communication between train watchers and railroad employees. Compare those friendly waves to the kinds of hand gestures sometimes exchanged between automobile drivers! For those of you who remember railroads in their prime, I hope this book brings back happy memories. For younger readers, who know railroads only as coal trains blocking their automobiles, you will find this book a pleasant surprise as you discover the many facets of railroading.

INTRODUCTION

CHAPTER ONE

The "Lightning Express" Trains: "Leaving the Junction." Currier & Ives.

THE RIGHT STUFF

Railroads built America and America built railroads. Politically, the railroads unified both the United States and Canada. The Industrial Revolution would have not taken root in the vastness of the North American continent without railways.

ENTER THE RAILROADS

Men had pushed and animals had pulled carts on wooden rails for hundreds of years. But on February 21, 1804, the world's first steam locomotive trundled along the rails at a mine in Cornwall, England. The world's first public railway, the Stockton & Darlington, opened in 1825. The real breakthrough, however, was made in 1828 when the Liverpool and Manchester Railway, also in England, sponsored a cash prize for the best steam locomotive design. At the Rainhill Trials, George and Robert Stephenson's *Rocket* revolutionized locomotive design. More importantly to America, a number of American observers attended the Rainhill trials and returned to the United States enthusiastic to launch the railroad age on this side of the Atlantic. Railroads in the Old and New Worlds would be quite different, both in technology and in social consequences. In densely populated Europe, railroads eased travel between existing population centers. In sparsely populated America, they were the driving force that created new population centers.

AMERICA BEFORE THE IRON HORSE

In the first half of the nineteenth century, Americans thought of "The West" as the land between the Appalachian Mountains and the Mississippi River. Because water provided the easiest transportation, American settlements were located on or near bodies of water. But rivers did not always flow where they were needed. Agriculture, mining, and logging spread far from rivers. Animals strained to haul freight wagons and passenger stagecoaches over primitive roads. Since water transport was already a developed technology, its obvious extension was the building of canals to locations not served by natural watercourses. Eventually, thousands of miles of canals were built. Although inexpensive to operate, canals were expensive to build.

Canal traffic was slow. Speed was limited by that of the animals that pulled the canal boats at about 3 miles per hour. Locks and ramps, needed to ascend and descend hills, slowed traffic even more. Except in the most temperate regions, canals suffered the same problem as rivers in the winter—ice completely halted traffic for months at a time.

The marvel of all U.S. canals was the Erie Canal, connecting Albany, New York, on the Hudson River with Buffalo, New York, on Lake Erie. Completed in November 1825, this 364-mile-long ditch provided a route from the port of New York City to the Great Lakes and, thus, to the resources and markets of the West. Ironically, this masterpiece of canal construction sowed the seeds of the extinction of its species. The prospect of a monopoly for the port of New York City so unnerved other ports that they made their own plans for access to the West. Pennsylvania and Washington, D.C., chose canals while Boston and Baltimore chose to hitch their future to the iron horse and build railroads.

FIRST AMERICAN RAILS

It is difficult to identify the first American railroads with certainty, but three railroads are usually chronicled as the first.

In 1826, horses of the Granite Railway of Massachusetts started hauling stone 3 miles from a quarry in Quincy, Massachusetts, to a wharf on the Neponset River from which it would be transported on water to the construction site of Bunker Hill Monument. The railroad sported wooden rails mounted on individual stone foundations called sleepers. A ramp, called an inclined plane, allowed cars to be hauled up or let down on an endless chain.

In 1827, coal was transported down a gravity railroad at Mauch Chunk in Pennsylvania. Mules hauled the empty cars back uphill to the mines and, loaded into one car, rode back down the hill with the coal. To save time, the mules were fed on the downhill ride. The speed did not agree with their digestive process, however, and the ride was slowed for their comfort—and probably also for the comfort of the men who worked around them! The single track could only be used in one direction at a time, limiting the railroad's capacity. A second track, the "back track," was constructed to return empties to the mine via cable-hauled, inclined planes, creating a large number of unemployed mules. As steam locomotives opened up access to coal mines, the gravity railroad evolved into a purely recreational attraction renamed the Switch Back Railroad. Sightseers rode the line up and coasted back down, no doubt drawn by the exhilaration of the 65-mile-per-hour top speed of the downhill trip! Operation ceased in 1933 and the rails were sold for scrap in 1937.

In 1823, the Delaware & Hudson Canal Company was chartered to build a canal from Honesdale, Pennsylvania, to Roundout on the shore of the Hudson River in New York. Coal would travel from Pennsylvania to the substantial market of New York City and beyond. The mines were connected to the head of the canal by a gravity railroad; loaded cars were hauled back to mines by cable. One of four steam locomotives imported from England in 1829, the *Stourbridge Lion* had the distinction of being the first commercial steam locomotive operated in America. Horatio Allen, one of the Americans that observed the Rainhill Trial, was at the controls as the locomotive rumbled 3 miles up the track. The 7-ton weight of this iron monster so deformed the track's wood supports that neither the *Lion* nor its three sister engines were ever run again. Allen's name appears often in early American railroad history.

FROM WATER TO WATER

Like the Erie Canal, the objective of early American railroads was to connect bodies of water and provide the missing links between existing water routes. Four of these primal railroads were especially important because of their geographic scope. Two were designed to connect the East with the Great Lakes; two to connect the East with the Ohio River. Thus, they were the long-distance trunk lines that provided a continuous transportation system between Atlantic ports and the economies to the West. Eventually, all four railroads built past their original watercourse destinations and rendered water transportation, if not completely obsolete, at least much less important. Those four railroads were the Baltimore & Ohio, the Erie, the Pennsylvania, and the New York Central.

BALTIMORE & OHIO RAILROAD

Projected to connect Baltimore with Wheeling, West Virginia, on the Ohio River, the Baltimore & Ohio's mission

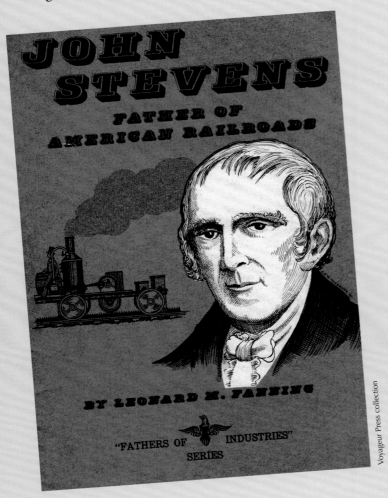

In 1825, at the age of 76, John Stevens designed and constructed a small steam locomotive—the first to operate in America—which ran around a circle of track on his estate in Hoboken, New Jersey. The locomotive was propelled by a gear that meshed with a toothed rail in the center of the track. Early inventors were not sure that friction between the locomotive's wheels and the track would be sufficient to prevent slipping.

Voyageur Press collection

was formulated by adventurous visionaries who foresaw an almost-400-mile-long rail line when the prototype Stockton & Darlington Railroad measured only 27 miles end to end. Construction on the first common carrier railroad in the United States began on July 4, 1828. A common carrier railroad transports all passengers and freight needing passage, not just the freight and employees of the company that owns the railroad.

Horses hauled the Baltimore & Ohio's trains until 1831, when the tracks extended barely 60 miles. It was clear, at least to some, that horses would not be a practical solution on a 400-mile transportation artery. Peter Cooper designed and constructed a tiny 1-ton experimental steam locomotive, the *Tom Thumb*, at his own expense. In August 1830, the diminutive *Tom Thumb* made a 26-mile round trip on the Baltimore & Ohio at the unheard of speed of 18 miles per hour.

After an almost-quarter-century construction ordeal, the Baltimore & Ohio reached Wheeling on January 1, 1853. Success only whetted appetites, and the rails reached St. Louis just four years later in 1857, thus opening the great Mississippi River to Baltimore's economy. Baltimore's business community clearly chose well in selecting the technology of railroads.

ERIE RAILROAD

The New York & Erie Railroad was the first of the four great trunk lines to reach western waters, but it did so at great cost. Opened from Piermont on the Hudson River to Dunkirk on Lake Erie on May 17, 1851, the Erie Railroad was a gift to southern New York State, a consolation prize in return for their support of the Erie Canal farther north. Serving an area lacking sufficient traffic and burdened with inexperienced management, the Erie found itself in bankruptcy in 1859. Its business model of "build a railroad and commerce will follow" was eventually used successfully by the great transcontinental railways in settling the far West. Future railroads would also emulate its pioneering bankruptcy all too frequently.

PENNSYLVANIA RAILROAD

The Pennsylvania Railroad was everything that the Erie was not. The Pennsylvania was so well constructed, well managed, and efficiently operated, it became know as the "Standard Railway of the World." The story of the Pennsylvania clearly demonstrates the superiority of railroads over canals.

The chief competitor of this privately financed railroad was the publicly financed Main Line of Public Works, an incredible Rube Goldberg combination of 3 canals, 2 cable-hauled railroads, 177 canal locks, 49 aqueducts, 11 inclined planes, and a 1,000-foot tunnel—all to connect Philadelphia to Pittsburgh, and then only when its waterways weren't frozen in the winter. The costly Main Line showed what could be done using yesterday's technology to build tomorrow's transportation system. Not only was it expensive to construct, it was slow to traverse.

Construction of the Pennsylvania Railroad began in 1847, and chief engineer J. Edgar Thomson's well-thought-out route concentrated the railroad's steepest grades in a single mountainous area. The Pennsylvania Railroad was completed from Philadelphia to Pittsburgh by November 1852, putting the Main Line on the sideline forever. To try to protect its archaic investment, the state of Pennsylvania included in its charter a tax on traffic moved by the railroad. Yet the railroad's efficiencies were such that even this desperate ploy could not save the old Main Line.

Site of First Railroad in the United States, Built 1825, Quincy, Mass.

America's first commercial railway was built at this site in Massachusetts. Three miles of track were laid to convey stone to the construction site of the Bunker Hill Monument in 1826.

NEW YORK CENTRAL RAILROAD

The easternmost section of the Erie Canal was exceptionally slow, with several locks and a pair of inclined planes. Early in the canal's history, a stagecoach company began service on a 17-mile route that bypassed 40 miles of canal travel. A year after the canal was completed, the Mohawk & Hudson Rail Road was incorporated to replace these stages. In a not-so-subtle comparison, the railroad's first locomotive was named the *DeWitt Clinton* after the man who promoted the construction of the Erie Canal. The Mohawk & Hudson was the third U.S. railroad to power its trains with steam locomotives.

It would have been logical to parallel the entire canal with a railroad, but vested interests—including the State of New York, which paid for the canal—did their best to prevent this with restrictive legislation. The result was a jumble of railroads paralleling segments of the canal. The railroads cooperated with each other, and travel from Albany to Buffalo declined from days via canal boat, to hours via railroad coach. In 1851, the little railroads were consolidated under the name New York Central Railroad, which would give the mighty Pennsylvania a run for its money.

BUILDING THE IRON TRAIL

Railroads were among the first truly big businesses. They dominated the stock markets in which their equities traded. They dominated the employment market with a large number of jobs, some of the best in the nation. And they dominated the political landscape by controlling so much wealth and employment. Small investors—as well as some wealthy capitalists—lost a great deal of money, as there was little regulation and most railroads went bankrupt at least once. Many railroads were built, deliberately or not, on business models that simply could never have resulted in profitability.

Also, management of huge railroad enterprises was a new science. Only the world's armies were of comparable size and the railroads were quick to adopt the layered management structure of the military. The military also provided key managers and construction engineers for early railroads.

Imagine the difficulty of choosing a route for a pioneer railroad. A surveyor would be sent into the mountains having heard only rumors about the lay of the land. In the very earliest years, little was known about how steeply a railroad should climb or how sharp its track should curve. There were scores of questions to be asked just ahead of the next rise in the land. What would be the best balance between the cost of constructing and the cost of operating the railroad? What lay up this canyon—a dead end? Should the tracks go this way or that? Should the track be laid on the ground or on a trestle above it? Should the rails be wood with iron straps or made entirely of iron? How far apart should the rails be spaced? How many wheels should a locomotive have? A passenger coach? A freight car? How long should they be? All these questions and more were answered by experiment. Some decisions were disastrously incorrect and some wonderfully successful. The knowledge accumulated from this experimentation created standards for railroads that have remained remarkably robust for over 175 years.

THE WAY WEST

The prototype railroads connected navigable bodies of water. Mines, timberlands, farms, ranches, and sources of traffic were not always near bodies of water, so smaller branch railroads were built to connect with the main trunk lines. Railroads began to bump into each other, creating a network of rail lines. Commodities came down the branches, onto the trunks, and then to market in major cities. Manufactured goods from those cities traveled up the trunk lines and out the branch lines to loggers, miners, and farmers.

People and goods could be moved from anyplace on the network to anyplace else on the network. In the United States, *everyplace* came to be on the railroad network—the world had never seen the fires of an economic engine stoked so fiercely. Growth fed off growth. In 1830, there were 23 miles of railroad track in the United States. By 1840, that total had risen to 2,800—more miles than in all of Europe. By 1850, the United States had 9,000 miles, half the *world's* total. By 1860, the U.S. total had risen to 30,000 miles. Railroad fever swept North America. Visionaries and crooks swarmed the country looking for opportunities.

CIVIL WAR

At the outset of the U.S. Civil War, most of the North's rails were British standard gauge, or 4 feet 8 1/2 inches apart, while the South's rails were spaced an even 5 feet. Two-thirds of the railroad mileage in the United States was in the North, much of it in the form of efficient trunk railroads. The South's haphazard railroad lines did not possess this strength of purpose. Most of the manufacturers of locomotives, cars, and rail were located in the North. In September 1863, 30 trains of 20 cars each moved 20,000 northern soldiers a distance of 1,200 miles in only 11 1/2 days. War would never be the same again.

Rapidly restoring train service in the wake of the enemy's destruction of railroads became paramount, and Herman Haupt of the U.S. Military Railroad excelled in devising systems to do so. Destruction of train service, on the other hand, was the specialty of General William Tecumseh Sherman. In his famous "March to the Sea," Sherman's army swept across Georgia, rebuilding railroads in front of it, but destroying them in its wake. Although the war devastated southern railroads, it gave birth to the great era of railroad expansion in the rest of the country. Northern railroads that served great industrial centers prospered with wartime traffic, as did manufacturers of all kinds.

EARLY CANADIAN RAILROADS

Canadian railroad development lagged behind that in the United States. In 1851, the United States could boast 10,500 miles of railroad track compared to the British province of Canada's 90 miles. Canada had yet to coalesce into the country it is today, and included only the area that now comprises the provinces of Quebec and Ontario.

Canada's population was smaller and lived, almost entirely, along navigable water. Not surprisingly, Canada's first railroad was a portage railway—a railroad between two waterways. The Champlain & St. Lawrence Railroad opened in 1836 as a link in a system to connect Montreal and St. Lawrence River traffic with the United States. The railroad began at La Prairie, across the St. Lawrence River from Montreal, and ran to St-Jean-sur-Richelieu. There, steamboats carried freight and passengers south to the United States on the Richelieu River.

The first Canadian trunk line linked Montreal with Portland, Maine, and was soon purchased by the Grand Trunk Railway, one of several important players in Canada's railroad history. By 1860, the Grand Trunk was 800 miles long, at the time the longest railroad under one management, and Canada's rail mileage had increased to 2,138 miles. Besides the railroads in the Province of Canada, this total included railroads in the British provinces of New Brunswick and Nova Scotia, where railroads had been built by the governments there as public works. By comparison, U.S. rail mileage had increased to 30,000 miles.

Switch Back Railroad showing return track at five mile tree, Mauch Chunk, Pa.

The second commercial railroad in America originally transported coal by gravity at Mauch Chunk in Pennsylvania. It was a tourist railway before its demise.

In 1867, the Dominion of Canada was formed from New Brunswick, Nova Scotia, and the old province of Canada. In this restructuring, the province of Canada was divided into the provinces of Quebec and Ontario. The country of Canada was born and the government-built railroads in New Brunswick and Nova Scotia were transferred to the new national government on the condition that they would be extended to join all the provinces by rail. This promise was fulfilled by 1876 with the Intercolonial Railway, which would later form the nucleus of Canadian National Railways.

Voyageur Press collection, courtesy of Bionik Media Photo lab, bionikmedia.com

This huge mortar, nicknamed the "Dictator," bombarded Petersburg, Virginia, with federal projectiles weighing 200 pounds. This image was also the basis for a comedic scene in the Buster Keaton movie *The General*.

BALTIMORE & OHIO

The 25-year construction of the Baltimore & Ohio's main line from Baltimore to the Ohio River may seem glacially slow in retrospect, but the railroad was busy experimenting. It learned that the vast distances of the United States and the uncertain markets of the wilderness required that railroads be built quickly and inexpensively, and upgraded only when traffic justified additional expenditures. Its network of rails reached Lake Erie at Cleveland and Toledo; Lake Michigan at Chicago; the Mississippi River at St. Louis; and the Ohio River at both Cincinnati and Louisville. At its largest extent in 1936, the B&O operated 6,396 route miles. In 1960, the Chesapeake & Ohio Railway began to acquire B&O stock, and in 1967 the two railroads jointly took control of the Western Maryland. The three railroads became subsidiaries of the Chessie System in 1973. The B&O and C&O merged in 1987 and, a few months later, became part of CSX Transportation.

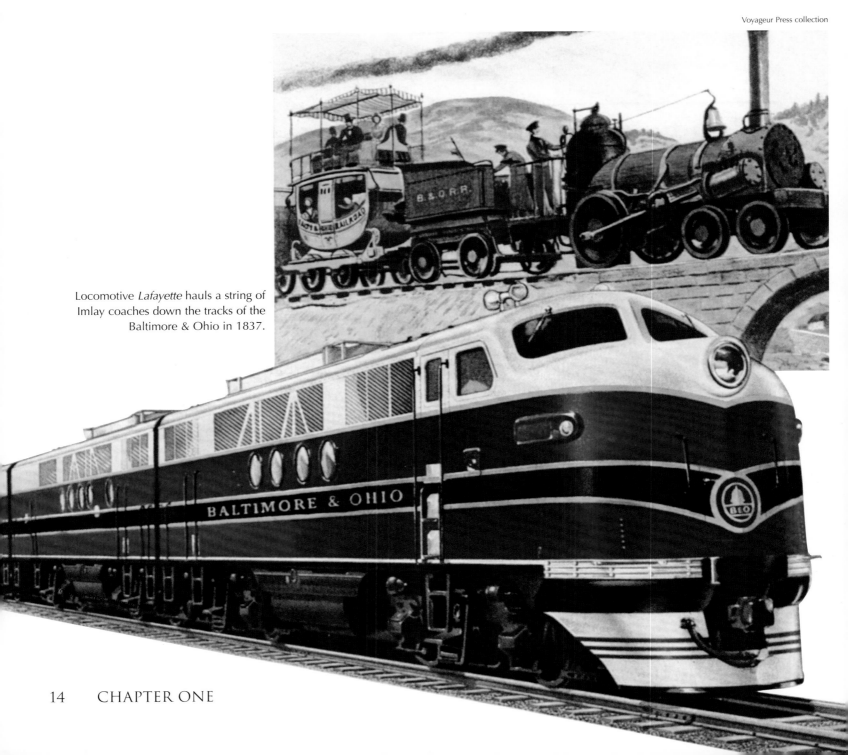

Locomotive *Lafayette* hauls a string of Imlay coaches down the tracks of the Baltimore & Ohio in 1837.

The reverse side of this postcard states, "CARILLON PARK, DAYTON OHIO. The *John Quincy Adams* is the oldest original Baltimore & Ohio locomotive in existence. It is of the 'grasshopper' type, was built in 1835, and saw active service for more than 50 years."

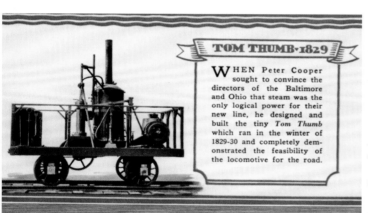

Visitors to the Fair of the Iron Horse in 1927 could purchase a packet of 15 postcards for 15 cents. The cards chronicled the history of Baltimore & Ohio locomotive technology from the tiny 1829 *Tom Thumb*, the first demonstration of steam locomotion on the B&O, to the magnificent *President Washington*, a modern 90-mile-per-hour passenger locomotive in a striking green and gold livery.

This April 1940 cover of *Railroad Magazine* features a hand-tinted photograph of passengers of a special excursion on the Baltimore & Ohio in either 1857 or 1858. As with many old photos, several descriptions exist. The most interesting is that it is a special train from Baltimore to Wheeling for journalists, artists, and photographers.

THE RIGHT STUFF   15

BOSTON & MAINE

The Andover & Wilmington Railroad started operation in Maine in 1836 and crossed into New Hampshire in 1840 to pioneer the route that merged into the Boston & Maine Railroad in 1842, taking the name of the New Hampshire railroad chartered in 1835. The B&M would absorb other railroads until its rails stretched north to Sherbrooke, Quebec; northeast to Portland, Maine; west to the Hudson River at Mechanicsville, New York; and south to New Haven, Connecticut. In 1900, the B&M acquired the Fitchburg Railroad, which owned the 4.75-mile Hoosac Tunnel in northwestern Massachusetts. The B&M was purchased by Guilford Transportation Industries in 1983.

The B&M operated the *Flying Yankee*, the nation's third diesel streamliner. Routed over the tracks of both the B&M and Maine Central Railroad, the *Yankee* could carry 140 passengers between Bangor, Maine, and Boston, with a stop in Maine's capital city, Portland.

The Boston & Maine published this 20-page booklet in the winter of 1929 extolling the virtues of a winter vacation in New England. Information includes winter resorts and sports, advice on what to wear (several pairs of socks), and special winter tourist fares.

Steam locomotive *Marlboro* chugs through Massachusetts' Berkshire Hills about the time of the Civil War.

Voyageur Press collection

Below: These two postcard views of the west portal of the Hoosac Tunnel show it before and after electrification. The tunnel was first proposed as a canal tunnel in 1819 and was finally completed as a rail tunnel in 1875, becoming part of the Boston & Maine in 1900. Electrification of the tunnel was completed by 1911.

Hoosac Tunnel, Looking out from West Portal, Mass.

Voyageur Press collection

WESTERN ENTRANCE TO HOOSAC TUNNEL, MOHAWK TRAIL, MASS.   56

Voyageur Press collection

One remnant of the steam era that could be reused was the roundhouse. In 1970, a Boston & Maine Alco RS3 diesel goes for a spin on a turntable previously reserved for steam locomotives.

G. V. "Jerry" Carson photo

DELAWARE & HUDSON

In 1828, the Delaware & Hudson Canal Company opened a 108-mile canal from Honesdale, Pennsylvania, to New York's Hudson River.

An Erie Railroad branch reached the D&H coal mines in 1868. In 1871, the canal company continued this track north to ensure its coal had access to Albany. The canal company continued to build railroads, reaching Scranton, Pennsylvania, in 1871, and Montreal by 1875. The canal was last operated in 1891. After a name change to the Delaware & Hudson Railroad, came a new mission. With oil replacing coal for heating, the railroad evolved from plodding coal trains to racing merchandise trains on the shortest and fastest line to New England and Montreal.

Trackage rights to Buffalo, Newark, Philadelphia, and Washington, D.C.—compensation for the formation of Conrail—could not stem the inevitable red ink, however. In 1984 Guilford Transportation Industries purchased D&H, intending to consolidate its operations with the Maine Central and Boston & Maine. Unsuccessful, D&H went bankrupt and was purchased by CP Rail in 1991. Today, Canadian Pacific trains have access deep into the U.S. eastern seaboard on those same tracks D&H obtained during the formation of Conrail.

G. V. "Jerry" Carson photo

Delaware & Hudson locomotive No. 708, a GE U33C, waits a call to duty at Mechanicsville, New York, in March 1970.

A Delaware & Hudson coal train rumbles past as an Erie train flies overhead on the massive Starrucca Viaduct. The year is 1947, and with coal a diminishing commodity, the cover wonders about the Delaware & Hudson's future.

This attractive map of the Delaware & Hudson highlights the summer vacation potential of the railroad's route.

The *Laurentian* was the Delaware & Hudson's crack passenger train between Montreal and New York City. This small booklet details the route with full-color strip maps and descriptions of some of the sights along the way.

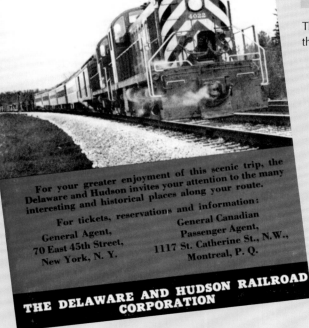

ERIE LACKAWANNA

MISS PHOEBE
again welcomes you to the

🄴 ERIE LACKAWANNA
The Friendly Service Route

Voyageur Press collection

Lackawanna locomotives burned anthracite coal, which produces little soot to rain down on passengers. Advertising underscored cleanliness through Miss Phoebe Snow, an imaginary woman in a white gown whose journeys were chronicled in advertising jingles: "Says Phoebe Snow/About to go/Upon a trip/To Buffalo/'My gown stays white/From morn till night/Upon the Road of Anthracite.'" This small brochure was issued after the merger of the Erie and the Lackawanna to explain the origin of the name of the streamlined passenger train called the Phoebe Snow.

To gain support for the Erie Canal, politicians promised a transportation artery to serve cities on New York's southern border. Thus, the New York & Lake Erie Railroad was chartered in 1832.

The original 1851 route from Dunkirk on Lake Erie to Piedmont on the Hudson River was soon revised to connect Buffalo with New York City. The Erie's trains arrived in Ohio in the 1870s, and 1880 proved pivotal as the railroad was narrowed to standard gauge and extended to Chicago.

Cooperation between the Erie and the Delaware, Lackawanna & Western Railroad evolved into a 1960 merger. Bankruptcy was at hand when the road suffered heavy damage from Hurricane Agnes in 1972. The Erie Lackawanna became a constituent of Conrail in 1976.

Voyageur Press collection

The Erie's great Starrucca Viaduct was built in Pennsylvania when American railroads still emulated the European practice of erecting monumental engineering works built to last the ages. Such practices were not unreasonable in the eastern United States where railroad traffic was fairly certain, especially on the first railroads to be built. It wasn't long before a crossing such as this would be made on an inexpensive wooden trestle or eliminated completely with switchback tracks to the valley floor.

This 1950 Lackawanna timetable lists passenger train schedules in New York, New Jersey, and Pennsylvania, but also includes connections as far west as Chicago and St. Louis on other railroads. Streamlined and diesel-powered trains are specifically identified.

Above: With a train of hopper cars in tow, Erie locomotive 3376, a 2-8-4, smokes it up near Hackensack, New Jersey, in 1951.

Opposite: The Erie celebrated the opening of America's longest rail line in 1851 with a 427-mile party. Guests included President Millard Fillmore and Secretary of State Daniel Webster. The 69-year-old Webster insisted on riding outside on a flatcar to better observe the sights. Webster was ahead of his time, as anyone who has ridden in an open car on a preserved railway will tell you it is the best experience of rail travel.

ILLINOIS CENTRAL

Congress passed the Land Grant Act in 1850. In return for land, the federal government was guaranteed reduced transportation rates from railroads. The Illinois Central Railroad would receive 2.6 million acres of land and fulfill a congressional desire for a railroad connecting Chicago with the Gulf of Mexico.

The Illinois Central's initial route stretched from the confluence of the Mississippi and Ohio Rivers to the city of Galena, Illinois. This main line and a branch to Chicago were completed by 1856.

Illinois Central tracks would saturate a broad corridor from Chicago to New Orleans, with side excursions crossing Iowa to reach Omaha and Sioux Falls, and serving Indianapolis, Louisville, and Birmingham to the east and south.

The Illinois Central merged with the Gulf, Mobile & Ohio Railroad in 1972. Disposing of unwanted routes, the newly named Illinois Central Gulf gave birth to 6 regional railroads and 11 short lines, and sold other routes to three Class 1 railroads. Having divested itself of almost all GM&O track, the Illinois Central Gulf was renamed the Illinois Central in 1988. A decade later, the Illinois Central became part of the Canadian National Railway.

G. V. "Jerry" Carson photo

An Illinois Central Mountain-type locomotive with a 4-8-2 wheel arrangement passes through Homewood, Illinois, in 1955. Railroad photographers would describe this image of No. 2604 as a "glint shot."

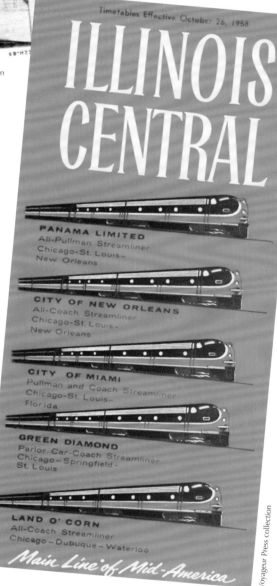

Illinois Central Passenger Train Crossing Kentucky Dam, Western Kentucky

An Illinois Central passenger train crosses Tennessee Valley Authority's concrete blockage of the Tennessee River that created 184-mile-long Kentucky Lake. The dam was completed in 1944 after six years of construction.

Companies that built streamlined passenger cars for railroads also advertised their customers' services. This ad boasted of a 29 1/2-hour schedule between Chicago and Miami. Departures, however, were every third day.

Another Great Streamliner for The Illinois Central

CITY OF MIAMI

BUILT BY PULLMAN-STANDARD

THE WORLD'S LARGEST BUILDERS OF RAILROAD AND TRANSIT EQUIPMENT

Timetables Effective October 26, 1958

ILLINOIS CENTRAL

PANAMA LIMITED
All-Pullman Streamliner
Chicago-St. Louis-
New Orleans

CITY OF NEW ORLEANS
All-Coach Streamliner
Chicago-St. Louis-
New Orleans

CITY OF MIAMI
Pullman and Coach Streamliner
Chicago-St. Louis-
Florida

GREEN DIAMOND
Parlor Car-Coach Streamliner
Chicago-Springfield-
St. Louis

LAND O' CORN
All-Coach Streamliner
Chicago-Dubuque-Waterloo

Main Line of Mid-America

Besides the named trains on its cover, numerous minor passenger trains undeserving of a fancy name are listed inside this timetable. By 1958, cracks were beginning to show in passenger service. Some trains no longer ran daily and timetables listed alternate bus services. A fair amount of this timetable is devoted to freight service, including piggyback routes.

MISSOURI PACIFIC

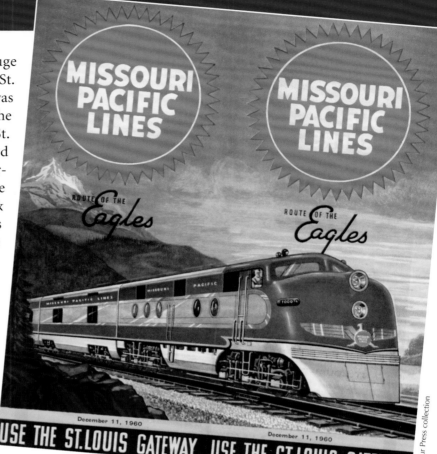

Ground was broken for the 5-foot, 6-inch–gauge Pacific Railroad in 1851 and the line between St. Louis and Kansas City was completed in 1865. It was standard-gauged in 1869 and its name changed to the Missouri Pacific Railroad in 1870. Merger of the St. Louis, Iron Mountain & Southern in 1917 extended the Missouri Pacific across Arkansas to the Texas border and added Memphis to its destinations. The Missouri Pacific bought the New Orleans, Texas & Mexico in 1924, obtaining its line from New Orleans through Houston to Brownsville, Texas. The NOT&M purchased the International-Great Northern that same year and its line from Longview to Laredo, Texas, with access to Mexico.

By 1967, the Missouri Pacific—sometimes called the MoPac—had accessed Chicago through control of the Chicago & Eastern Illinois, which it merged in 1976. Also in that year, it added the Texas & Pacific with its trunk line from New Orleans through Dallas to far western Texas at El Paso. The Missouri Pacific now occupied a corridor southwest from Chicago to the Mexican border. In 1982 it was merged into the Union Pacific.

This 1960 timetable lists a round-trip fare from St. Louis to San Antonio of $34.79 and a round-trip to Denver for $53.50. Both fares included sleeping accommodations.

If this ten-wheeler looks a little tired, perhaps it is because it was built by Rogers Locomotive & Machine Works in 1898. Rogers could trace its origins to 1831 and was purchased by Alco in 1905. Its erecting shop is now a museum in Paterson, New Jersey. Perhaps, the most famous locomotive that Rogers constructed was the *General* of Civil War fame.

The Missouri Pacific's first locomotive is unloaded from a river boat in 1852 and will be the first to run west of the Mississippi River. When that river was bridged, the railroad had second thoughts about its wide gauge and converted to standard gauge in 1869 to allow interchange with railroads in the eastern United States.

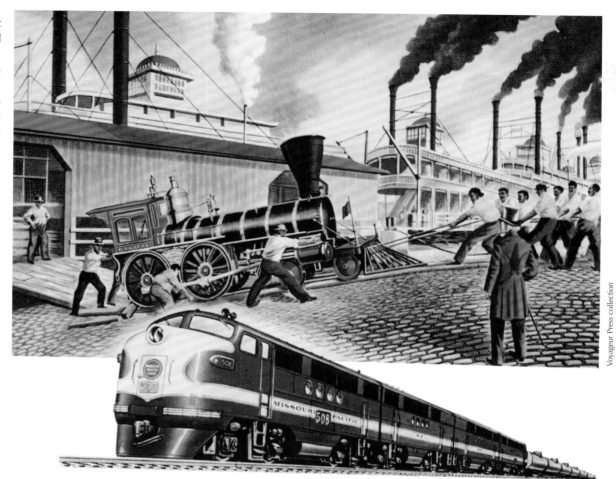

Voyageur Press collection

A giant-size car wash cleans a Missouri Pacific streamlined locomotive at Choteau Yard in St. Louis in 1970.

G. V. "Jerry" Carson photo

READING COMPANY

The Philadelphia and Reading Rail Road was chartered in 1833, but the cost of acquiring anthracite coal deposits forced bankruptcy in 1880. A new strategy of controlling coal transport by leasing railroads—the Lehigh Valley, the Central Railroad of New Jersey, and others—ended in another bankruptcy, and after separation of coal operations, the railroad became the Reading Company in 1924.

Its physical size was modest—it served southeastern Pennsylvania, New Jersey, and touched Delaware at Wilmington. Excess passenger capacity from Philadelphia to Atlantic City was addressed in 1933 when the Reading Company and Pennsylvania Railroad consolidated operations between those points under the name Pennsylvania-Reading Seashore Lines.

As the use of coal for domestic heating ended, the Reading developed bridge traffic between the Midwest and the Northeast. This bridge route, between Shippensburg and Allentown, Pennsylvania, was comparatively tiny as the age of mega-railroads dawned. Because they were classified as commuter trains, the Reading's money-losing passenger routes did not go to Amtrak in 1971. The railroad entered bankruptcy for the final time in 1971 and became part of Conrail in 1976.

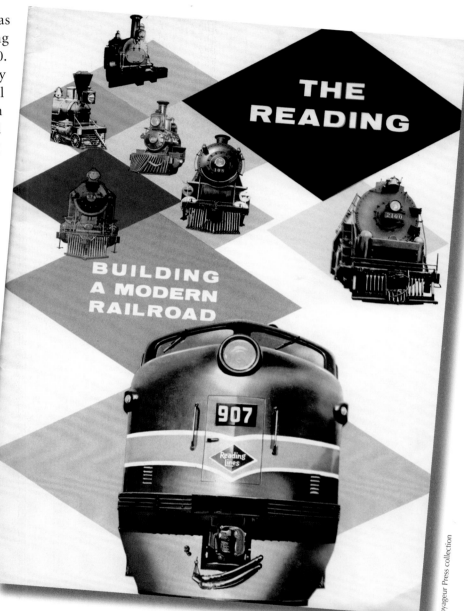

The Reading published this
60-page booklet in 1958 to celebrate 125 years.

Reading's streamlined *Crusader* leads a parade of steam locomotives. Published in 1941, the 108-page book includes exquisite photographs of Reading locomotives.

READING COMPANY NO. 3017   READING, PA.
2-10-2 REBUILT FROM 1800 SERIES MALLETS   1940

READING COMPANY NO. 178   PHILADELPHIA, PA.
4-6-2 SEMI-STREAMLINED PASSENGER LOCOMOTIVE   1940

READING COMPANY NO. 348   DRIVERS 90" - BOILER PRESSURE 200 LB.
4-4-2 PASS. LOCO.-ATLANTIC TYPE   A VERY FAST ENGINE

All three of these locomotives show Reading's characteristic wide firebox at the back of the boiler, which allowed anthracite coal to be burned efficiently.

ROCK ISLAND

The Chicago & Rock Island Rail Road was incorporated in 1851 and trains were running between its namesake cities by 1852, connecting Lake Michigan with the Mississippi River, which was bridged in 1856. A more ambitious, never-realized goal was announced with an 1866 name change to Chicago, Rock Island & Pacific, whose rails would reach as far west as Colorado and New Mexico.

The Rock Island, as it was popularly known, was the quintessential agricultural railroad, with its tracks stitching together the agricultural heartland from Illinois to Colorado and Minnesota to Louisiana. A dozen indecisive years of delaying western railroad mergers exemplified the failure of the Interstate Commerce Commission to reasonably regulate the nation's railroads. One consequence was the final bankruptcy of "The Rock" in 1975. Operated temporarily by other railroads, train service on Rock Island tracks ended in 1980. Over 7,000 miles of railroad fell silent—the nation had never seen anything like it. Although the Rock disappeared, its infrastructure was too important to the nation and most of its routes were incorporated in other railroads.

ROCKY MOUNTAIN ROCKET
At the Foot of Famous Pikes Peak

Above: The 1948 Rock Island timetable still includes a large number of passenger routes. An ad encourages the traveler to visit the railroad's exhibit at the Chicago Railroad Fair. Name trains included the *Golden State* from Chicago to Los Angeles (via the Southern Pacific from New Mexico west), the *Rocky Mountain Rocket* from Chicago to Colorado Springs and Denver (the train split at Limon, Colorado), the *Corn Belt Rocket* between Chicago and Omaha, and several others.

The Rock Island's *Rocky Mountain Rocket* arrived at the foot of Pikes Peak in Colorado Springs but never climbed into the pine-clad foothills as shown in this postcard. The Rock Island came close to purchasing the Colorado Midland Railway and, if it had, a scene like this would have actually been possible.

Above: The United States' entry into World War II and the railroad traffic it would bring was a year in the future as this Rock Island Northern-type locomotive passes Silvis, Illinois.

Left: A 1955 Rock Island ad from *Railway Age*.

A Rock Island streamliner passes through Joliet, Illinois. The EMD E8 locomotive is followed by a baggage car and a dome observation car hauled "backward" in the consist.

SIGNALING: WHAT HAD MORSE WROUGHT?

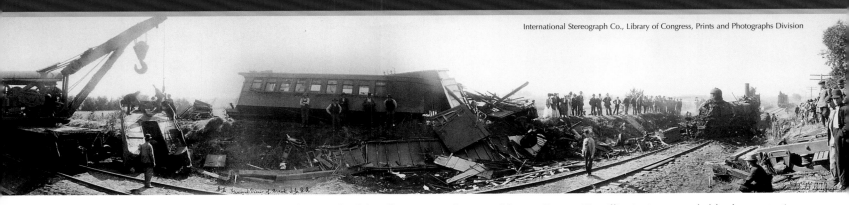

International Stereograph Co., Library of Congress, Prints and Photographs Division

The twisted steel locomotive and splintered wooden coach of this Illinois Central 1909 mishap at Farmer City, Illinois, is a remarkable demonstration of a moving train's energy. It is no wonder the public finally demanded that the railroads incorporate the telegraph and other safety measures.

When a second locomotive was added to a railway's roster, that railway was faced with the problem of preventing the two locomotives from colliding. The earliest solution was to give each train written orders based on a timetable. Besides the risk of error in devising and interpreting such orders, trains were often obliged to wait for hours, delaying passengers and freight. Even so, train orders were not foolproof and collisions could and did occur due to unforeseen circumstances—there was no communication method faster than the trains themselves. That changed with the invention of the electric telegraph and its instantaneous communication.

Although Samuel Morse telegraphed the message "What had God wrought" on May 24, 1844, the first telegraphic train order was not sent until September 22, 1851. Charles Minot, superintendent of the New York & Erie, was faced with holding a westbound train for hours at Turner's station when the eastbound train failed to show up. Telegraph wires paralleled the railroad but were not used to control trains. Minot telegraphed the operator at the next station to the west, Goshen, inquiring about the whereabouts of the eastbound train. Upon receiving a reply that the eastbound train was nowhere in sight, Minot acted. A surprised operator copied Minot's Morse code message to hold the eastbound train at Goshen should it arrive. Minot then asked the westbound train's conductor to tell the engineer, Isaac Lewis, to proceed to Goshen. Lewis refused, believing he was obligated by the timetable to wait for the eastbound train. Minot operated the locomotive himself for this first-of-a-kind run to Goshen. Showing his confidence in the telegraph. Lewis retreated to the last row of the last car to wait for the inevitable collision that never happened.

Minot's telegraphic dispatching of trains was so obviously effective that railroads everywhere should have adopted the procedure. It wasn't until a half-century later, however, that public outrage over avoidable fatalities in train wrecks finally convinced railroads to use telegraphs to coordinate train movements.

Voyageur Press collection

Operators hooped up orders to the locomotive and caboose while the train continued moving. Train orders frequently depended on the correct time, and the regularly checked accuracy of railroad watches was critical.

Left: When the station agent needed to stop a train, he lowered the ball on its rope. The engineer knew to stop to pick up an order or for some other purpose. If the ball were high on the mast, the engineer called out "highball," the fireman confirmed the signal by repeating "highball," and they rolled through the station without stopping.

Below: Modern train dispatching integrates functions that once required many men stationed at remote locations along the railroad.

Bottom left: This World War II–era New York Central ad touted the railroad's state-of-the-art signaling system and the railroad's role in the war effort.

STEAM LOCOMOTIVES

It is a remarkable experience to watch a steam locomotive given life by the lighting of a fire. Slowly, steam begins to escape from this pipe or that. As the pressure builds, steam gushes up the stack, creating a draft that makes the fire hotter, faster. Finally, the locomotive moves itself and thousands of tons of train cars behind it—all from a simple fire, the first energy source harnessed by mankind.

Early American locomotives followed British patterns and, in fact, around 100 were imported from England. It soon became clear that American locomotives had to be special. American track was lighter and more uneven, for New World financiers had to stretch their meager funds to North America's larger dimensions. Better suspension systems would keep American locos from derailing on uneven track. Extra front wheels guided engines around sharp curves. America's tracks were not fenced so the pilot—also called the cowcatcher—was invented to brush obstructions from the tracks, though it was none too successful with cows! Night trains on unfenced rights-of-way required a headlight. (The first headlight was a flatcar, pushed ahead of the locomotive, upon which a bonfire was lit.) By the 1850s, American locomotives' wooden cabs protected crews from the elements. The rear of the cab was left open for the next 70 years so the fireman could shovel coal from the tender to the boiler's firebox. Canadians finally developed enclosed cabs to protect crews from subzero temperatures. Other early additions included bells and whistles for signaling crewmembers and for warning the public.

By 1850, there were over three dozen U.S. locomotive manufacturers. Designers and the craftsmen who constructed them took great pride in creating these technological marvels. Attention was paid to creating pleasing proportions. Shiny multihued paint schemes were augmented by brightly polished brass and ornamental scrollwork. Artists painted pictures on the sides of headlights and cabs. An engineer was assigned his own locomotive and almost always customized its appearance to his own tastes. Locomotives were named and not just numbered. Names implied speed or size, honored important men or mythological figures, or identified someone's girlfriend! By the 1890s, all locomotives were black, ornamentation had disappeared, and engineers were no longer assigned a personal locomotive.

Locomotive manufacturers coalesced into larger and larger firms. In the United States, three manufacturers emerged: Baldwin, Alco, and Lima. Jeweler Matthias Baldwin started building locomotives in 1831, became the largest U.S. locomotive builder, and exported steamers of all gauges to the entire world. To compete with massive Baldwin, Alco (American Locomotive Company) was formed in 1901 from eight smaller builders. Two more builders joined in 1905, including Canada's Montreal Locomotive Works. Lima was a smaller builder that, nonetheless, had a big impact on steam locomotive technology. Not only did it build the geared Shay-type locomotives essential to railroad logging, it created the concept of superpower locomotives in 1925. Superpower locomotives incorporated a number of technologies that allowed them to travel faster and pull heavier trains at lower costs.

Smaller manufacturers built specialized steam locomotives. Porter and Davenport, for example, built very small locomotives for industrial applications such as road construction and rock quarrying. Larger railroads built their own—or at least some of their own—steam locomotives. The Pennsylvania Railroad and the Norfolk

A December morning in 1942 finds Chicago & North Western steam locomotives positioned over the ash pit in Chicago. Coal was loaded from the large tipple in the background and ashes from the burned coal eventually had to be dumped in a pit located between the rails.

This angled steam locomotive was designed to climb the steep grades of the cog railroad that travels up Colorado's Pikes Peak. In addition to propelling itself via a gear that meshes with a toothed rail, this unusual locomotive is also a "Vauclain compound," meaning it uses the steam twice to extract as much energy as possible before exhausting it up the stack.

This rare 1906 exposure shows an early prototype of the Shay geared locomotive on a logging railroad in Michigan. Invented of necessity by a local mechanical genius, the locomotive was eventually mass-produced by the Lima Locomotive Works in Lima, Ohio. Snappily dressed ladies and gentlemen attest to this train being used for a short holiday excursion into the woods.

This American Locomotive Company advertisement asks, "Which one is the freight locomotive?" In 1948, average Americans still cared enough about steam locomotive technology to be impressed by a single design that could race along with a passenger train in tow or pull thousands of tons of freight.

Required after every run, the considerable routine servicing of steam locomotives was performed in a roundhouse. There were many roundhouses across America but few survive. Light repairs also were completed here. Major maintenance and heavy repairs were completed in a "back shop."

and Western were notable in this regard. N&W constructed the last new steam locomotive for a major railroad in the United States.

Around 1900, Frederic Whyte devised a system to categorize steam locomotives by their wheel arrangements. A string of digits represents the number of wheels starting with the front of the locomotive. Perhaps six-dozen wheel arrangements were tried with only a dozen or so gaining significant success. Locomotive types were also given nicknames. Here are some examples:

Whyte System	Pilot Wheels	Driving Wheels	Driving Wheels	Trailing Wheels	Nickname(s)
4-4-0	4	4	-	0	American
Exceptionally well-adapted to American railroad conditions (hence the name), tens of thousands were built starting in 1837. In the 1870s, 85 percent of all U.S. locomotives were Americans. By 1900, they were obsolete in the United States.					
2-8-0	2	8	-	0	Consolidation
Built in 1865, the first of this type was named the Consolidation. Replicated in large numbers, they replaced Americans, especially in freight service.					
4-8-4	4	8	-	4	Northern Pocono Dixie Niagara Potomac
Most call this locomotive a Northern because the first of its kind was produced for the Northern Pacific in 1927. Eastern and southern railways did not appreciate its nickname, however, and devised many others. It was popular until the demise of steam locomotives. Union Pacific Northern No. 844 is the only U.S. steam locomotive never retired by a Class 1 railroad and still operates on special trains.					
4-8-8-4	4	8	8	4	Big Boy
A second set of driving wheels requires another number in the Whyte system. Twenty-five Union Pacific Big Boys were the largest locomotives built. The front set of eight driving wheels had to swivel to go around curves, making these locomotives part of a class of locomotives called *articulateds*.					
2-8-8-2	2	8	8	2	Y6b
Built by the Norfolk and Western, these articulated locomotives used the same steam twice, first for the rear set of driving wheels and again for the front. Such locomotives are called Mallets, after a French designer. The terms Mallet and articulated were interchangeable in the United States, though they described different technologies.					

This odd-looking locomotive, sometimes called a Camelback or a Mother Hubbard, was developed to allow the boiler's firebox, to the left of the cab, to be as wide as possible, a necessity for burning anthracite coal. The fireman actually stood outside between the tender and firebox to shovel that coal, while the engineer sweltered in the cab atop the boiler. Eventually, a suitable mechanical arrangement allowed the cab to be placed in its customary position even on locomotives that burned anthracite coal.

From 1909 to 1943 Southern Pacific purchased 256 articulated steam locomotives with the cab in front of the boiler. Improved visibility was certainly a benefit of these "cab-forwards," but the primary reason for the design was to keep crews from being asphyxiated by exhaust gases in the 38 miles of snowsheds that sheltered the railroad in the Sierra Mountains. The only other railroad to use the design was California's North Pacific Coast, which built a tiny cab-forward in 1901.

HOW STEAM LOCOMOTIVES WORK

Fuel is burned in the firebox of a boiler that turns water into steam. In a modern locomotive that steam is passed through superheater pipes exposed to the fire's hot exhaust gases, increasing the steam's temperature and the energy in it. Steam is then piped to a cylinder on each side of the locomotive. Its pressure pushes pistons back and forth in the cylinders. A main rod connects each piston to one driving wheel, converting reciprocating motion to rotary motion. Side rods transfer the motion to other driving wheels.

The valve gear—a second mechanical system—starts and stops steam flow into the cylinders at the correct times. A "Johnson bar" in the locomotive's cab controls the length of time steam is admitted to the cylinders (as well as the direction of the locomotive). For starting a train, steam is admitted for most of the cylinder's stroke to provide maximum force. As the train's speed increases, steam is admitted for a shorter time and natural expansion continues to power the cylinders. Without this function, a steam locomotive would use too much water and fuel to be useful.

Cylinder exhaust steam is directed up the same smokestack through which the fire's exhaust gases are expelled. If the locomotive works harder, more steam exits the stack, pulling more exhaust gases from the firebox, creating suction that pulls more air through the fire, making it burn hotter. This feedback system is critical for practical operation. The harder the locomotive works, the hotter its fire and the more steam it generates.

Water and fuel is carried in a tender behind the locomotive. A modern locomotive tender might carry tens of thousands of gallons of water and tens of tons of coal.

Steam locomotives run on anything that will burn. In the United States, early locomotives burned wood. Coal, with a much higher energy density, replaced wood and on some railroads oil replaced coal. Even the lowest quality, least expensive oil could be burned, and was easier to transport than coal and created less smoke.

Claude Wiatrowski photo

A fireman hoses down the boiler of a helper locomotive that has just assisted the regular passenger train up Cumbres Pass from Chama, New Mexico, in July 2001. The fireman is responsible for the mechanical well-being of machinery from the boiler up while the engineer cares for everything below.

Jack Delano, LC-USW361-646, Library of Congress, Prints and Photographs Division

Steam locomotive driving wheels have steel tires. Just like rubber tires, these need to be replaced when worn. A circular gas-fired burner heats a steel tire in the Santa Fe shops at Shopton, Iowa, in 1943. The tire expands and can be slipped over the driving wheel. As the tire cools, it contracts to secure itself to the wheel.

WESTERN MARYLAND RAILWAY

The Western Maryland Railway's history begins in 1852 with a charter to build west from Baltimore. Its early construction was marred by the Civil War. Jay Gould's 1902 purchase of the line began many improvements, including the construction of Port Covington, a major marine terminal at Baltimore. Coal-laden trains ran from Durbin, West Virginia, to Baltimore. Lines from Shippensburg, Pennsylvania, to Hagerstown and Cumberland in Maryland and back across the Pennsylvania border to Connellsville were important links in the Alphabet Route, an amalgam of smaller railways cooperating to compete with the large carriers.

Eventually, the Western Maryland came under the control of John D. Rockefeller, and in 1921 the Baltimore & Ohio bought Rockefeller's share. As larger railroads coalesced around it, the relatively small (about 1,200 miles) Western Maryland found a home in the Chessie System in 1973 and eventually CSX Transportation.

Voyageur Press collection

1852 – 1952
100th
Anniversary

MODERN TRANSPORTATION

FOR one hundred years, Western Maryland has successfully geared its service to the ever-changing requirements of industry and commerce . . . attaining a standard of transportation excellence which ranks it as one of the nation's outstanding freight carriers.

With a proud backward glance the Western Maryland reaches toward new vistas of achievement with enduring faith in America's future.

WESTERN MARYLAND Railway

G. V. "Jerry" Carson photo

Western Maryland locomotive No. 3579, an EMD GP35, stands ready at Hagerstown, Maryland, in 1969. Most photographers preferred this color scheme to Western Maryland black.

Voyageur Press collection

This is one side of a brochure titled *Western Maryland Railway in Miniature*. Extended, the flyer measures 2 1/2 inches x 3 1/2 feet. The brochure's cover is at left.

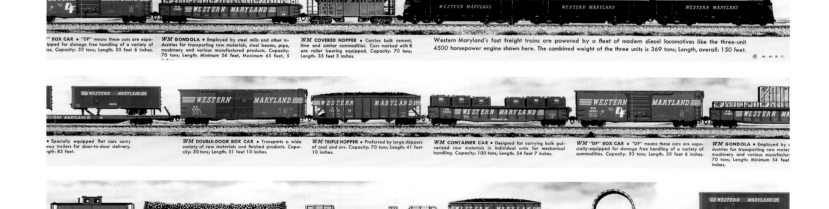

CHAPTER TWO

In 1952, the New York Central celebrated the 50th anniversary of the *20th Century Limited* with this recreation of famous passengers who rode the train in 1902. From left to right are actors representing William Jennings Bryan, Booth Tarkington, Theodore Roosevelt, Lillian Russell, J. P. Morgan, Mme. Schumann-Heink, and "Uncle Joe" Cannon.

www.archivesofadvertising.com

ROBBER BARON BOOM

After the Civil War, the railroad's effect on American life was nothing short of revolutionary. When animals and wind-driven watercraft provided painfully slow methods of transportation in a large nation, one's sphere of experience was limited to places within a day's travel. After the iron horse made its high-speed appearance, America became more unified and Americans less provincial. Newspapers, carried by train, delivered the news to small towns when it still *was* news. Instead of weeks or months, mail was delivered in days. The telegraph wires that followed the rails delivered information literally at the speed of light.

Pleasure travel, previously nonexistent, now gave rise to entire secondary industries providing lodging, meals, and travel information. Travel for business became efficient, as did the delivery of goods ordered from traveling salesmen. Sears, Roebuck and Company, would deliver merchandise from their catalog to any house near a railroad track in days. If you had no house, they would deliver a kit of parts so you could build one.

Perishable foods moved quickly and *fresh* foods, vegetables, and meats were added to Americans' diets, no matter where those Americans lived. Cost-effective transportation allowed large factories to produce goods that were sold anywhere near those steel threads across the continent. Former luxuries now became necessities. The impact on the day-to-day lives of Americans, especially on rural residents and especially on women, was immeasurable.

SONG OF THE ERA: A VERSE OF STANDARDIZATION

The maturation of the railroad system required standardization. Perhaps, the most critical standard was the distance between the rails, called the gauge. Railroads must have the same gauge if cars of one railroad are to travel over the tracks of another. Before the Civil War, there were several popular gauges in North America, including 6 feet (the Erie), 5 feet (in the South) and 4 feet 8 1/2 inches (in the North). Legislation enabling the construction of the first transcontinental railroad required that it be built with a gauge of 4 feet 8 1/2 inches—partly to freeze the South's 5-foot gauge railroads out of the picture. Following the war and the completion of the first railroad to the Pacific, almost all railroads standardized on the gauge of 4 feet 8 1/2 inches, now known simply as standard gauge.

If trains could now operate across multiple railroads, railroads would have to coordinate their schedules, so time itself was standardized when the railroads adopted a system of time zones (four across the continental United States).

Railroad cars from different railroads would have to be coupled together to run and brake together to stop. Eli Janney patented an automatic coupler in 1873 to save the fingers of brakemen who coupled those cars; George Westinghouse developed the automatic air brake in the 1860s to relieve those same brakemen from the task of running from car top to car top to manually set brakes.

Finally, because railroad cars could wander all across America, a system was devised by which a railroad using the car of another would pay a daily fee to the owning railroad.

SONG OF THE ERA: A CHORUS OF GROWTH

Given the innovations on America's railroads, it is no surprise that growth was substantial. Not quite 31,000 miles of track in 1860 became 93,000 in 1880. Ninety-three thousand miles became 193,000 miles by 1900. U.S. railroads reached their peak in 1916 with enough track, about 254,000 miles, to reach the moon. The peak rate of construction of new railroad track occurred in 1886 and 1887.

The railroads were keys to the development of natural resources, to the success of the Industrial Revolution, to the development of management techniques, to never-before-seen methods of finance, to the growth of agriculture, to the new practice of labor relations, and to the rise of urban centers. Yet, there was a dark side. The railroads dominated the American economy and the men who financed them dominated America. By 1906, two-thirds of railroad miles were in the hands of just seven syndicates controlled by a small number of entrepreneurs. Depending on one's vision of the past,

This cartoon illustrates the struggle between Jim Fisk and Cornelius Vanderbilt for control of the Erie Railroad. If Vanderbilt could add the Erie to his New York Central & Hudson River Railroad, he would have a monopoly on much of the traffic within and through New York State.

A steam locomotive of the Fremont & Elkhorn Valley Railroad poses in front of the grain elevator at Hooper, Nebraska. Farmers led the rebellion against the excesses of the robber baron railroads.

these entrepreneurs were either railroad barons or robber barons. The truth is that a few played each role and many both. Railroad barons raised money, built track, and operated railroads that benefited Americans. Robber barons manipulated stocks to enhance their personal wealth and power regardless of the negative effects on the railroad or its constituents. Greed sowed the seeds of government regulation, which eventually strangled the once all-powerful railroads almost to their demise.

"COME, YE SINNERS, POOR AND NEEDY"

"Come, Ye Sinners, Poor and Needy" was said to be Cornelius Vanderbilt's favorite hymn. Some certainly classify Vanderbilt as a sinner; others say he had little interest in the poor and needy. The life of this prototype railroad baron was more complex. Vanderbilt made his first fortune as a ferry boat operator and was thereafter called Commodore Vanderbilt. Starting at age 69 with the New York & Harlem Railroad, he became a collector of railroads. Through large investments and high performance standards, Vanderbilt's railroad collection became the great New York Central Railroad from New York City to Chicago, with eventual service to Boston, Cincinnati, and St. Louis.

Although Vanderbilt was certainly a wily manipulator of railroad securities when necessary, he at least created real value in profitable railroads. Others had no interest at all in running railroads, only in manipulating their stock price. Daniel Drew, Jay Gould, and Jim Fisk all fell into that latter category. They operated under the principle that good press releases and political contributions were more effective at fortune-building than running trains on time. The three participated in such fortune-building using Erie Railroad stock.

The Big Four—Charles Crocker, Mark Hopkins, Leland Stanford, and Collis Huntington—built the Central Pacific Railroad, the western end of the nation's first transcontinental railroad. Their political friends declared that the Sierra Nevada foothills began on the flatlands near Sacramento, California, thus qualifying for more federal construction aid.

The eastern end of the first transcontinental was the Union Pacific Railroad. After particularly scandalous affairs of graft and corruption during construction, the Union Pacific was purchased by Edward Harriman in 1897. Harriman already owned the Illinois Central and added the Southern Pacific (formerly the Central Pacific) to his empire in 1901. Like Vanderbilt, Harriman spent much effort creating efficient railroads that would be profitable and useful businesses.

James J. Hill built the Great Northern Railway, another transcontinental railroad. His railroad portfolio would also include the Burlington and Northern Pacific, and it was instrumental in the development of the Pacific Northwest.

The shenanigans of these and other robber barons have filled volumes that only accountants could love. Railroad magnate and banker J. Pierpont Morgan consolidated railroads into what would become the Southern Railway, instrumental in the development of the United States Southeast. Morgan's own words, "I owe the public nothing," summed up the era of the robber barons.

Morgan turned out to be disastrously wrong about owing the public nothing. He and his contemporary railroad entrepreneurs made a critical error while they were intoxicated with the wealth flowing from the cornucopia of the nation's railroad boom: at least four constituencies—investors, workers, customers, and voters—believed they *were* owed something.

This flower-covered locomotive is decorated to pull President Teddy Roosevelt's train in 1903 at Santa Cruz, California.

INVESTORS

The robber barons looked upon railroad treasuries as their own personal piggy-banks. Construction companies—owned by corporate insiders—would profit handsomely from a railroad's construction even while the railroad itself went bankrupt and its stockholders lost everything. (A never-completed tunnel west of Denver was to be a link in a transcontinental railroad. If any investor had stood at the tunnel mouth, as has the author of this book, they would have realized that the only way a train could get to the tunnel was to fly through the air!) Nevertheless, it took the collapse of the stock market in 1929 to bring about the establishment of the Securities and Exchange Commission in an effort to regulate abuses against public stockholders.

WORKERS

After struggling to coax a reluctant train over a snow-covered landscape for days, crews might get a couple hours of rest before being called for a return train. Refusal meant loss of their jobs. Railroad accidents were frequent as dog-tired workers stumbled over heavy equipment bereft of the most

basic safety appliances. A slip meant death and a token payment to a railroader's widow. If there was money enough for the grandest mansions, surely there was money enough to pay for train brakes.

Railroads were the stage for the world's first industrial unions. Organizations such as the Brotherhood of Locomotive Engineers began as insurance pools because railroaders could not otherwise obtain insurance in their dangerous occupations. It was inevitable that such unions would attempt to improve working conditions and wages.

The first railroad strike in the United States occurred in 1877. At the end of the nineteenth century, federal troops took the side of the railroad's owners. At the beginning of the twentieth, government regulations increasingly protected the rights of railroad workers.

CUSTOMERS

Did railroads exist only to maximize owners' profits, or did they have an obligation to the public good? If railroads had not become indispensable to America, this question would never have been voiced. The first serious insurrection against railroads came not from wild-eyed radicals but from Midwestern farmers. With railroads free to collude to fix rates and to discriminate against individual shippers who happened to rub them the wrong way, it is no wonder that huge shipments of grain became the catalyst for change. The vehicle for that change was the National Grange, an association of farmers. Grangers were the first to lobby for federal legislation to control railroad freight rates.

Because of the railroads' political power, the first federal attempt at regulation—the creation of the Interstate Commerce Commission in 1887—was a dismal failure. The ICC was a toothless tiger until Congress started expanding its powers in 1903. Eventually, the ICC would wield much greater regulatory power against railroads than ever imposed on any other industry.

VOTERS

By the end of the Civil War, Jefferson's vision of a rural nation of small farms and businesses was

World War I saw the nationalization of U.S. railroads. Little promotional material appeared partly because of the nationalization and partly because U.S. involvement in the war was much shorter than in World War II.

quickly disappearing. Americans reveled in stories of railroad entrepreneurs whose hard work, cunning, and ability propelled them from obscurity to wealth and power. At the same time, voters were increasingly alarmed by these same men who had more power than their elected government. With a tradition of freedom from government intervention, how was America to deal with entrepreneurs who exercised unlimited power? Could America remain a democracy under such circumstances? It was Vanderbilt himself who said, "Law! What do I care about law? Hain't I got the power?" This arrogant attitude eventually gave rise to anti-trust laws limiting anticompetitive behaviors of big business, and laws taxing the income of the wealthiest Americans.

WORLD WAR I

The performance of the nation's railroads was less than stellar during World War I. The United States entered the war in April 1917 and legislation to nationalize the railroads was passed on December 26 after a little more than eight months of unacceptable performance. U.S. railroads were brought almost to a standstill by congestion that some blamed on the railroads' incompetence and others attributed to factors beyond the railroads' control. Whatever the reason, the United States Railroad Administration would temporarily operate the railroads until hostilities ended. Germany surrendered on November 11, 1918, but the railroads were not returned to their owners for another 16 months, and then not until the Interstate Commerce Commission was strengthened in anticipation of their return. Railroads were so disliked and distrusted that consideration was given to keeping them in the government's hands.

A GLIMPSE OF THE FUTURE

As the twentieth century dawned, growth of the railroad network slowed. It had been that breathtaking growth that had motivated the robber barons. Even before James J. Hill—the last of his kind—died in 1916, swashbuckling entrepreneurs were being replaced by professional managers. The Colorado Midland Railway closed in 1917, and in 1921, unfamiliar scenes of this major railroad being dismantled were a precursor to events that would become all too familiar. The failure of the Colorado Midland was often blamed on the nationalization of the railroads in World War I. While this was the immediate cause, the Colorado Midland would have eventually fallen, as did many other railroads, to technological change and regulatory excess.

CANADA IN THE ROBBER BARON AGE

At first glance, Canada's railroad history may look similar to that of the United States but it is actually quite different. Great distances and few residents meant that the Canadian government either built or financed many of its railroads and thus exerted more control over them than in the United States. Although the United States eventually came to view its railroads as quasi-public works and control them by regulation, Canada had this view of railways from the start and believed in using them to affect social policy.

In 1871, British Columbia was induced to become part of Canada on the promise of a Pacific railway—to be constructed in 10 years—that would connect this far-west province with Canada's eastern provinces. However, the Canadian government found itself pressed for funds; it had also committed to build another railroad, the Intercolonial Railway, binding its eastern provinces together. In 1880, just one year before the promised completion date of the Pacific railway, the Canadian government struck a deal with private entrepreneurs to construct that line—to be called the Canadian Pacific Railway. The agreement specified that the Pacific railroad be completed by 1891, 10 years past the date originally promised to British Columbia. The privately financed Canadian Pacific was completed in 1885 and began service in 1886—five years ahead of its second promised completion date.

In the 1890s, a small local railroad—the Canadian Northern—began to expand both east and west from its origins in western Manitoba, which had become a province in 1870. Both the Grand Trunk Railway and the Canadian Northern had ambitions to become Canada's second transcontinental railroad. After unsuccessfully trying to broker a partnership between these two railroads, the Canadian government decided to back the transcontinental aspirations of the Grand Trunk by constructing the eastern portion of the new line as far as Winnipeg. The government-built portion was to be called the National Transcontinental Railway. The Grand Trunk would build the western portion, called the Grand Trunk Pacific, from Winnipeg to a new Pacific port named Prince Rupert. Both railroads were constructed but the Grand Trunk had exhausted its funds and was unable to lease and operate the National Transcontinental as it had promised. As a result, Canadian Government Railways—successor to the Intercolonial Railway—was given the task of operating the National Transcontinental.

Meanwhile, the Canadian Northern also completed its Pacific extension to Vancouver. After the start of World War I in 1914, the Canadian Northern went bankrupt and was absorbed by the federal government. In 1918, all railroads of the Canadian government were consolidated under the name Canadian National Railways.

By the end of 1914, Canada's railroad network had mushroomed to 30,000 miles. By way of comparison, U.S. railway mileage reached its peak of 254,000 miles in 1916.

BURLINGTON ROUTE

The Burlington's yard in Keokuk, Iowa, bustled with activity in 1907. Milk cans are unloaded from the baggage section of the passenger train's combine and transferred to horse-drawn wagons. Beyond the passenger train is a carload of Falstaff beer. A sternwheeler is tied up on the bank of the mighty Mississippi River, no doubt engaged in intermodal transport. At far left, a switch engine waits for its next call to action.

In 1850, the Aurora Branch Railroad was opened from Aurora, Illinois, to a connection with the Galena & Chicago Union Railroad. With its name changed to the Chicago, Burlington & Quincy Railroad, its tracks would bridge both the Mississippi and the Missouri. Its trains would call on Kansas City, Denver, and St. Paul; traverse Wyoming's coal fields to reach Billings, Montana; and chug through South Dakota's Black Hills on narrow gauge tracks.

In 1901, James J. Hill, who had had built the Great Northern and acquired the Northern Pacific, added the Burlington to his empire. The Burlington gained access to Dallas and connections to the Gulf of Mexico after it purchased the Colorado & Southern in 1908. By 1934, the Moffat Tunnel and the Dotsero cutoff gave the Burlington a direct connection to the Pacific from Denver.

The Great Northern, Northern Pacific, and Burlington were merged in 1970 to form the Burlington Northern. The Burlington Northern and the Santa Fe Railway would become BNSF Railway.

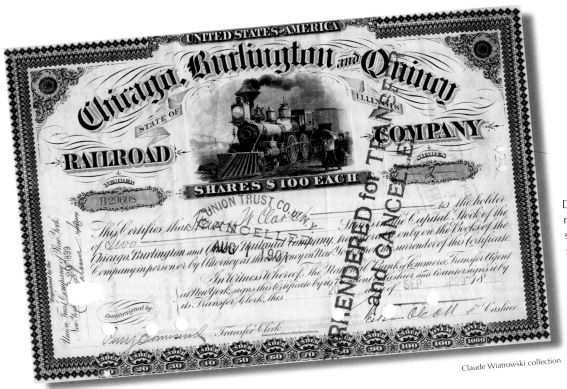

During the last decades of the nineteenth century, there was little securities regulation. Stockholders small and large lost fortunes in railroad bankruptcies while insiders amassed great wealth through devious means.

Claude Wiatrowski collection

Though the Burlington was a pioneer of diesel streamliners, it had streamlined steam locomotives as well. No. 4000, the *Aeolus*, awaits its next assignment in West Burlington, Iowa, on August 8, 1937.

In 1925, six daily passenger trains traveled along the Burlington's Mississippi River Scenic Line between Savanna, Illinois, and Minneapolis. Most were passing through Savanna, either starting or ending their journeys in Chicago. This 16-page tour guide describes the river's 1539 discovery by explorer De Soto and the sights to be seen along the 300 miles of river paralleled by the railroad.

Voyageur Press collection

General Electric U28B near Pueblo, Colorado, leads a Burlington freight train in July 1971.

G. V. "Jerry" Carson photo

CHICAGO & NORTH WESTERN

In 1859, the Chicago, St. Paul & Fond du Lac was reorganized as the Chicago & North Western Railroad. In 1865, C&NW merged with the Galena & Chicago Union, which had operated Chicago's first train in 1848. In 1866, C&NW leased—and later bought—the Chicago & Milwaukee Railway running between its namesake cities. C&NW now included lines running north, northwest, and west from Chicago.

By 1884, C&NW trains ran to Council Bluffs, Nebraska, and continued to the Pacific via the Union Pacific and Southern Pacific. Westward progress was halted in Wyoming by an agreement with the Union Pacific, which faced being bypassed completely by this C&NW line. The North Western continued expansion in the Midwest.

The C&NW had been the Union Pacific's most important eastern connection at Omaha, and in 1995, the Union Pacific merged the C&NW into itself.

Voyageur Press collection

Above: The cover of this booklet lists the diverse destinations of the Chicago & North Western in 1908. The booklet is mostly blank paper with a light-blue grid. Several pages of this copy include penciled entries of names and amounts. There is also a list of Chicago & North Western agencies in cities served by the railroad and the agent's names, and a locomotive speed schedule converts the elapsed time between mileposts and the speed at which the train is traveling. The table starts at 12 miles per hour and ends at 120 miles per hour.

Left: Chicago & Galena Union's *Pioneer* has just arrived with a load of agricultural products to be transferred to a ship waiting on Lake Michigan. *Pioneer*, the first locomotive to operate in Chicago, is displayed at the Chicago Historical Society's museum. The Chicago & Galena Union was a predecessor of the Chicago & North Western.

Voyageur Press collection

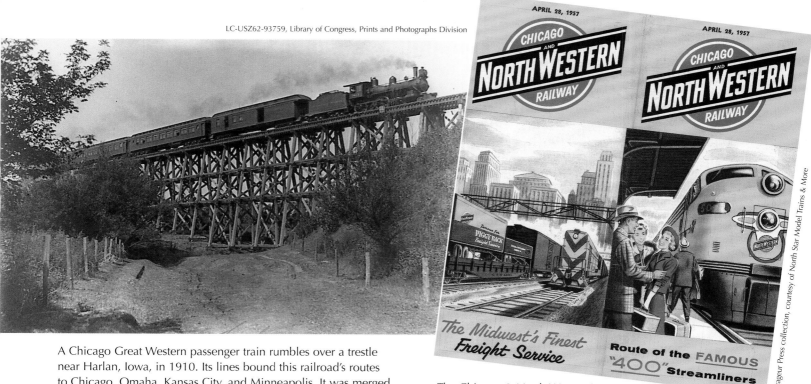

A Chicago Great Western passenger train rumbles over a trestle near Harlan, Iowa, in 1910. Its lines bound this railroad's routes to Chicago, Omaha, Kansas City, and Minneapolis. It was merged into the Chicago & North Western in 1968.

The Chicago & North Western's 1957 timetable featured both diesel-powered freight and passenger trains on its cover. Listings included not only passenger trains but freight-only and mixed (freight and passenger) train schedules.

In December 1942 at least 19 steam locomotives are visible in a Chicago & North Western yard in Chicago. At left are four switch engines ready for assignments in front of a line of 11 road locomotives waiting their turn. These counts do not include locomotives obscured or identified by wisps of steam on this frosty morning.

ELECTRIC LOCOMOTIVES

Ernst von Siemens demonstrated the first electric locomotive at the Berlin Industrial Exposition of 1879. The history of electric locomotives is the history of the individual railroads that used them.

In 1895, the Baltimore & Ohio Railroad electrified 3 miles of its main line through the Howard Street Tunnel that served its namesake city of Baltimore. The city had granted its approval for the tunnel on the condition that smoke from trains would not annoy its citizens.

Smoke was also the reason for the Great Northern's 1909 electrification of its Cascade Tunnel in the state of Washington. As traffic grew on this transcontinental railroad, hot, poisonous locomotive exhaust gases left engine crews unconscious; electric locomotives produced no exhaust at all.

The only other major main-line electrification in western North America was that of the Milwaukee Road. In 1916, 440 miles were electrified in Montana and Idaho. Next, 207 miles followed in Washington State in 1920. The Milwaukee's electrification was atypical for two reasons. First, it powered its trains with direct current and at a relatively low 3,000 volts, somewhat unusual for a long mountainous railroad. Second, it purchased 12 of 20 locomotives built for Russia as World War II was ending. Never delivered as the Cold War developed, these were the most powerful electric locomotives built.

Eastern railroads also had problems with tunnels and mountains. The Norfolk and Western electrified 40 miles of its coal-hauling line over the Appalachian Mountains in 1915. The Virginian Railway was built primarily to haul

G. V. "Jerry" Carson photo

The bright new "McGinnis" color scheme couldn't help the New Haven survive, though it did sell a lot of Lionel toy locomotives with the same—though cleaner—colors.

coal over those same mountains, and it electrified 134 miles of track by 1926. Eventually, the Great Northern, Milwaukee, Norfolk and Western, and Virginian electrifications succumbed to the onslaught of diesel locomotives.

The extraordinary costs of erecting and maintaining the wires of electrification are exceeded by economies of operation only where there is a great deal of traffic to haul. On this criterion, the Pennsylvania Railroad placed 2,800 miles of track under wire, including 800 miles of main-line routes starting in 1928. The Depression simplified the task of erecting the wires as fewer trains interfered with construction. Everything needed—from wages to copper wire—was less expensive. By 1937, electric trains roamed the Pennsylvania from New York City to Washington, D.C., and as far west as Harrisburg, Pennsylvania.

In an era when most electric locomotives looked like shoeboxes on wheels, the Pennsylvania's model GG1 was astonishing for its beautiful streamlining. The first GG1 was delivered in 1934 and 139 units would be built. The Pennsylvania's electrification survives to this day and electrically powered trains race between New York City and Washington on Amtrak's most traveled route.

COMMUTER RAILROADS

In 1897 and 1898, electrical engineer F. J. Sprague converted Chicago's South Side elevated trains from steam to electric propulsion. Electric trains are especially suited to

"SEE WASHINGTON FIRST." 2 ELECTRIC ENGINES JUST EMERGING FROM THE CASCADE TUNNEL ON THE GREAT NORTHERN RAILWAY

Voyageur Press collection

Perhaps, the most famous and beautiful American electric locomotives were the Pennsylvania Railroad's GG1s, this one shown in 1969. One hundred thirty-nine were built during the 1930s and some operated until 1983.

Chicago, North Shore & Milwaukee "steeple-cab" locomotive 452 sits alone in Highwood, Illinois, in 1960. The North Shore was famous for its high-speed interurban service from Chicago to Milwaukee, although freights trundled along behind locomotives like this.

the frequent stops and starts of commuter railroads. They can start a heavy train quickly but also pull it at high speed—a perfect combination for getting commuters to and from work expeditiously. Sprague went one step further: he put electric motors under *every* car in a commuter train. No matter how long the train, it could accelerate at the same rate and travel at the same top speed. Sprague had invented the technology that made interurban railroads a roaring success.

HOW ELECTRIC LOCOMOTIVES WORK

Power for the electric locomotive's motors comes from a generator in a stationary power plant. A huge stationary power plant can be made more efficient and have fewer emissions than a small mobile diesel engine.

Power from the stationary power plant can be transmitted to the moving locomotive in two ways. Both use the two steel rails upon which the train operates as one electrical conductor. A third rail is the second electrical conductor for urban railways such as subways and elevated lines where people and animals are unlikely to touch—and be electrocuted by—this third rail. Where accidental contact is a concern, an overhead wire, the *catenary*, is the second electrical conductor.

The motors of an electric locomotive generate electricity when coasting downhill. This electrical energy can be sent back into the overhead wire, thus slowing the locomotive's descent. These *regenerative brakes* can actually power another locomotive that is going uphill somewhere else on the railroad!

The Milwaukee Road and the South Shore Railroad both acquired locomotives built for Russia when the U.S. government prohibited export to the Soviet Union. These huge locomotives were built to the Russian standard gauge of 5 feet and had to be re-gauged to run on U. S. standard gauge track. The South Shore was an interurban railroad—it must have been quite a sight to see one of these monsters creeping down a street!

The Illinois Terminal was an interurban with substantial freight service. This unusual electric freight locomotive waits for a train at Springfield, Illinois, in 1960.

ROBBER BARON BOOM   49

FAIR OF THE IRON HORSE

To celebrate the centenary of its founding in 1927, the Baltimore & Ohio held the Fair of the Iron Horse. Created on 1,000 acres at Halethorpe, a suburb of Baltimore, the fair was on the B&O's main line to Washington. Trains—as well as automobiles—carried revelers to the fair, which would entertain 1.3 million visitors in a scant 23 days!

Exhibits were plentiful but the fair's pageant, with the uninspiring name of the Pageant of Inland Transportation, was its roaring success. A grandstand faced an 800-foot-long stage—actually three traffic lanes. One was a railroad track upon which full-sized trains and railroad-wheeled floats performed. Another carried motor vehicles, while a third was reserved for pedestrians and horsedrawn vehicles. Two bands played for the pageant's 67 scenes, while actor Charles Coburn narrated, a feat possible only because a high-tech, public-address system made him audible to 12,000 people. No one had ever seen railroad locomotives perform as part of a drama before and the addition of music proved a stroke of genius. Planned for only four days a week, the pageant was rescheduled as a daily event after an incredible response to its first performance. When a third week was later added to the fair, the pageant was performed twice daily but still could not accommodate the crowds.

Staging full-size trains required a mile-long loop of track and 2 miles of sidings and service tracks. In an era when locomotives still excited the masses, the fair over-flowed with iron dragons. The pageant's climax saw an enormous modern steam locomotive, the *President Washington*, haul the six-car *Capitol Limited* on stage. The crowd went wild.

This was the celebration of the very first public railway in the North America so it was not surprising that other railroads sent locomotives to perform, including the New York Central's *DeWitt Clinton* and the Pennsylvania's *John Bull*, both built in 1831. The longest journey of all was that of the Great Western Railway's *King George V*, which traveled across the Atlantic Ocean for the celebration.

Many of the B&O's rare old locomotives that participated in its 1927 centennial celebration later formed the basis for the Baltimore & Ohio Railroad Museum. That museum, located in Baltimore, planned on celebrating with its own fair in 2003. The museum's collection was housed in its centerpiece building, an 1884 covered roundhouse complete with interior turntable. But at the height of a February 2003 storm, snow and wind combined to bring down a large portion of the building, which collapsed onto the historic railroad locomotives and cars it sheltered. The resources required for the monumental effort to restore both the roundhouse and the artifacts on which it collapsed forced the museum to cancel its celebration. The roundhouse was reopened in November 2004 and work continues on restoring damaged railroad equipment.

NEWEST of Baltimore and Ohio locomotives are the Presidents—4-6-2, which made their appearance in this centenary year, 1927. These engines, with their 80-inch drivers, are distinguished not alone by their rare beauty but also by their unusual power. Weighing 525,000 pounds, they are capable of hauling heavy express-passenger trains at upwards of ninety miles an hour. In their handsome liveries of green and gold they present a striking appearance.

Visitors to the Fair of the Iron Horse in 1927 could purchase a packet of 15 postcards for 15 cents. The cards chronicled the history of Baltimore & Ohio locomotive technology from the tiny 1829 *Tom Thumb*, the first demonstration of steam locomotion on the B&O, to the magnificent *President Washington*, a modern 90-mile-per-hour passenger locomotive in a striking green and gold livery.

THE FAIR
of the
IRON HORSE

BALTIMORE & OHIO R.R. ATLANTIC

The
CENTENARY
PAGEANT
of the
BALTIMORE & OHIO
RAILROAD
★ ★ ★

Additional copy
of this Brochure
10c
Centenary Director
The Baltimore & Ohio Railroad
Baltimore, Maryland

The pageant's program cover features a scene that shows how stagecoach construction influenced early railroad passenger cars.

An aerial photo of the Fair of the Iron Horse shows its immense size. An Indian village is at the lower right. Above the village are several display tracks. The one closest to the building supports six tiny antique locomotives. At upper right are four tracks of the Baltimore & Ohio's main line between Washington, D.C., and Baltimore. Below the main line is a queue of 10 large steam locomotives "backstage" before entering the pageant area. A rail-mounted float parades past the pageant grandstand at upper left.

THE AIRMEN SAW THE FAIR OF THE IRON HORSE
A view, from an aeroplane, of Halethorpe Field, showing the buildings, reviewing stands and grounds of the Centenary Exhibition and Pageant of the Baltimore & Ohio Railroad. The Teepees of the Indian Village may be seen at the lower right-hand corner of the picture, the Coffee House at the left.

HARVEY'S RESTAURANTS

After Fred Harvey's 1850 arrival from London and a less-than-successful start in the restaurant business, he became a Burlington freight agent in 1876. While working there, he operated three restaurants along the Kansas Pacific Railway. His proposal to operate restaurants along the Burlington was rejected but they suggested he present a similar proposal to the Santa Fe Railway, which was interested and placed Harvey in charge of its Topeka eating house. The restaurant began serving 5,000 meals daily.

Soon, Harvey was operating a chain of restaurants, one every 100 miles, along the Santa Fe's track west of Kansas City. The Santa Fe operated dining cars east of Kansas City, but trains heading west stopped at eating houses for meals. Harvey's formula was hard to beat. The ambiance of the establishments was above average and the food was first-rate. Service was efficient and became the province of attractive, young unmarried women. Harvey even coordinated menus so travelers would not be forced to eat the same dish twice on an extended journey.

The Santa Fe gave Harvey an exclusive contract to operate restaurants, lunch counters and even hotels along its route. Santa Fe advertising boasted of "Meals by Fred

H-1936 NAVAHO BLANKET WEAVERS, FRED HARVEY INDIAN BUILDING, ALBUQUERQUE, NEW MEXICO

William J. Lock collection

Fred Harvey's tours did much to promote local artists and familiarize Americans with Native American and Spanish cultures.

Harvey." Harvey kept all the profit and the Santa Fe agreed to haul his employees, supplies, and equipment for free. The railroad also supplied coal, water, and ice at no charge.

Reservations were taken on the moving passenger cars and wired ahead at the station stop just before arrival at the eatery. The wailing of the train's whistle warned that the diners were close, and the first course was on the tables before a single passenger walked in the door! Full meals were served and eaten in 25 minutes. With a string of Harvey hotels in the Southwest, travelers were encouraged to break their trips and spend a few days exploring the nearby natural and cultural wonders.

Harvey made an accidental discovery in 1883 that would change the American West forever. After firing a group of waiters at Raton, New Mexico, for fighting, he hired young women to replace them. You can imagine the response of mostly male passengers in a land where most women were "ladies of the evening." So successful was this experiment that Harvey began recruiting young women to work at his establishments.

Wanted: Young women 18–30 years of age, good character, attractive and intelligent, as waitresses in Harvey Eating Houses. Good wages with room and board furnished.

Here was the chance of a lifetime: experience the adventure of the American West, make great money, and get married. Get married? Harvey Girls had to sign a contract that required them to remain single for one year. It must have been a failure since Fred

"THIRTY MINUTES FOR SUPPER" BY WALTER RICHARDS

Voyageur Press collection

This highly romanticized illustration graced the cover of the 1952 Fred Harvey menu at the Chicago Union Station Building Restaurant. It's doubtful that passengers of the era portrayed were the happy travelers shown here, even when confronted by a 30-minute respite at a Harvey House. The gong player was historically accurate, as every restaurant near a depot was apt to send a gong virtuoso to attract passengers.

himself would congratulate any girl who was still single after six months! Harvey Girls were an important part of civilizing the American frontier.

Eventually, dining cars began operating west of Kansas City and faster trains made "breaking the trip" with a hotel stay less important. It seemed that the Harvey operations were doomed. Fred responded with an innovative plan to build elegant destination hotels. Starting in 1900, he built the La Fonda in Santa Fe and El Tovar at the Grand Canyon. These hotels, and others, still shelter travelers today! Other former Harvey buildings now harbor museums, art galleries, bus stations, railroad offices, and storage buildings. Coming full circle, still others are used as new hotels and new restaurants.

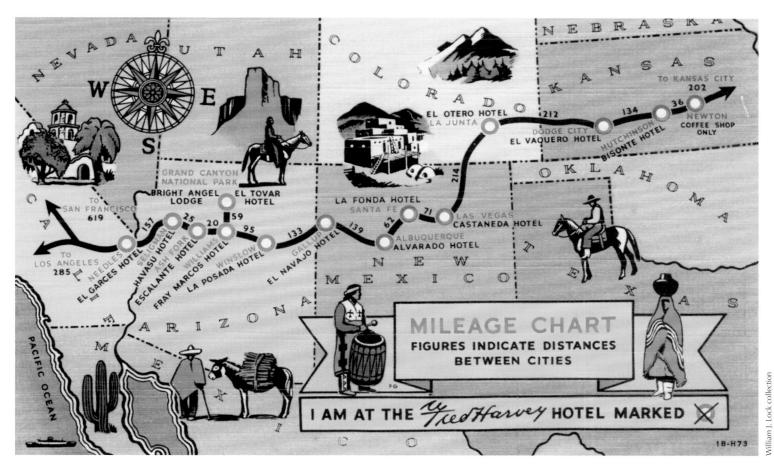

Harvey Girls pose in front of the Chanute, Kansas, Harvey House about 1900. The substantial building contained the Santa Fe's depot as well as the eating house.

HEROES OF THE IRON TRAIL

In an age when few traveled outside the county in which they were born, the most glamorous jobs belonged to train crews. Here were men (and almost all were men) who traveled a hundred miles every day!

Working for the railroad was a lifelong occupation. You started in a lowly job and spent your entire life working up the ladder. Most executives, including railroad presidents, started their careers this way. Railroading jobs frequently exceeded one lifetime, for fathers passed the calling to their sons, who often passed it to their sons.

Engineers were the idol of every young boy. When most people traveled a few miles an hour by horse, whistle-blowing, rod-clanking, steam-spouting locomotives roared through town at 10 times that speed—and the engineer controlled it all. Sometimes, *hoggers*—an old slang term for steam locomotive is "hog"—even stepped down onto the ground at small towns to mysteriously oil the machinery and clank away at it with a small hammer, listening for the telltale sound of a hidden crack.

Firemen were a necessary step away from becoming engineers. The *tallow pot*—named for the archaic task of lubricating a locomotive with tallow—was responsible for the proper operation of the boiler as it made steam. He shoveled more than 2 tons of coal an hour into its firebox—before federal law mandated mechanical stokers on all large locomotives—and made sure that there was enough water in the boiler to keep it from exploding. Skilled and experienced, he had to anticipate the load placed on the locomotive to ensure its efficient operation.

Conductors were the captains of the train. The conductor, not the engineer, had the final word. Ideally, conductor and engineer consulted with each other about important issues such as the meaning of a train order. On passenger trains, conductors also collected tickets and hollered "All aboard!" as the train departed the depot. On freight trains, they spent their time at a desk in the caboose tending to the waybills, the paperwork for the shipments in their charge.

Brakemen had the most difficult and dangerous job on the train. Before automatic train brakes, the brakeman set the brakes individually on each car. They walked across the top of each rocking car along a slim wooden strip and jumped from car to car, in the dark, with ice covering

Fathers often passed their railroad calling to their sons, who often passed it to their sons. Just such a family is pictured outside the Milwaukee Road roundhouse in Minneapolis in the 1930s. From left to right are Al, Phillip, and Tom Bowler.

Courtesy Karen Bowler Dougherty

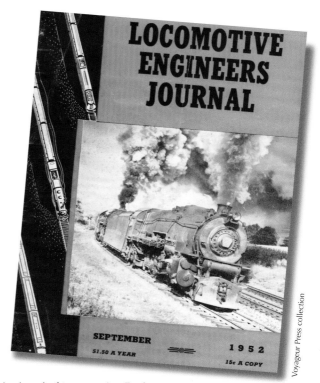

The Brotherhood of Locomotive Engineers published this journal. The content of this issue included everything from wedding anniversaries and obituaries to railroad history, and from technical issues and union administration to railroad fiction.

Voyageur Press collection

A locomotive engineer oils around the running gear of his locomotive. He was responsible for its mechanical care, for its safe and efficient operation, and for the safety of everyone on his train and other trains it might meet. In an era where most employees were closely supervised, train crews were on their own. It is no wonder that railroads were run like military units and many early railroad managers were former military officers.

AS IMPORTANT AS THE "President"

everything, in the howling wind. Before automatic couplers, a brakeman also stood between cars and guided the coupling mechanism with his hand. If things went wrong, a few fingers might be left behind.

CASEY JONES

Surely the most famous railroad hero is Casey Jones. By age 15, he was an apprentice telegrapher for the Mobile & Ohio and was a fireman on the same road at age 18. Just short of his 24th birthday, he signed on as a fireman with the Illinois Central and passed the exam to become an engineer at the ripe old age of 26. His career as an engineer was launched running fast freights between Jackson, Tennessee, and Water Valley, Mississippi.

Casey was offered the job of running the most prestigious of the Illinois Central's passenger trains: Nos. 1 and 2, the Chicago–New Orleans *Cannonball*. Casey moved to Memphis on January 1, 1900, when he was assigned to the Memphis–Canton segment of the run, and began what would be a short career on the IC's crack passenger trains.

Then on April 30, 1900 at 12:50 a.m., running 95 minutes behind schedule, Casey and Simm Webb, his fireman, eased locomotive 382 out of Memphis southbound with six cars of train No. 1 in tow. Casey's orders were to make up all 95 minutes by the time he reached Canton, 190 miles to the south. Two southbound trains were ahead of Casey's train and three trains were headed north, including north-

A fireman releases thousands of gallons of water into the tender of his locomotive. He also loaded coal or fuel oil into the tender and was responsible for the operation and well-being of the boiler, a complex task. Occasional proposals still surface for designing and building new steam locomotives with the boiler controlled by microcomputers instead of a fireman.

The June 1932 issue of *Railroad Magazine* honors the conductor. They had the final authority in the operation of the train. When a train stopped unexpectedly, the conductor or a brakeman had to walk back to protect the rear of the train. Before radio communications, there was no other way to warn following trains.

In May 1980, a retired conductor in his original uniform welcomed Manitou & Pikes Peak passengers aboard a rare steam train excursion.

9407. Y. M. C. A. Building, Colorada Springs, Colo.

Voyageur Press collection

PENNSYLVANIA RAILROAD
YOUNG MEN'S CHRISTIAN ASSOCIATION
OF GREATER NEW YORK

RICHARD CARROLL

is a member of this Association

PENNSYLVANIA STATION
NEW YORK

SUNNYSIDE YARDS
NEW YORK

Train crews could be called on a moment's notice, and they could be away from home for days at a time, staying in a fleabag boarding house or just bunking down in some straw in a boxcar. In this environment, alcoholism, prostitution, and other vices flourished, with consequent disruptions to family life and to productivity of the employees. William H. Vanderbilt, the Commodore's son, established the first Railroad Young Men's Christian Association (YMCA) facilities to provide a wholesome alternative for men away from home.

bound No. 2. Most of them would pass each other at Vaughan, Mississippi, which had few sidetracks, but a delay in the complex switching procedure left a caboose and four freight cars on the main line when Casey's train was due. A flagman walked back to warn Casey with a lantern. He also fastened a torpedo, an explosive signaling device, to the track. Casey roared by the flagman at 70 miles per hour and hit the torpedo. At the sound of the explosion, his train began to slow. Its speed was estimated at 50 miles per hour when Simm jumped—and lived to tell about it. Casey stayed with his train, still attempting to stop it when it slammed into the caboose. Legend has it that Casey's body was found in the wreck with one hand gripping the whistle cord and the other on the brake.

Why has Casey become an icon of the heroic railroad worker? Wallace Saunders, an African-American roundhouse worker at Canton, had known Casey and cared for his locomotive. Soon after the crash, he composed the words and lyrics to a song honoring Casey as the "brave engineer" (many felt that by staying with the train and trying to stop it he had helped save his passengers' lives). The song was transcribed by another IC engineer and adapted by others. In 1903, T. Lawrence Siebert further adapted the lyrics and Eddie Newton the music in a version that is still sung today and which has been recorded by dozens of musicians. Millions of copies have been sold, helping to enshrine Casey in railroad history.

KATE SHELLEY

A great storm bore down on the valley of the Des Moines

J. E. France photo, Bruce Gurner collection, Water Valley Casey Jones Railroad Museum

Casey Jones poses in the cab of his favorite locomotive, Illinois Central No. 638.

River on July 6, 1881. Usually tranquil Honey Creek overflowed its banks as it roared past the home where Kate Shelley and her mother remained awake. The Shelleys were no strangers to danger—Kate's father, a railroad worker, had been killed just three years prior.

A lone Chicago & North Western locomotive ventured out into the storm from Moingona, Iowa, with four men anxiously peering out to inspect the track for washouts—an eastbound passenger train was due shortly. The locomotive crawled across the huge wooden trestle straddling the Des Moines River without incident, but as it crossed little Honey Creek Bridge, the timbers gave way. The Shelleys knew exactly what had happened when they heard the crash. Fifteen-year old Kate could not be restrained from venturing out into the storm to try to help the men on the locomotive.

She found that only two of the four men had survived and were clinging to trees in the flood. Unable to help them, she struggled westward to warn the oncoming passenger train, which was due to stop at Moingona before continuing east over Honey Creek. With only a makeshift lantern, she crawled across the damaged bridge in the rain and the dark and arrived at Moingona, to the surprise of the railroad personnel. The signal was set to stop the passenger train arriving from the west and a locomotive whistle called everyone in town to help rescue the two men at Honey Creek.

As the sun rose on the days following Kate's heroic deed, newspapermen showed up at her door and accounts of her bravery appeared all over the country.

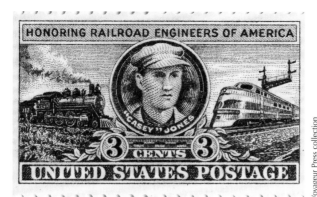

In 1950 the U.S. Postal service issued a stamp commemorating Casey Jones.

Kate Shelley crawls across a stormy Des Moines River bridge to save a passenger train from almost certain destruction. Women did appear in early railroad history but it is only recently that the number of women in railroading, especially on train crews, has begun to slowly increase. The International Society for the Preservation of Women in Railroading collects and distributes information about women in railroading.

Of the many engineers who died heroically in train wrecks, Casey Jones stands out perhaps because of the song written about him by an African-American engine wiper, Wallace Saunders, who was Casey's friend. It was performed and modified by others. When finally published in 1902, the sheet music listed T. Lawrence Seibert as the lyricist and Eddie Newton as the composer. No mention is made of Saunders. Millions of copies were sold and Casey became an American folk hero.

Sim Webb, Casey's fireman, and his widow, Janie Brady Jones, were guests of the St. Francois Railroad Club in October 1949 when this photo was taken at Bonne Terre, Missouri. The whistle is from Casey's locomotive and a model of that locomotive sits next to the whistle.

LEHIGH VALLEY

In 1855, the Lehigh Valley Railroad completed a line from Mauch Chunk's coal mines to the Delaware River at Easton, Pennsylvania. Trains connected with the Erie Railroad at Waverly, New York. After the Lehigh Valley paid to lay a third rail in 1876, its standard gauge cars could travel to Buffalo on the wide gauge Erie.

As eastern connections were devoured by competitors, the Lehigh Valley was forced to build through New Jersey, arriving in Perth Amboy in 1875 and in Jersey City, across from New York City, in 1899. Under a new name, Lehigh Valley Rail Way, the road completed its own iron artery to Buffalo in 1892.

But highways captured business, oil replaced coal, and a huge explosion devastated Jersey City. The government forced the Lehigh Valley to divest its Great Lakes shipping line and its coal mines. The Great Depression struck and after bobbing to the surface in World War II, the LV again began to sink. In an act both prophetic and practical, the New York State Thru Way usurped the Lehigh Valley's right-of-way to Buffalo. In 1976, the LV was added to the stew that became Conrail.

Courtesy Milton A. Davis collection

This Lehigh Valley Ten-wheeler is a "camelback" locomotive with its cab astride the boiler, allowing the firebox to extend the full width of the locomotive for efficient combustion of the anthracite or hard coal that it burned. The fireman had the job of shoveling coal under the miniscule sheltering roof between locomotive and tender.

White was not the best choice for a locomotive, but these Lehigh Valley locomotives are clean and bright near Waverly, New York, in 1972.

Three Lehigh Valley diesel locomotives display three different color schemes.

LOUISVILLE & NASHVILLE

The Louisville & Nashville Railroad sprang from the concern of Louisville merchants that their city would be bypassed. Its main line was completed in 1859 and the Civil War struck the railroad with all its fury. Kentucky was a northern state, while Tennessee's allegiance was to the South—the L&N's main line connected the two.

Recovering from the war, L&N arrived at the gulf ports of Mobile and Pensacola. St. Louis and Cincinnati were added to the timetable, and the line to Atlanta included a spiral of track that crossed over itself called the Hiwassee Loop. Under J. P. Morgan's direction, the Atlantic Coast Line obtained control of L&N, which, jointly with the Southern Railway, would purchase the Monon.

After World War II, L&N accessed Chicago by buying part of the Chicago & Eastern Illinois. The Monon was merged in 1971, but in 1982, L&N disappeared in a merger with the Seaboard Coast Line that created the Seaboard System Railroad. Well, it almost disappeared. Advertising called the combination "The Family Lines" and frequently listed all constituent railroads. In 1980, the holding company of the Seaboard Coast Line merged with the Chessie System to form CSX Corporation.

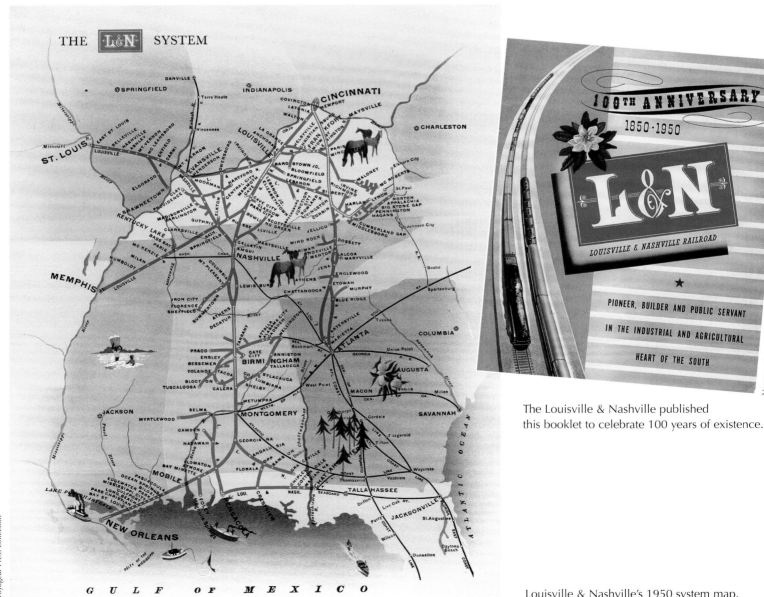

Voyageur Press collection

The Louisville & Nashville published this booklet to celebrate 100 years of existence.

Voyageur Press collection

Louisville & Nashville's 1950 system map.

Louisville & Nashville M-1 Class 2-8-4 No. 1954 starts an Atlanta-bound fast freight from DeCoursey Yard near Cincinnati in 1956. Crews referred to the M-1s as "Big Emmas."

The *Tippecanoe* crosses the Tippecanoe River at Monticello, Indiana. Until 1959, this streamliner made a daily journey between Chicago and Indianapolis on the Monon Railroad. The Monon's official name was the Chicago, Indianapolis & Louisville. Its four tentacles of track reached Chicago, Michigan City in Indiana, Indianapolis, and Louisville. All four converged at the town of Monon, Indiana, from which the railroad derived its colloquial name.

"THE TIPPECANOE" CROSSING THE TIPPECANOE RIVER AT MONTICELLO, IND.

Two Alco RS3 locomotives pull a train of auto racks through Covington, Kentucky. Hopper cars of coal define the primary industry of this region. Railroads still carry new automobiles but in covered railroad cars to protect them from vandalism.

MAINE CENTRAL

The Maine Central Railroad was created in 1862 to combine two existing 5-foot 6-inch gauge rail lines that provided service from Portland to Bangor. It narrowed these lines to standard gauge in 1871.

Thereafter, Maine Central began a long period of growth fueled by its leases of existing railroads. The 1888 lease of the Portland & Ogdensburg provided an important connection with the Canadian Pacific at St. Johnsbury, Vermont. The line became the mountain division of the MC as it assaulted New Hampshire's White Mountains. Two unusual acquisitions were the 2-foot gauge Sandy River & Rangeley Lakes and the Bridgton & Saco River.

After World War I, the MC started to contract and by the 1980s was left with a main line from Portland, through Bangor, to Mattawamkeag, where it connected with the Canadian Pacific; and with its mountain division from Portland to St. Johnsbury. The railroad's routes were not much different than they had been in 1888! Guilford Transportation Industries purchased the MC in 1981.

In 1899, a short documentary film showed a train crossing Frankenstein Trestle in New Hampshire's White Mountains. Although Maine Central trains no longer tread these rails, you can still ride across the 500-foot-long and 80-foot-high trestle on the Crawford Notch train of the Conway Scenic Railroad.

Voyageur Press collection

M. C. R. R. TRAIN CROSSING FRANKENSTEIN TRESTLE

Voyageur Press collection

Presenting Our New Babies

Twelve Sets of Twins

Left and below: In a joint effort with the Boston & Maine, the Maine Central introduced new streamlined passenger service between Boston, Massachusetts, and Bangor, Maine. A total of 24 cars were purchased (thus the "twelve sets of Twins" referenced on the brochure's cover). This is part of a 38-inch-long brochure about the new cars. Individual headrests allowed passengers to sleep in their reclining seats on air-conditioned cars. Special sound insulation made sleep easier. Meals and drinks were served in the restaurant-lounge cars, and glass-enclosed smoking sections were part of each coach. New England workmen built the cars at a total cost of $2 million.

A Maine Central EMD GP7 idles in South Portland, Maine, in February 1972.

G. V. "Jerry" Carson photo

Voyageur Press collection

Above: In 1935, the Maine Central Railroad timetable listed every transportation mode except ship. The government's concern about railroads monopolizing passenger transportation delayed the development of integrated transportation systems in the United States for decades.

Left: Maine Central locomotive No. 702 leads a double-headed freight train out of town.

G. V. "Jerry" Carson photo

NARROW GAUGE BONANZA

The distance between the inside edges of the rails is called the gauge. In North America, standard gauge is 4 feet 8 1/2 inches, adopted from the English who approximated the distance between the ruts of Roman roads, enough room for two horses abreast. The Ohio legislature mandated 4 feet 10 inches, but this gauge was forbidden in Pennsylvania. The New York legislature required the Erie Railroad be laid with 6 feet between its rails. Canada required 5 feet 6 inches. In the United States, 23 different gauges were in use in 1871, from 3 feet to 6 feet. Within 15 years, two *more* gauges were added. Two-foot gauge railroads were constructed in Maine. The longest, the Sandy River & Rangely Lakes, operated more than 120 miles of main line. An Oregon logging line was laid with an astounding 8 feet between the rails.

Congress fixed the gauge of the first transcontinental railroad at 4 feet 8 1/2 inches to exclude the rebellious South, most of which was laid with 5-foot gauge. In a few days in mid-1886, 13,000 miles of 5-foot gauge track was narrowed by 3 1/2 inches, and 4 feet 8 1/2 inches would forever be standard gauge in North America.

Immediately after the Civil War, the notion circulated that a railroad could be profitably constructed almost anywhere. If traffic could not justify constructing a standard gauge line, then a narrow gauge track could be built less expensively. Much less dirt would have to be excavated. Bridges would require less material. Locomotives and cars would be built smaller and less expensively. Grades could be steeper and curves sharper, further reducing the amount of earth to be excavated, especially in mountainous terrain.

As routes for profitable standard gauge railroads were already occupied, the narrow gauge message was irresistible to would-be railroad entrepreneurs. In 1876, the United States had 81 narrow gauge railroads in 26 states and the boom was just getting started. Pennsylvania had 11 narrow gauge railways. Colorado peaked at about 1,800 miles of narrow gauge track. As late as 1942, the nation still had 1,400 miles of narrow track, of which 900 miles were in Colorado. In the end, some lines were widened to standard gauge and others abandoned as the cost and inconvenience of transfers between trains of different gauge became too burdensome.

Claude Wiatrowski photo

Above: As traffic and costs increased, larger narrow gauge locomotives were built to operate trains more economically. One common technique was to build locomotives with frames outside their wheels, allowing wider locomotives with bigger boilers. Without close inspection, outside-frame locomotives seem to have no driving wheels, with only counterweights and rods visible as shown here.

Right: Three-foot-gauge Denver & Rio Grande locomotive No. 496 was constructed from an old standard gauge locomotive. It waits in Salida, Colorado, on three-rail track that allows both standard and narrow gauge trains to travel the same track.

Courtesy Milton A. Davis collection

Narrow gauge railroads were irresistible in mountainous, remote terrains serving a natural resource market whose longevity was in question. The White Pass & Yukon was completed in 1900 to serve the Klondike gold rush in Canada. Trains still travel through Tunnel Mountain, with its adjacent trestle. Soon after the railroad opened in 1900, it became an intermodal carrier providing steamship service from Seattle to Skagway, train transport from Skagway to Whitehorse, and sternwheeler transport on the Yukon River from Whitehorse to Dawson, the hub of the Klondike gold rush.

A substantial network of narrow gauge railroads flowered near Nome, Alaska. Collectively, they have become known as the Wild Goose Railroad. Traffic had declined considerably when this photo was taken in 1912 and locals were using "pupmobiles" to travel on the tracks of the Seward Peninsula Railroad. Many remnants of these railroads, including steam locomotives, dot the tundra of the Seward Peninsula because of the extreme difficulty of scrapping a railroad in this remote location.

The Tanana Valley Railroad in Alaska was built to 3-foot gauge to serve mines near Fairbanks. The U.S. government purchased it and converted a portion to standard gauge to complete the Alaska Railroad from Seward through Anchorage to Fairbanks.

A locomotive of the Durango & Silverton Narrow Gauge Railroad waits at Silverton for its return trip to Durango. The rocky crags are Colorado's San Juan Mountains.

PENNSYLVANIA RAILROAD

In 1861, a lease initiated in 1847 brought the rails between Philadelphia and Pittsburgh under the management of the Pennsylvania Railroad. Expansion blanketed its namesake state, and Pennsy train whistles could be heard as far away as St. Louis. Its red passenger cars also reached Buffalo, Baltimore, Washington, Wilmington, and Atlantic City. Pennsy rails served the industrial heartland: Chicago, Indianapolis, Cleveland, and Detroit.

Pennsylvania Station broke the New York Central's Manhattan monopoly in 1910. Its Hell Gate Bridge over the East River carried the first direct passenger rail service from New York to Boston in 1917. In an industry where investors frequently lost everything, the Pennsy paid dividends for a *century* and became the largest U.S. railroad in revenue and traffic.

It aggressively pursued the economies of standardization. Hundreds of passenger cars, freight locomotives, passenger locomotives, and switching locomotives were built to the same plans, as were thousands of boxcars. Its most heavily used main lines were electrified.

Perhaps the conservative, methodical management that served the Pennsy so well in good times was slow to react in hard times. In 1968 it merged with the New York Central to create the Penn Central, which went bankrupt in 1970.

The Pennsylvania Railroad celebrated its centenary in 1946. The image shows its modern diesel, steam, and electric locomotives. In 1946, the railroad operated 3,170 daily freight trains and 1,340 daily passenger trains.

A 1903 photo of the Pennsylvania Railroad's shop at Altoona, Pennsylvania, shows why steam locomotives were expensive to maintain. In 1903, there was no practical alternative motive power. Altoona would grow to enormous size and build as well as maintain the Pennsylvania's fleet of steamers.

This 1907 photo shows all four tracks of the Pennsylvania Railroad's main line occupied. The rightmost train is a work train most likely hauling rock from the embankment on which the men are working. The first car of this train carries the men to and from work. The third train is pulled by two steam locomotives, while the fourth and leftmost train demonstrates one of many reasons why brakemen's jobs were the most dangerous. As two men walk across the tops of the cars, each of the four stacks of semaphore blades controls train movements on the track below it.

Pennsylvania Railroad locomotive *Tiger* crosses the Upper Juniata Canal, a mode of transportation it would soon replace. The *Tiger*, an American-type locomotive built at Baldwin in 1857, shows brightly painted colors in an era before the predominant color of steam locomotives was black.

Stormy or Starry the night...

...THIS GREAT ALL-WEATHER FLEET GOES THROUGH!

Serving the Nation

A Pennsylvania Railroad advertisement on the inside cover of the January 12, 1941 issue of *Time* stressed the reliability of railroads in all weather. Today, railroad technology still provides the most reliable transportation in bad weather.

In 1945, the Pennsylvania featured an articulated steam locomotive and its 26,000-mile railroad system—serving half the U.S. population—in an ad that emphasized the railroad's importance to the transportation of war freight. The Pennsylvania was one of a few railroads that built articulated locomotives that had different numbers of driving wheels in each engine. The locomotive shown here has a 4-4-6-4 wheel arrangement with four drivers in the lead engine assembly and six in the second.

The *Liberty Limited* speeds between Washington, D.C., and Chicago. Its name is clearly inspired by the Allied victory in World War II, which ended eight years before this ad ran.

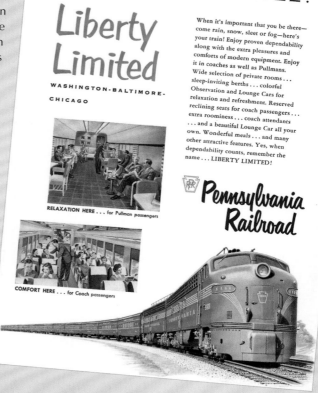

This 1952 timetable featured an image of Horseshoe Curve with passenger trains pulled by streamlined diesel locomotives. Inside was a joint schedule with the *California Zephyr* that allowed travelers to venture from New York to San Francisco.

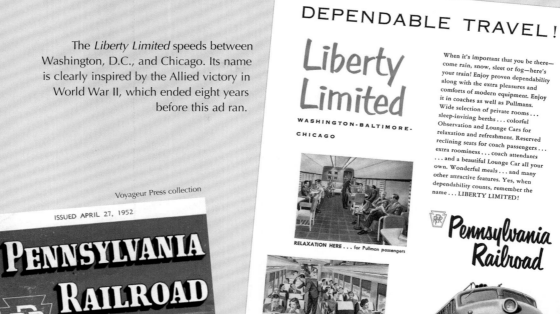

A streamlined GG1 electric locomotive leaves Washington, D.C., for a trip to New York City that might well exceed 100 miles per hour. These locomotives were built decades prior to this 1952 advertisement. When electric locomotives were simply boxes on wheels, the Pennsylvania chose a Raymond Loewy design featuring futuristic compound curves that remained "modern" for the life of the locomotives.

SANTA FE RAILWAY

Chartered in 1859 and renamed the Atchison, Topeka & Santa Fe in 1863, this railroad's construction commenced at Topeka, Kansas, in 1868. Only a branch line would reach Santa Fe, New Mexico, the second oldest European city in the United States. The railroad reached the Colorado border in 1872 and was instrumental in recruiting Mennonite colonists from Russia to settle western Kansas. Santa Fe trains would also serve Colorado's Front Range cities of Pueblo, Colorado Springs, and Denver. Its rails crossed Raton Pass into New Mexico and sliced through Albuquerque to Deming, where they joined with Southern Pacific rails in 1881.

The Santa Fe and Frisco jointly built west from Albuquerque through the vehicle of the Atlantic & Pacific Railroad. Eventually coming under sole ownership of the Santa Fe, this line provided its trains access to the Pacific at San Diego, Los Angeles, and San Francisco. Its lines reached Galveston, Texas, in 1887 and Chicago in 1888. The Santa Fe became a component of the Burlington Northern Santa Fe in 1995.

www.cabincreekcds.com

The Santa Fe was one of a few railroads that used the Prairie-type steam locomotive with its 2-6-2 wheel arrangement. One wonders about the economics of this passenger train with one "combine" car, half devoted to passengers and half to baggage and express.

Voyageur Press collection

Above: The Santa Fe emphasized the cultural history along its southwestern route. Here, passengers imagine Francisco Coronado on his fruitless search for the seven lost cities of Cibola.

Left: Four diesel locomotives sporting Santa Fe's famous warbonnet paint scheme head up the westbound *Super Chief* at Winslow, Arizona, in the 1960s. This stop was scheduled for 8:35 p.m. for a crew change and inspection.

Image Archives

Clouds of steam testify to Chicago's bitter cold as a Santa Fe freight train prepares to leave Corwith Yard at the height of World War II in 1943.

Santa Fe's early diesel locomotives were painted blue and yellow for freight service instead of the red, yellow, and silver of its passenger locomotives. Instead of a historic image of the Santa Fe, this EMD ad art featured a Currier & Ives print of a train near Jersey City.

Be carefree, be comfortable and enjoy a

New World Standard in Travel

The new Santa Fe

Super Chief

Advanced ideas for your travel luxury... new cradled smoothness in the ride... daily between Chicago and Los Angeles

From the flanges on the wheels to the tip of the Pleasure Dome, the Super Chief is new—entirely new.

To give you the smoothest ride of your life on rails, this new Super Chief glides on cushioned springs . . . revises any ideas you ever had about any train.

The keynote is comfort.

You find it in the distinctive Turquoise Room in the lounge car—a delightful place to relax, enjoy a cocktail or entertain your friends at dinner—the first time such a room has been provided on any trains.

You find it in the Pleasure Dome—"top of the Super," next to the stars"—that brings you an unobstructed view of wonderful southwestern scenery.

You find it in the new dining cars where Fred Harvey chefs present new and exciting menus.

Accommodations in this beautiful all-room train are designed to pamper you every mile of the way. "Push-button" radio or music in your room when you want it . . . beds you just can't help sleeping in . . . charming apartments by day.

From the engineers who glide you across this great country to the porter who answers your bell, this is the train of thoughtful service.

For your next trip between Chicago and Los Angeles say "Super Chief." Now, more than ever, it is America's train of trains. Consult your local ticket or travel agent.

SANTA FE SYSTEM LINES
Serving the West and Southwest

Santa Fe

The *Super Chief* was Santa Fe's most famous luxury train. From the warbonnet color scheme of the locomotive to the Turquoise Room lounge car, it was an icon of the greatest in American passenger railroading. Passengers were pampered with an ultra-smooth ride, dining provided by Fred Harvey, comfortable beds, and pushbutton radios in every room to lull you to sleep with relaxing music.

SOUTHERN PACIFIC

El Paso & Southwestern Railroad employees pose by the 14-stall roundhouse and shop buildings in Douglas, Arizona, in 1909. The El Paso & Southwestern was a little-known railroad connecting El Paso with Tucson. Built by the Phelps Dodge Corporation to facilitate their copper-mining business and later merged into Southern Pacific, most of its tracks are now gone. Beautiful depots remain in Tucson and Douglas.

Voyageur Press collection

Theodore Judah found backing for his transcontinental route from Sacramento merchants Collis Huntington, Mark Hopkins, Charles Crocker, and Leland Stanford. Remarkably, these local merchants, who would become known as the "Big Four," undertook construction of the Central Pacific Railroad, the western portion of the first U.S. transcontinental. Starting in 1863, the line was constructed over the rugged Sierras by 10,000 Chinese laborers. So deep were the winter snows that the track was eventually covered with wooden snowsheds for much of its length. The last spike holding the rail connecting the Central Pacific with the eastern transcontinental, the Union Pacific, was driven home on May 10, 1869 in Utah.

By 1870, the Big Four also controlled the Southern Pacific, projected to connect California with New Orleans. In the 1880s, the Southern Pacific leased the Central Pacific, formalizing their joint control. The Union Pacific purchased control of the Southern Pacific in 1900 but was later forced to sell its stake due to federal antitrust concerns.

The physical extent of the Southern Pacific was remarkable. Lines it controlled were bounded by Portland, Oregon, Los Angeles, New Orleans, and Chicago. The Denver & Rio Grande purchased the Southern Pacific in 1988 but the combined railroad retained the Southern Pacific name. In 1996, the Southern Pacific name disappeared when Union Pacific again purchased the Southern Pacific.

These three views of passenger trains on the Southern Pacific's Shasta Route from San Francisco to Seattle explain its popularity with tourists.

Below: The *Sunset Limited* crosses through the cotton fields on its way from Los Angeles to New Orleans. The locomotive color scheme is similar to that used on the Southern Pacific's *Daylight* steam locomotives. In the postwar optimism about passenger train travel, the Southern Pacific purchased five trainsets for the *Sunset* at a total cost of $15 million. The trip was scheduled for 42 hours, a number that shows why airlines were unbeatable competitors for long-distance passenger travel in the 1950s.

7160. Overland Limited Crossing Great Salt Lake, Utah, at Sunset.

540 WESTWARD BOUND, CROSSING THE DESERT, CALIFORNIA

In 1904, the Southern Pacific completed a 12-mile trestle across the Great Salt Lake. This Lucin Cutoff was eventually replaced with earthen fill. The original trestle's wood, pickled in the lake's salty mineral-laden water, is prized for its varied colors and has been salvaged and used as paneling in new construction.

Southern Pacific passengers enjoy spring-time wild flowers of the California desert.

Passengers arrive at Shasta Springs in 1905. In California's far north, the resort was one of several that were popular summer destinations for overheated Californians. Naturally carbonated spring water was bottled and shipped to markets over the railroad's Shasta Route from San Francisco to Portland and Seattle.

The *City of San Francisco* has just departed its namesake western terminus for a direct trip to Chicago via Southern Pacific, Union Pacific, and Chicago & North Western rails. The trip featured a daylight crossing of Donner Pass high in the Sierra Nevada Mountains. In 1939, the *City of San Francisco* was wrecked in Nevada with the suspected cause being sabotage of the rails. In 1952, 226 people, cold, hungry and miserable, were stranded on the train in 12-foot snows on Donner Pass. That same storm saw one SP engineer killed and four of its five rotary snowplows immovably buried in the white powder. The fifth and oldest rotary plow finally rescued the stranded train after three days.

Voyageur Press collection

Modern diesel locomotives of the railroads that formed America's first transcontinental stand side by side at California's Portola Railroad Museum. The Southern Pacific absorbed the Central Pacific, the western portion of that transcontinental railroad route, and is now part of the Union Pacific, the eastern portion of the first transcontinental.

Claude Wiatrowski photo

ROBBER BARON BOOM   75

TOURIST RAILWAYS

There are hundreds of tourist railways in North America today. These are discussed in this book under the heading of "Preserved Railways and Museums" (see page 174). Tourist railways are not a new phenomenon and many railways were built for the purpose—sometimes the sole purpose—of carrying tourists. Frequent destinations were the tops of mountains, amusement parks, picnic groves, and resort hotels. Some tourist railways were just slightly above the category of carnival rides, while others were clearly major railroad projects. A few continue to operate but most succumbed to the automobile.

Manitou & Pikes Peak trains reached the summit of Colorado's Pikes Peak in 1891 and still travel this route pioneered solely for transporting tourists to the top of "America's Mountain." At Mountain View, an antique diesel streamliner waits for a regularly scheduled passenger train. Pikes Peak is visible above the trains.

Two incline (cable-hauled) railways were built up Chattanooga's Lookout Mountain. The first brought patrons to a hotel at the summit; the second provided general transportation to anyone who wanted to view the valley 1,600 feet below. The second incline was opened in 1895 and still operates today.

Claude Wiatrowski photo

Claude Wiatrowski collection

SCENE ON NEVERSINK MOUNTAIN, READING, PA.

Voyageur Press collection

Someone has dotted the route of the Neversink Mountain Railway on this old postcard. Opened on June 30, 1890, Pennsylvania's Neversink was the third electric railroad in the United States. It closed in 1917.

6608 Devil's Gateway, Mt. Lowe, California "On the Road of a Thousand Wonders"

6607 Circular Bridge, 400 ft. above lower track, Mt. Lowe Railway. California
"On the Road of a Thousand Wonders"

Claude Wiatrowski collection

Above and right: The Mt. Lowe Railway included several segments. Near Los Angeles, a Pacific Electric trolley snaked up Rubio Canyon, where an incline railway climbed the hillside to the Alpine Division, pictured here. A tavern, hotel, and casino were some of the attractions along the rail lines. The railroad ceased operation in 1937.

8144. Observation Car in the Royal Gorge, Colo.

Claude Wiatrowski collection

The Denver & Rio Grande routinely added an outdoor observation car to its regular passenger trains traveling through the Royal Gorge. The Royal Gorge Route now operates tourist trains, including an open-air car, through the gorge.

Summer stops in the snow were popular with tourists on any railroad that reached high into the mountains. The Moffat was not a tourist railroad, but plenty of tourists rode its line over Rollins Pass before it was bypassed by the Moffat Tunnel.

8487. Snow Banks on Continental Divide, Altitude 11,660 Feet, Denver, Northwestern & Pacific,
"The Moffat Road," Colo.

Claude Wiatrowski collection

UNION PACIFIC

In 1850, California became the 31st state. In 1859, Oregon became the 33rd. Their isolation was the motivation for a transcontinental railroad. The Pacific Railroad Act of 1862 chartered the Union Pacific Railroad to build west from Omaha, Nebraska, to meet the Central Pacific, which would build east from Sacramento, California.

On May 10, 1869 at Promontory, Utah, two last spikes were driven, celebrating completion of the transcontinental route. From Ogden, Utah, Union Pacific trains reached the copper mines of Butte, Montana, and the Pacific Ocean at Portland and Los Angeles.

In 1897, E. H. Harriman purchased the Union Pacific at public auction. He controlled and made improvements to the Union Pacific, the Southern Pacific (successor to the Central Pacific), the Illinois Central, and the Chicago & Alton. In 1912, federal regulators required that the Union Pacific sell its ownership in the Southern Pacific.

In the 1980s, merger with the Western Pacific gave the Union Pacific a third Pacific terminus at Oakland. Merger with the Missouri Pacific added Texas and Chicago. The Missouri-Kansas-Texas Railroad joined in 1988. In 1995, the Chicago & North Western was folded into the Union Pacific with its straight-line route from Omaha to Chicago. Coming full-circle, the Southern Pacific again became part of the Union Pacific in 1996.

508—Union Pacific Streamliner "City of Los Angeles" Crossing the Desert

© CURT TEICH & CO., INC.

OB-H680

Voyageur Press collection

Streamlined diesels generating 5,400 horsepower rocket the *City of Los Angeles* across the flower-carpeted desert after the end of World War II.

Sherman Hill is the Union Pacific's original crossing of the Continental Divide. Although the line has been relocated and additional tracks added, the route still crosses the divide between Cheyenne and Laramie, Wyoming.

Claude Wiatrowski photo

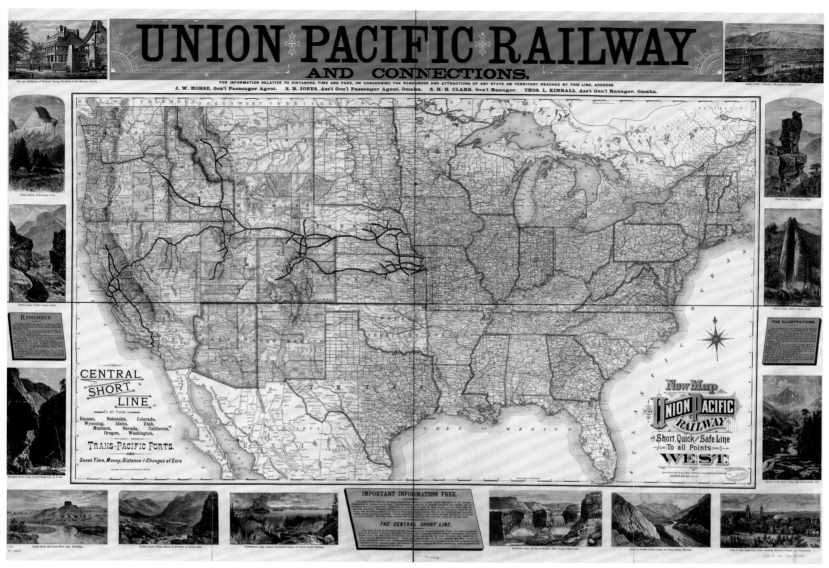

Probably the most famous scene in American railroading is the ceremony at which the first transcontinental railroad was completed. Central Pacific locomotive *Jupiter* is at left while Union Pacific's No. 119 is at right. Many photographic copies and this artist's rendition were altered from the original image. In the original photograph, the two men reaching toward each other from the locomotives hold whiskey bottles. The National Park Service regularly recreates the scene at this very spot in Utah.

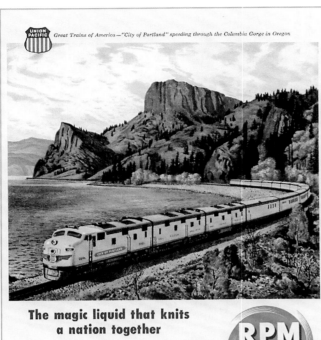

Great Trains of America—"City of Portland" speeding through the Columbia Gorge in Oregon

The magic liquid that knits a nation together

Portland and Chicago are just 2400 minutes apart on Union Pacific's "City of Portland." And the power that speeds it across the continent is a team of high-speed Diesels. These mighty engines practically never stop. They're on the job more than 90% of the time —and one secret of their rugged endurance is a special chemical developed by

Standard of California to keep carbon off engines. Added to RPM DELO oil this magic liquid eliminates stuck rings, enables Diesel trains to run as far as the distance to the moon without overhaul. So today, with RPM DELO oil in their Diesels, streamliners run far and fast to knit the nation together with finer transportation.

RPM DELO

DIESEL ENGINE LUBRICATING OIL

From the laboratories of

STANDARD OIL COMPANY OF CALIFORNIA

Subsidiaries: THE CALIFORNIA COMPANY · STANDARD OIL COMPANY OF TEXAS
THE CALIFORNIA OIL COMPANY

UNION PACIFIC RAILROAD

In any season, for many reasons all signs favor . . .

UNION PACIFIC

Railroad

Serving eleven western states with the finest in travel comfort and dependable freight service

---

Above left: The Union Pacific's *City of Portland* meanders down Oregon's Columbia River Gorge.

Above right: A postwar Union Pacific ad draws a parallel between its passenger services and the seasons of the year, via the signs of the zodiac.

Let 'Big Boy' speed your freight

A gigantic, rolling power-house . . . the 600-ton locomotive "Big Boy" speeds the heaviest freight loads. Equipment designed to handle any freight shipment . . . large or small . . . backed by modern facilities and men who know their jobs are assurance of dependable performance.

Union Pacific traffic experts are located in metropolitan cities from coast to coast. They offer you complete cooperation in handling any traffic problem.

UNION PACIFIC RAILROAD

BE SPECIFIC: *Ship* UNION PACIFIC

Although the Union Pacific Big Boy—a locomotive with 4-8-8-4 wheel arrangement— was the world's largest, it was more than a tool to enhance operational efficiency. Union Pacific advertising stressed that this 600-ton behemoth sped the shipper's freight to its destination.

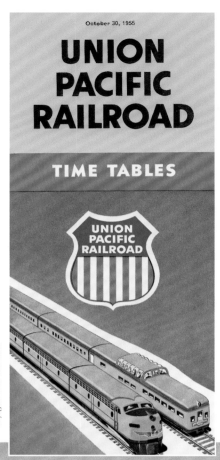

Above: "We can handle it" underscores this scene as Union Pacific's last two operational steam locomotives, 8444 and 3985, thunder past a Wyoming billboard in May 1981. "Thunder" is an understatement for a pair of steam locomotives weighing about 1,000 tons and running at 70 miles per hour.

Left: This 1955 Union Pacific timetable listed passenger service from named high-speed streamlined trains down through self-propelled motorcars, ending with, remarkably, mixed freight and passenger trains.

This 1979 photo of a leased Union Pacific locomotive at Martin, Utah, predicted the future. The Union Pacific now owns the track that passes Martin, and its yellow trains climb past this spot regularly.

WHY STEAM LOCOMOTIVES ARE BLACK

Anyone who has seen lithographs of very old American steam locomotives or has ridden preserved steam locomotives in England knows that locomotives were a kaleidoscope of bright colors and ornate decoration. Early American railroads would assign a locomotive to a single engineer who frequently augmented the already ornate iron steed. Additions such as deer antlers over the headlight were not uncommon.

Sometime after 1875, Commodore Vanderbilt began a trend among American railroads by requiring all his locomotives be painted black and that ornamentation be removed. Both moves saved money—when railroads switched from wood to coal as primary fuel, soot from the coal was difficult to clean from the locomotives. Under protest from his crews, Vanderbilt relented somewhat but the pattern had been set, and with few exceptions, modern steam locomotives were all black. Fortunately, that pattern did not continue into the diesel age, when brightly painted locomotives advertised brand awareness to the viewer waiting for a train to clear a road crossing.

Resting by the depot in Silverton, Colorado, locomotive *Eureka* shows some of the colorful and ornate detail common to steam locomotives before the all-black era.

Claude Wiatrowski photo

Georgetown Loop Railroad No. 40 illustrates the all-black look. The polished bell and white striping provide some ornamentation. Not all railroads adopted the all-black look, especially for steam locomotives used on passenger trains. The diesel-era brought exciting color schemes back to the railroads.

Claude Wiatrowski photo

WORLD'S COLUMBIAN EXPOSITION

Chicago's Columbian Exposition hosted 27 million visitors in 1893. It featured a fast, smoke-free electric railway to transport guests who gawked at displays of locomotives and included soon-to-be railroad legend Casey Jones, whom the Illinois Central had assigned the temporary duty of running shuttle trains to the fairgrounds. Jones found Illinois Central locomotive 638 on display at the expo and had it assigned to him on his return to Water Valley, Mississippi.

J. E. France photo, Bruce Gurner collection, Water Valley Casey Jones Railroad Museum

Illinois Central No. 638 was displayed at the 1893 Columbian Exposition in Chicago where Casey Jones was assigned to run shuttle trains carrying visitors to the fair. Casey was so impressed with locomotive No. 638 that he managed to have it assigned to him in Water Valley, Mississippi. He even convinced management to allow him to run the locomotive all the way from Chicago to Water Valley across five divisions of the railroad. Normally, an engineer assigned to each division would have piloted the locomotive across that division. In this photo, Casey relaxes in the cab just north of Water Valley in 1898.

CHAPTER THREE

Jack Delano, LC-USW36-584, Library of Congress, Prints and Photographs Division

The Depression brought a steep decline in orders for new locomotives, with railroads making worn-out locomotives last. With the coming of huge transportation demands in World War II, the railroads were caught in an exceptionally difficult position. Here, the Chicago & North Western repairs a steam locomotive in 1942 at its Proviso Yard shops in Chicago.

FADED GLORY

As the nation's primary mode of transportation, railroads rode the wave of prosperity following World War I. While railroad traffic and profits increased, ownership of private automobiles increased as well. Automobile owners complained about the poor state of the roads and the government embarked on its never-ending program to build, maintain, and improve them. Better roads and improved vehicle technology increased commercial trucking. Trunk railroads welcomed trucks, which served just like branch-line railroads, feeding goods to the main-line trains. They never dreamed that trucks would compete with long-haul freight railroading. As markets grew, all carriers prospered even as the railroad's market share began to decline, ever so slowly at first.

BLACK THURSDAY

October 24, 1929—Black Thursday—is generally acknowledged as the start of the Great Depression. By 1932, 25 percent of the American workforce—13 million—was unemployed. A year later saw an additional 2 million without work. At the Depression's low point, 50 percent of the adult males in Canada were without work.

The economy's reliance on trains made the railroads especially vulnerable to dislocations of that economy. Railroad passenger service showed its first annual loss in 1930. It got worse. In the decade from 1928 to 1938, railroad employment was nearly halved from 1.7 million to a little more than 900,000. The still-employed railroader worked fewer hours and those low on the seniority list might get a few hours of work a week—if that. This monster fed on itself. Unemployed and underemployed railroaders couldn't afford to purchase goods that the railroads carried or to ride passenger trains. The economy swirled into an ever-deepening whirlpool. Elimination of money-losing train services and redundant railroad facilities was made difficult by the regulations of the Interstate Commerce Commission. Even the Emergency Railroad Transportation Act of 1933, essentially a three-year relaxation of these regulations, did little to help.

Passenger traffic in 1932 was only 61 percent of what it had been in 1929. The Great Depression marked the end of the golden era of railroad passenger service. In 1929, 20,000

This railroad yard holds the 75 trains—passenger and freight—that were required to move a single armored division of 12,000 men during World War II. It is no wonder that the war gave the railroads a temporary reprieve from their long-term decline.

ROLLING TO VICTORY IN MILL.. ON RAIL!

Voyageur Press collection

Steel was an essential component of winning World War II. Aluminum aircraft, radar, and even television-guided bombs made their first appearance in this war, but steel was still the foundation of victory.

What it takes to move a division

Voyageur Press collection

Uncle Sam pitches in to help the wartime activities of the Pennsylvania Railroad and the industries it served.

passenger trains polished the steel rails *each day*. In 2005, U.S. airlines operated 27,000 daily flights. In 1929, one daily passenger train ran for every 600 Americans. In 1995, one daily airline flight operated for every 1,100 Americans. By these measures, transportation services in 1929 were almost double those in 1995. In addition, those 20,000 trains in 1929 served numerous small, rural towns. Today, most airline flights operate between hub airports in large cities. Rural America, especially, lost out when passenger trains started to slide toward oblivion.

In the United States, 1932 freight tonnage was less than half of what it had been in 1929. Canada fared worse. Canadian grain shipments in 1935 were an eighth of what they had been in 1928. Recovery had been almost nonexistent when another economic decline in 1937 and 1938 must have convinced Americans that the world was coming to an end. By 1939, a full third of U.S. railroad trackage was in the hands of court-appointed trustees of bankrupt railroads.

The excesses of the robber barons motivated government regulations that limited the railroads' ability to respond to the changing conditions of the Depression. Although railroads may have done better had they been allowed to adapt, it would have been impossible for them to have done well. The North American economy had collapsed and the railroads were intimately intertwined with that economy. Stock manipulations begun in the days of the robber barons reached their zenith in the 1920s. The Great Depression motivated the establishment of the Securities and Exchange Commission and the first attempts at regulating the securities industry.

None of this had any substantial immediate effect on ending the Great Depression. Entry into World War II and the enormous demands the war made on the economy put Americans back to work and the railroads on the right track. But time would prove that the war was only a temporary respite from more basic structural causes for the railroads' woes.

WORLD WAR II

Railroads proved themselves the primary domestic transportation mode in World War II. Gone were the missteps of World War I. The railroads moved freight and passengers as never before: over 80 percent of all freight traffic during the war years and close to a billion passengers in 1944. What makes this record all the more remarkable is that the railroads' capital resources were spent. Through over a decade of Depression, the railroads had limped along with old locomotives, old cars, deferred maintenance, and inadequate infrastructure. With the outbreak of war, the country's resources were stretched to the breaking point and the railroads delivered magnificent service with the resources they had. With young men away at war, old-timers were brought out of retirement and for the first time women played a substantial role in railroad operations. Wooden railroad cars emerged from what had been expected to be

During World War II, the Pennsylvania Railroad lost 48,000 male employees to the armed forces while it gained 23,000 women to help run the railroad. War's end spelled dissatisfaction for many women who wanted to continue in careers. Molly Pitcher was a Revolutionary War heroine and became associated with the women who went to work during World War II.

A 1945 advertisement by the American Locomotive Company illustrates the key decision to be made by the nation's railroads at the time: steam or diesel or both? Alco manufactured both and the ad illustrates some of the company's most successful products.

permanent retirement and antique locomotives chugged down the rails.

THE GREAT MOTIVE POWER DEBATE

By the war's end in 1945, the American locomotive fleet was worn out. Most locomotives had been built in the 1920s prior to the Great Depression and they were at the end of their useful lives. After the war, railroads saw a dramatic drop in business even as their labor costs remained high. Solutions were limited by constraints imposed by the Interstate Commerce Commission and union labor agreements. This set the stage for an important decision about technology. Should the new locomotives be steam-powered or diesel-powered?

One important player on that stage was the Electro-Motive Division of General Motors (EMD). Formerly the Electro-Motive Corporation (EMC) and a pioneer manufacturer of diesel locomotives, the company was purchased by GM in 1930 and became EMD. (In 2005, the company

was purchased yet again but retained its EMD initials when it was rechristened Electro-Motive Diesel. This book will use the letters EMD to refer to this company.)

The purchase of a new fleet of steam locomotives seemed virtually guaranteed. At war's end, U.S. railroads operated 40,000 steam locomotives and only 3,000 diesels. The railroads had massive investments in steam locomotive infrastructure. Perhaps most importantly, a steam locomotive cost half as much as a diesel locomotive with the same horsepower. On the other side of the equation, many more men were required to service and maintain steam locomotives.

DIESELS AND STANDARDIZATION

Each railroad had different operating conditions to which steam locomotives were custom-designed. Diesels were much more adaptable than steam locomotives and one design would work as well amid the grain elevators of the flat Midwest as it would on the steep climb through the western mountains.

An unexpected consequence of standardized diesel designs was ease of financing. Since steam locomotives were unique to a specific railroad, banks knew that they would be difficult to sell and were loath to use the locomotives as collateral for loans. Diesel locomotives were standardized and easy to sell to another railroad if a purchaser defaulted on a loan. Much like an automobile loan today, approval was almost automatic since the loan financed the purchase of the very item that would act as collateral.

DIESELS AND PASSENGERS

As servicemen returned from the war, the railroads saw an expanding market for passenger business and were determined to get their share. The automobile had already become formidable competition and commercial aviation would soon be unstoppable. With their sleek, modern, colorful styling, and fast, smooth rides, streamlined diesel locomotives caught travelers' imaginations. In a reversal of Henry Ford's philosophy of delivering Model T autos in any color as long as it was black, EMD delivered the flashiest color schemes but only on standardized diesel locomotives.

This 1957 advertisement prophetically predicted that within a few decades containers and trailers on flatcars would become the fastest growing segments of railroad revenue.

Voyageur Press collection

DIESELS AND THE UNIONS

In 1937, railroads agreed to station a fireman in the cabs of diesel locomotives, even though these locomotives had no boiler for the fireman to tend. Management's decision to include a fireman was made primarily for labor peace. It was not until a 1963 U.S. Supreme Court decision that firemen gradually started to disappear.

When the modern freight diesel, EMD's model FT, arrived just before World War II, those locomotives could be connected together to form one multiple-unit (MU) locomotive, all of which could be controlled by a single engineer in the first unit. Unions demanded a second engineer on multiple-unit diesels. The railroad resisted and strikes ensued.

THE UNIMAGINABLE

The considerations that governed the selection of the technology for the next generation of railroad locomotives were compelling:

- New diesel servicing facilities would have to be built, but old steam facilities would have to have been upgraded.
- Employees would have to be trained in diesel maintenance and operations but only a fraction of the current steam-knowledgeable employees would be required for a dieselized railroad.
- Although diesels were expensive, financing was easy and the savings from operations and maintenance would quickly make up the difference.
- Diesels spent much less time being serviced than did steam locomotives so they could spend more time pulling trains. Also, fewer diesels would be required.
- Maintaining both technologies simultaneously would be prohibitively expensive.

It was clear that not only was the future in diesel locomotives, but that the best course of action was to convert as quickly as possible. Change swept the railroad yards like wildfire. Steam had almost disappeared by 1958. That postwar fleet of 40,000 steam locomotives was completely replaced by 27,000 diesel units. The last large U.S. railroad to use steam locomotives was the Norfolk and Western, a major coal-hauling railroad. Even on this railroad, steam lasted only a few years more until 1963. Major Canadian railroads used steam locomotives as late as 1962.

NO MORE PASSENGERS

During the war, a surplus of Depression labor became a shortage of war labor. As a consequence, wages increased. Gas was rationed and automobile production halted. New highways were not constructed and maintenance of existing roads was minimal. Is it any wonder that when the war ended railroads carried more freight and passengers than ever? Railroads invested heavily in diesel-hauled streamlined trains, and dome cars gave vacationing families spectacular views of western America.

As the standard of living rode the tide of postwar prosperity, Americans wanted the convenience of a personal automobile. Politicians scrambled to build and improve highways. The Interstate Highway System was begun in 1956 and gasoline was inexpensive. World War II had produced great strides in aircraft technology that was now transferred to civilian use. Plane trips were not just for the wealthy adventurer anymore.

By 1960, it was clear that passenger train travel in the United States was doomed and that the railroads' massive postwar investments had been a waste.

ANOTHER TEAR IN THE FABRIC OF RURAL LIFE

Though the demise of steam locomotives and passenger service occurred for very different reasons, they both had consequences that were especially difficult for small-town America, where steam locomotives no longer stopped to quench their thirst. The roundhouse was deserted and railroad employees' salaries no longer contributed to the local economy. Outside of agriculture, mining, or logging, the main source of wealth for many small towns was the salaries of railroad workers. Their departure left holes in the social and economic fabrics of towns.

Without the passenger train, it was a long drive to Grandma's house or to the nearest big city to board an airplane. The town didn't seem as connected to the outside world without its passenger train. It was more isolated and more of its younger residents moved to the nearest metropolis.

END OF AN ERA, BEGINNING OF ANOTHER

By 1962, railroad freight traffic dropped to its lowest level since the Great Depression. On newly improved highways, truckers more easily competed with railroads not just over short and medium distances but on long-distance hauls as well. These changes have been recorded by historians as both good and bad. They have been attributed to the success of the free market system and to the failure of the government's biased intervention in that system. It seems that conclusions are in the eye of the investigator. One thing that was certain: The railroad age—central to the development of America from the 1840s—was over. The railroads were no longer central to the economic, political, social, and cultural life of the nation. As the story unfolded, railroads would retain their importance but in a different and more invisible role.

TOUGH TIMES IN CANADA

By 1919, the Canadian government controlled the Grand Trunk Pacific, and it took control of the Grand Truck Western in 1920. Both were integrated into Canadian National Railways in 1923. Now there were only two major railways in Canada: one—Canadian Pacific—was owned by private investors, and the other—Canadian National—was government-owned.

Both spent much of the 1920s—perhaps too much—expanding connecting lines, especially in the prairie provinces. Rail also reached northern waterways in 1929 at Churchill, Manitoba, and in 1932 at Moosonee, Ontario. Though there was much less railroad track in Canada than the United States, Canada's rail system had more excess capacity for the meager amount of traffic available. In many ways, Canada was hit harder by the Great Depression than was the United States. Canadian Pacific actually proposed integration and management of Canadian National, a proposal that was politically unacceptable even though logical. By a 1933 agreement, the two railroads did manage to eliminate some parallel lines and share some duplicate facilities, efficiency-enhancing moves that would be implemented by mergers in U.S. railroading in the 1960s and 1970s.

Newfoundland was added to Canada in 1949 and brought with it a government-owned network of 700 miles of narrow gauge (3 feet 6 inches) track that became part of Canadian National Railways.

Each group of travelers enjoys a different view from the dome car of Santa Fe's *San Francisco Chief*. From left to right: Cattle roam the Texas panhandle; the red rocks of New Mexico and Arizona brighten the landscape; the San Francisco Peaks, the highest in Arizona, crest at 12,000 feet; and the Oakland Bay Bridge signals imminent arrival in San Francisco.

CABOOSE

In the 1840s, a converted boxcar at the end of the train became an office for the conductor to complete paperwork. That last car, called a caboose, became a logical place for an extra set of brakes to augment the locomotive's brakes. An observation post, the cupola, was built on the top of the caboose. Stoves were added for warmth, and facilities for eating and sleeping were crowded into the cramped little car. Crews personalized their caboose, making the days they sometimes spent getting their trains across the road more comfortable. Although the caboose was a warm place away from the storm, one of the train crew's favorite nicknames for it was "crummy," indicating another opinion about this car.

Second only to the locomotive, the caboose symbolized the romance of railroading. Normally, the conductor and rear brakeman were stationed in the caboose and a friendly wave from a child would always bring a wave in return.

Improvements in technology, changes in work rules requiring fewer crewmembers, and the cost of maintaining and operating cabooses led to the demise of this famous bright-red car. It was displaced by the decidedly less romantic end-of-train device, also called a "flashing rear end device" or FRED.

Except in railroad museums or at preserved railways, the caboose is rarely seen on trains. With the end of its use, thousands of cabooses became surplus, and many are used today as restaurants, gift shops, motels, summer cabins, and even lawn ornaments!

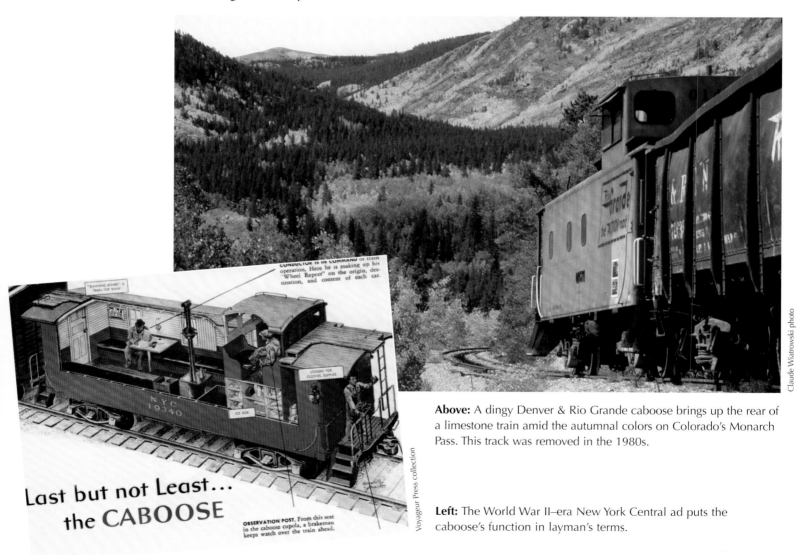

Claude Wiatrowski photo

Voyageur Press collection

Above: A dingy Denver & Rio Grande caboose brings up the rear of a limestone train amid the autumnal colors on Colorado's Monarch Pass. This track was removed in the 1980s.

Left: The World War II–era New York Central ad puts the caboose's function in layman's terms.

Above: When increasing freight car heights made the roof-mounted cupola useless as an observation post, some railroads built bay-window cabooses such as this one at the Carbon County Railway in Utah.

Left: As freight car heights increased, some railroads widened the cupola to improve sight lines. This "extended vision" caboose is displayed at the Collis P. Huntington Railroad Historical Society museum in Huntington, West Virginia.

The Nevada Northern's cabooses were painted bright yellow, which was more visible than traditional red against the rock backgrounds in the copper mining area.

A CENTURY OF PROGRESS

In seasons of roughly five months each, the Chicago World's Fair hosted 22 million visitors in 1933 and 1934. The Wings of a Century Pageant of Transportation celebrated not only railroads but automobiles, boats, and airplanes. One hundred and fifty performers aided by 10 trains—in addition to the boats, autos, and a model of the Wright brothers' airplane—mesmerized the audience.

On May 26, 1934, the Burlington's *Pioneer Zephyr* broke the world's long-distance nonstop speed record, traveling from Denver to Chicago, averaging 77.6 miles per hour and reaching a top speed of 112.5 miles per hour. A half hour after it came to a halt in Chicago, it appeared on stage at the Wings of a Century pageant. It was a remarkable experience even as the country was mired in the depths of the Great Depression.

The Burlington's exhibits in the Century of Progress Travel and Transportation building included dioramas of Colorado's Front Range and the Black Hills of South Dakota. Outside was a six-car modern passenger train. This brochure invited fairgoers to "use the six cars as headquarters . . . and relax and rest in comfortable soft-cushioned seats." Headed by locomotive No. 3000, a 4-6-4, the display train consisted of a Railway Post Office car, a chair car, a dining car, a Pullman (half sleeper and half lounge), a standard 14-section Pullman, and a lounge car. The Burlington's *Pioneer Zephyr* was also exhibited at the 1934 season of the fair.

The Baltimore & Ohio's Century of Progress exhibits featured interior sections of three passenger cars, including an 1890 coach. The other two cars were replicated outside the building as full-size passenger cars, part of the *Capitol Limited* headed by steam locomotive *President Cleveland*. Of the many antique locomotives displayed there, the original 1832 *Atlantic* and a train of Imlay coaches also starred in the pageant at the 1948 Chicago Railroad Fair and are pictured on that fair's program.

Much importance was attached to the air conditioning of trains, and B&O was a pioneer in that technology. The dining car *Martha Washington* was air conditioned in 1930 and was the first railroad car to be mechanically refrigerated. By 1931, B&O had its entire St. Louis–New York City train air conditioned. By 1932, several more trains were also equipped.

Additionally the public could order "at cost" china celebrating B&O's centenary for later delivery.

This aerial view of Chicago's A Century of Progress, from about 13th Street on the right to 31st Street on the left, shows the Sky Ride dividing the north and south lagoons. The round building closest to the bottom of the photo is the Adler Planetarium. The stadium at right is Soldier Field. The substantial railroad yards of the Illinois Central are easily seen just above the fairgrounds passing from upper left to lower right. The dark cylindrical shape at the far left of the fairgrounds is the rear of the Travel and Transport Building.

CHICAGO 1934 WORLD'S FAIR
BIGGER, BRIGHTER, BETTER

Illinois Central
A STATION AT EVERY GATE

Adjoins Fair Grounds from End To End

The Illinois Central's main lines and heavily used electric suburban service were adjacent to the Chicago Railroad Fair. Fair-bound passengers arriving on through trains detrained at the Illinois Central station near the Roosevelt Road fair entrance. Locals visiting the fair arrived at one of five suburban service platforms, each adjacent to one of the five fair entrances. This stylized cover shows numerous Illinois Central suburban trains and their stations at every fair entrance. The heights of the fair buildings are greatly exaggerated.

CHESAPEAKE & OHIO

The Chesapeake & Ohio Railroad was formed from a merger of the Virginia Central and Covington & Ohio in 1868. Bankrupt by 1869, it was acquired by C. P. Huntington, who saw it as a link in a transcontinental connecting the Atlantic with the Pacific. Huntington lost ownership when the road was reorganized in 1875.

By 1882, the railroad did reach the Atlantic at Newport News, Virginia. Reorganized yet again in 1888, it was acquired by the Vanderbilts. Soon, C&O trains were whistling into Louisville and the nation's capital. Acquisitions brought the railroad to the shores of Lake Erie at Toledo in 1903 and to Lake Michigan at Chicago in 1910. Like its competitors, the C&O would profit from hauling coal across the Appalachian Mountains to the Midwest.

In 1960 C&O began to purchase the Baltimore & Ohio, which owned half of the Western Maryland, which controlled the Reading, which controlled the Central Railroad of New Jersey, all of which became part of the Chessie System in 1973. By 1987, the C&O, Baltimore & Ohio, Western Maryland, Seaboard Air Line, Atlantic Coast Line, and Louisville & Nashville had all become part of CSX Transportation.

Introduced in 1933, the Chesapeake & Ohio's new crack passenger train, the *George Washington*, featured mechanical refrigeration instead of using ice as a coolant. Ads for the cool sleeping cars soon included the words "Sleeping Like a Kitten" and an image of a cat named Chessie. So successful was the advertisement that Chessie remained the railroad's advertising spokescat for decades. She even found time to acquire a husband and give birth to kittens. Millions of calendars were printed with her likeness, as well as countless advertisements. In this ad, a chorus sings Chessie to sleep to the tune of a popular song "Let Me Call You Sweetheart."

Chessie's kittens watch *The Chessie* roar past while Chessie herself chooses to sleep through the passage of the train named for her. To kick off the railroad's postwar passenger revival, the Chesapeake & Ohio ordered a steam-turbine-powered Vista Dome streamliner named *The Chessie* for daylight service between Washington, D.C., and Cincinnati. Even before the train arrived, the railroad had discovered there was no market for the planned service. As with other railroads, passengers never returned. After ordering almost 300 new passenger cars (in addition to *The Chessie*) the C&O sold off new passenger cars after delivery and canceled orders for those not yet delivered.

"Here comes your train, Chessie"

Ride a Postwar Wonder Train!

It's lounge car luxury at coach fares
on the new PERE MARQUETTES
—best way to travel between
Detroit, Lansing, and Grand Rapids

Voyageur Press collection

Chesapeake & Ohio extended into Michigan when it merged the Pere Marquette. The "wonder train" in this ad cut 40 minutes off the trip from Detroit to Grand Rapids. It featured a lounge-like environment in every coach, a novel dining car, and seats designed by a university to maximize comfort.

A 1943 wartime ad shows tanks loaded on flatcars behind an Allegheny-type locomotive with a 2-6-6-6 wheel arrangement, a new innovation first built in 1942. Company executives are urged to request a booklet describing the advantages of locating their manufacturing plant along the Chesapeake & Ohio.

Voyageur Press collection

Claude Wiatrowski photo

Though Chessie the Cat had retired by 1973, she was called back to active duty by the railroad as a stylized image that appeared, among other places, on Chessie System locomotives. Chessie adorns a diesel locomotive while a Kentucky Central steam locomotive prepares to depart with a special passenger train for the Tourist Railway Association.

CHICAGO

143   NEW UNION STATION, CHICAGO

All Voyageur Press collection

291   ILLINOIS CENTRAL STATION, CHICAGO

Chicago was the railroad hub of the nation and nowhere was that more evident to the average citizen than in the many monumental railroad stations that served the city. Chicago was a small grain port on Lake Michigan when railroad tracks of the Galena & Chicago Union were spiked down westward in 1848. By 1850, Chicago was home to 29,000 souls. A brief decade later, 109,000 resided here, with its economy stoked by the fires of steam locomotives pulling 70 daily trains on 11 railways. This railroad center of the nation would host 1.7 million residents by the close of the nineteenth century, an incredible 75 percent of whom had emigrated from other countries, frequently responding to railroad promotions to settle and prosper in the American West.

159—Dearborn Street Station, Chicago

BIRDS EYE VIEW BUSINESS DISTRICT OF CHICAGO
NEW PASSENGER TERMINAL, NORTH WESTERN RY. IN FOREGROUND

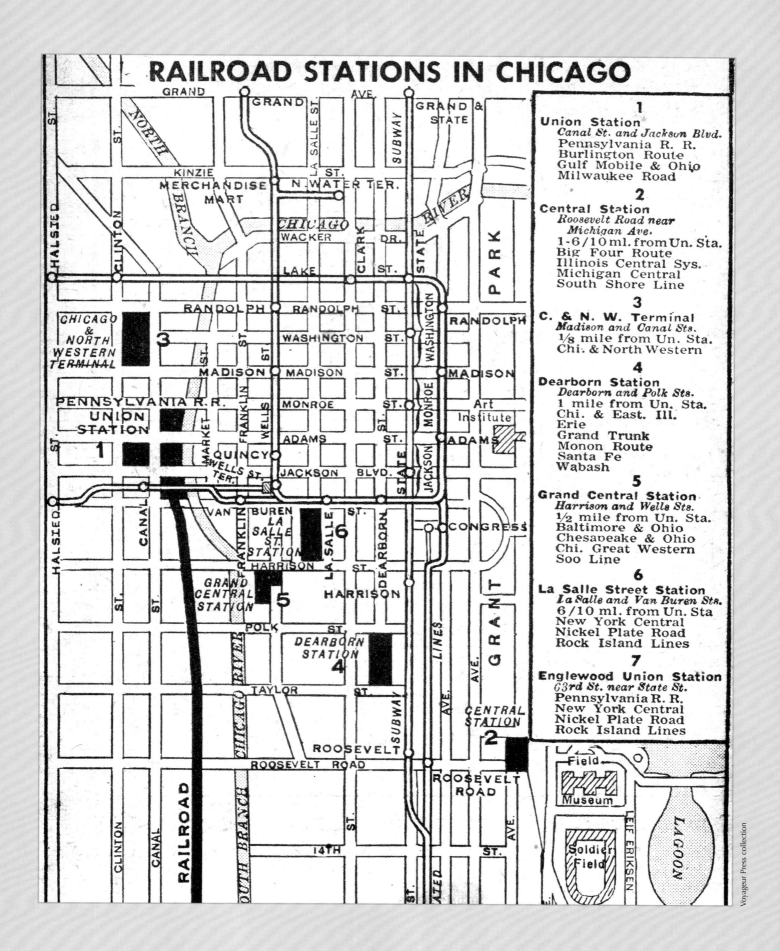

RAILROAD STATIONS IN CHICAGO

1
Union Station
Canal St. and Jackson Blvd.
Pennsylvania R. R.
Burlington Route
Gulf Mobile & Ohio
Milwaukee Road

2
Central Station
Roosevelt Road near Michigan Ave.
1-6/10 ml. from Un. Sta.
Big Four Route
Illinois Central Sys.
Michigan Central
South Shore Line

3
C. & N. W. Terminal
Madison and Canal Sts.
1/8 mile from Un. Sta.
Chi. & North Western

4
Dearborn Station
Dearborn and Polk Sts.
1 mile from Un. Sta.
Chi. & East. Ill.
Erie
Grand Trunk
Monon Route
Santa Fe
Wabash

5
Grand Central Station
Harrison and Wells Sts.
1/2 mile from Un. Sta.
Baltimore & Ohio
Chesapeake & Ohio
Chi. Great Western
Soo Line

6
La Salle Street Station
La Salle and Van Buren Sts.
6/10 ml. from Un. Sta
New York Central
Nickel Plate Road
Rock Island Lines

7
Englewood Union Station
63rd St. near State St.
Pennsylvania R. R.
New York Central
Nickel Plate Road
Rock Island Lines

CIRCUS AND CARNIVAL TRAINS

Imagine that you are 12 years old again and you are waiting by the railroad track in 1925 to watch the technological centerpiece of the age rumble past. You know the schedule of every train through town, so the sound of an unexpected whistle starts your blood pumping. You hear the chugging of a steam locomotive before it comes close enough for you to see its white flags signaling that it is an "extra" or unscheduled train. That would be exciting enough, but instead of the usual dark-green passenger cars or dull-red boxcars, the locomotive is chased by a parade of brightly painted circus cars. Gold. Red. White. Blue. The rainbow train passes in review. Flatcars shoulder gaudily painted circus wagons. Passenger coaches shelter clowns, acrobats, and lion tamers. Stock cars hold horses, elephants, lions, tigers, and bears. Such was the pageant as the circus train passed, and it was no accident: the train was an advertisement for the performances to follow.

If you lived in the town at which the circus would perform, you could rise early in the morning and go down to watch the unloading. With only a single day in each town, unloading started early and proceeded rapidly. Horses, sometimes elephants, and later tractors unloaded one circus wagon after another. No opportunity for advertising was wasted. All the wagons and animals crossed town to reach the circus grounds, and this explosion of color was always routed down Main Street.

As soon as the parade reached the circus grounds, tent poles, canvas, stakes, seats, flooring, rope, and everything needed to set up the circus tent was removed from those wagons and the canvas arena hurriedly assembled. Excursion trains from nearby hamlets began to arrive at the depot. Never before had so many passenger trains paused here at one time.

Even as the show was enthralling the audience, much of the menagerie had served its purpose and was loaded back on the train along with anything else that was now superfluous to the actual performance. As the last reveler left the grounds, the tent was being struck and reloaded into the

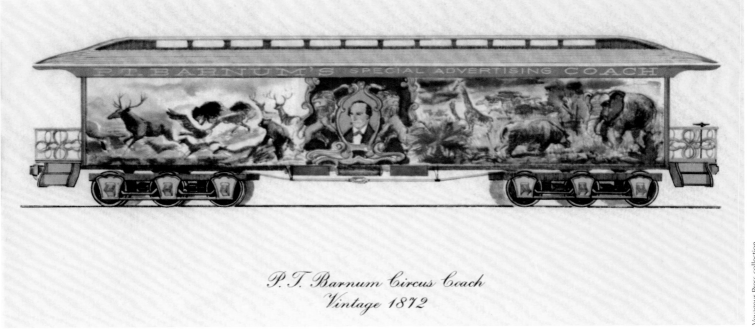

P.T. Barnum Circus Coach
Vintage 1872

The year of this lithograph, 1872, indicates it is a representation of the first true railroad circus organized by Coup, Castello and Barnum. Not all advance cars included elaborate murals but they all were rolling billboards advertising the circus. Advance cars were loaded with advertising bills, posters, and everything needed to customize them and paste them up. Men called "billers" worked out of the car and slept in it at night. The biggest shows had two, three, or even four such cars. Since a circus played most towns for just one day, the advance cars did their work in one day too. Sometimes, 5,000 or even 10,000 sheets could be posted in a single day. Billers also traveled to nearby towns on regular passenger trains to post bills, and an excursion agent operating out of an advance car arranged for the railroads to run special trains to bring patrons from nearby towns. He sent small advertising bills and large advertising posters to nearby station agents to be posted "in the interest of the railroad." Two free tickets to the circus accompanied the advertising posters just to be sure the agent complied.

wagons for transport back to the railyard. It was late. Tired performers removed their costumes and climbed into their sleeping-car bunks as the train whistled off for the next town and the next day's performance.

Dan Castello had moved his circus west in 1868 and 1869 on the first transcontinental railway, almost on the heels of the construction trains. His experience, combined with that of showman William Coup and legendary impresario P. T. Barnum, created the first modern railroad circus in 1872. Coup developed the system of

advance agents who peppered the town with advertising bills pasted on all available surfaces. Advance agents convinced railroads to run special excursion trains on the day of the performance to increase the size of the area from which the circus could draw customers, allowing railroad circuses to skip small towns and play only larger cities. By September of that first 1872 season, circus advertising emphasized for the first time that this was a *railroad* circus.

The railroad network was starting its golden years of expansion, and opportunities for showmen were unparalleled. Railroad circuses reached their zenith at the beginning of the twentieth century when 32 such shows rode the rails. Giant Ringling Bros. and Barnum & Bailey rolled along in a train that peaked at 100 cars in the mid-1920s.

The Great Depression spelled trouble. By 1939, only two railroad shows remained. By the 1950s, circuses moved by truck as tents disappeared in favor of performances in arenas. Ringling Bros. and Barnum & Bailey called a halt to both tents and trains in 1956. By 1960, it was back on the rails, and in 1968 the Ringling family sold the circus to Irvin Feld, who created

two independent units of the same circus. Each unit travels in a circus train of 40 cars.

OTHER SHOW TRAINS

Circuses weren't the only entertainment ventures that used the railroads. Minstrel shows, Wild West shows, orchestras, Chautauquas, theater companies, traveling museums, and ice shows all have moved by train. One kind of train stands out as being different, however, and that is the carnival train.

GENERAL VIEW OF THE TWELVE COLOSSAL WATER PROOF CANVAS PAVILIONS, EXACTLY THE SAME AS WILL BE ERECTED, BENEATH WHICH TWO GRAND EXHIBITIONS ARE GIVEN EVERY WEEK DAY. THEY ARE THE LARGEST AND FINEST CANVAS PAVILIONS EVER ERECTED ANYWHERE ON EARTH.

THE WORLD'S LARGEST, GRANDEST, BEST AMUSEMENT INSTITUTION.

Carnivals are conglomerates of shows, concessions, and rides. Shows might include a movie theater, a side show, or even a small circus. Concessions supply food and entertain with games. Rides were few at first but became more numerous in the 1920s.

Traveling carnivals appeared before the turn of the nineteenth century and soon were traveling by rail. Rail transport made the traveling carnival practical since carnivals carry a large amount of equipment.

Superficially, a carnival train looked a lot like a circus train. Both were brightly painted to attract attention. However, carnival trains were mostly flatcars of wagons loaded with equipment. Sleeping cars were not included since carnivals moved once a week or less. Circuses moved daily and employees had to sleep while traveling to a new destination. Circus trains included stock cars for animals, while a carnival train most often did not.

As roads and truck technology improved, carnivals abandoned trains. In 1981, Royal American Shows—which once operated a 90-car carnival train—switched to trucks, leaving only one carnival operator, James E. Strates Shows, using a train.

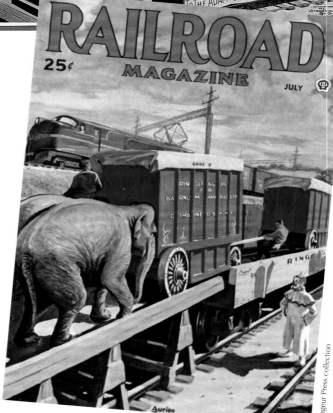

The cover of this magazine dated July 1946 depicts an elephant loading circus wagons onto a train to be moved by the New Haven Railroad.

Carnival wagons are unloaded with a tractor in the 1960s.

James E. Strates Shows operates the last carnival train, shown here at its winter quarters in Taft, Florida, in 1994.

DENVER & RIO GRANDE

In 1870, the Denver & Rio Grande Railroad built south from Denver with rails laid 3 feet apart as a cost-saving measure. Projected to cross the Rio Grande River on Mexico's border, the line would connect Denver with Mexico City. But the Santa Fe blocked its route over Raton Pass and its trains never arrived in Mexico City. Instead, its web of narrow gauge tracks would cover the Colorado Rockies and even reach Salt Lake City. Competition from the standard gauge Colorado Midland forced the Denver & Rio Grande to widen its most important routes; narrow gauge backwaters struggled on until 1968.

The Denver & Rio Grande's *Scenic Limited* pauses at Pueblo Union Station in 1935. Today, the station has been beautifully restored as part of Pueblo's historic downtown. A railroad museum displays its collection next to the building.

In 1934, the renamed Denver & Rio Grande Western Railroad built 40 miles of track connecting its own main line with that of the Denver & Salt Lake. This allowed "Rio Grande" trains to travel through the recently completed 6-mile Moffat Tunnel, shortening their trip between Denver and Salt Lake City by 200 miles. The Denver & Rio Grande merged the Denver & Salt Lake in 1947.

The Rio Grande purchased the Southern Pacific in 1988 but retained the name Southern Pacific. In 1996, the Southern Pacific would be merged into the Union Pacific.

351—West Portal of the Moffat Tunnel at the Foot of Berthoud Pass in Middle Park, Colorado

This is the west portal of the Moffat Tunnel. Its 6-mile plunge under the Continental Divide is still an important part of the national railroad system—trains of the Union Pacific use this shortcut through the mountains.

This 1953 timetable features both the Moffat Tunnel and Royal Gorge routes. The two tracks merged at Dotsero, Colorado, and continued west to Salt Lake City. This timetable still listed many narrow gauge freight services but only narrow gauge passenger service on the Silverton Branch.

As the Rio Grande's narrow gauge lines contracted, there were fewer places such as Salida, shown here, where three-rail track could accommodate trains of either width. The locomotive is a Challenger type with a 4-6-6-4 wheel arrangement. Large articulated, standard gauge locomotives were necessary to running a mountain railroad.

In this art from a GM Electro-Motive Division ad, two narrow gauge locomotives struggle with a short passenger train over Veta Pass between Walsenburg and Alamosa in Colorado. In 2006, the Rio Grande Scenic Railroad began carrying passenger over Veta Pass from Alamosa.

THE CURTAIN LIFTS ON TOMORROW'S RAILROADING

Voyageur Press collection

Claude Wiatrowski photo

Converted from narrow gauge steam to standard gauge diesel operation in the mid-1950s, Colorado's Monarch Pass branch passed into oblivion in the 1980s. Here, a Denver & Rio Grande train carries limestone from the quarry for which the line was built to Salida and then Pueblo, where the limestone was used in the steelmaking process.

DIESEL LOCOMOTIVES

The first successful uses of internal combustion engines on railroads were in self-propelled, gasoline-powered passenger cars. The Erie Works of General Electric even constructed a gas-electric locomotive in 1913. Although gasoline engines would have limited use as power sources for railroads, GE's pioneering transfer of power to the wheels by electricity would become key to future diesel locomotive technology.

By 1924, a diesel-electric switching locomotive was distributing cars in a railyard of the Central Railroad of New Jersey. In 1933, internal combustion engines were powering the first streamlined passenger trains. By 1936, almost 200 switchers were puttering around railyards in the United States and Canada.

In 1923, a small entrepreneurial company named Electro-Motive Corporation introduced its first gas-electric motorcar. That company became the Electro-Motive Division of General Motors in 1930. In 1939, EMD's first diesel freight locomotive, model FT, began a two-year demonstration tour, operating on 21 railroads in 37 states. Each of its four units generated 1,350 horsepower from a 16-cylinder diesel engine. Coupled together, all 5,400 horses could be controlled by a single engineer.

After World War II, EMD routinely advertised the benefits of traveling in trains hauled by their diesel locomotives. In the case of the legendary *California Zephyr*, the ad featured the three railroads that cooperated to run the train: the Burlington, the Denver & Rio Grande, and the Western Pacific.

Norfolk Southern locomotive 9807 glides through the dusk. General Electric built their model C40-9W, commonly called a Dash 9 series locomotive. The two low-mounted lights are called "ditch lights" and their purpose is to illuminate the ground just ahead of the locomotive.

Courtesy Milton A. Davis collection

Claude Wiatrowski photo

Though diesel locomotives did not generate as much smoke as steam locomotives, their exhaust was still dangerous in the confined space of a tunnel, requiring mechanical ventilation. A string of Denver & Rio Grande freight diesels leaves the 6-mile-long Moffat Tunnel.

In a peacock display of color, these four locomotives are displayed at the Illinois Railway Museum, along with many others. From right to left, they are painted for the Santa Fe, the Columbus & Greenville, the Green Bay & Western, and the Union Pacific.

Claude Wiatrowski photo

Unquestionably the most unusual postwar diesel experiment was the General Motors *Aerotrain*. Although their appearance was spectacular, their performance was not.

Voyageur Press collection

The Verde Canyon Railroad moves freight from Clarkdale, Arizona, with the EMD model GP7 locomotive at right. It also carries passengers with the EMD FP7 on the left. The railroad owns two of these rare streamlined passenger locomotives, which feature a spectacular illustration of an eagle on their sides.

Diesels required fewer crewmembers and fewer skills to operate, and ran hundreds of miles without servicing. Diesel locomotives also reduced track-maintenance costs by eliminating the pounding forces of the heavy reciprocating rods that drove steam locomotive wheels.

Diesel locomotives are more energy-efficient than steam locomotives, their efficiency and power output constant over a wide range of speeds. Steam locomotives were designed for maximum output and efficiency in a very narrow range of speeds, so railroads needed many different kinds of steam locomotives designed for different uses.

Repairs and maintenance required that an entire steam locomotive be taken out of service and parts custom made by experienced craftsmen. Diesels are assembled from interchangeable parts. Mechanics remove a damaged assembly, replace it with an identical premade assembly, and send the original to a specialized shop to be repaired or rebuilt for later use.

Today, only two major U.S. diesel locomotive manufacturers are left. They are also the two most important pioneers

of diesel-electric technology: General Electric Company and Electro-Motive Diesel, formerly the Electro-Motive Division of General Motors.

HOW DIESEL LOCOMOTIVES WORK

Diesel engines are called internal combustion because fuel is burned—really exploded—inside their cylinders, forcing their pistons to move. Power must be transmitted from the engine to the wheels. This transmission can be mechanical, hydraulic, or electrical. Most modern locomotives have electrical transmissions and are called diesel-electrics. The diesel engine rotates a generator that creates electricity, which powers electric motors in the locomotive's axles.

Brakes controlled by pressurized air take skill to operate. Air brakes use the frictional force between brake shoe and steel wheel to slow the train. Wheel and shoe wear away and need to be replaced. In addition to standard air brakes, some diesel-electric locomotives incorporate a *dynamic brake* system that does not use friction but instead dissipates braking energy as heat in electrical resistors to slow the locomotive, greatly reducing wear on wheels and brakes shoes.

RAIL MOTORCARS

Although they look like ordinary passenger cars, rail motorcars can move themselves with engines concealed inside or underneath the car. Only one crewmember is required and they are very economical to operate when only light traffic is expected on a railroad route.

The first rail motorcar was powered by steam—the only technology available—and ran in 1851. The economic advantage of a motorcar was magnified with the advent of the internal

Allan Hunt, Iowa Interstate Railroad

Both of these Iowa Interstate locomotives are variations of EMD's GP38. No. 603 is a GP38, while No. 700 is a GP38-2.

CN photo

Twin Canadian National locomotives stand side by side at Symington Yard in Winnipeg, Manitoba. GE built them as model C44-9W.

Claude Wiatrowski photo

This self-propelled car was built by the Edwards Railway Motor Car Company for the Butte, Anaconda & Pacific in 1925. It last served on the Butte, Montana, tourist railroad Neversweat & Washoe. Since that railroad ceased operation, the car is seldom displayed.

combustion engine. The two most important early manufacturers were McKeen Motor Car and General Electric. Neither company resumed production after World War I.

The Edward G. Budd Company pioneered construction of stainless-steel streamlined passenger trains. In 1949, it introduced a phenomenally successful line of streamlined diesel-electric rail motorcars, called RDCs (Rail Diesel Cars). In an era when passenger rail travel was declining, Budd sold 398 cars. Perhaps, it was because rail passenger travel *was* declining that railroads sought a more economic alternative for smaller numbers of passengers. The last great RDC route ran from Vancouver to Prince George in British Columbia and the last RDC made this journey for BC Rail in 2002. Five models of the RDC included combinations of passenger, baggage, and Railway Post Office compartments. They could be connected together and controlled by a single engineer when needed.

Budd tried to introduce a replacement, the SPV2000, but was unsuccessful. Colorado Railcar Manufacturing, a builder of luxurious passenger cars, currently builds a rail motorcar, the DMU (Diesel Multiple Unit). Available as both single- and double-decked models, they are marketed to commuter railroads.

Budd RDC cars successfully competed with airlines on shorter routes such as the Los Angeles–San Diego route to which these cars were assigned.

Self-propelled railcars were not restricted to standard gauge railroads. Narrow gauge Galloping Goose No. 5 crosses the Animas River on a special excursion on the Durango & Silverton Narrow Gauge Railroad. Several of these vehicles were constructed by the long-abandoned Rio Grande Southern to carry both freight and passengers. Their economy of operation was said to have delayed bankruptcy of the Rio Grande Southern for decades.

DINNER IN THE DINER

There may be no better memory from the era of great passenger trains than eating dinner while rolling through the countryside. Those memories start with the mellow sound of chimes calling passengers to the dining car and continue with a multi-course repast on par with dinners in the best restaurants.

Early railroads did not concern themselves with their passengers' need to eat, but as railroads got longer, passengers got hungrier. Even on short trips, delayed trains would disgorge famished riders. The knowledgeable traveler brought lunch. It wasn't long before entrepreneurs met trains at brief station stops and sold food to their passengers. In the 1840s, "news butchers" began roaming the aisles of passenger cars selling not only food but also books, newspapers, and medicines—any item that a traveler might need.

In addition, restaurants opened near depots. Travelers would step out onto the station platform to have their ears assaulted by the sound of gongs rung to attract attention to these dining establishments. Twenty minutes of bedlam ensued as passengers rushed to devour a meal. Eventually, railroads built their own eating facilities. A small country depot would incorporate a correspondingly small lunch counter. A large city might merit a railroad-built hotel with a dining room for hundreds. Although an improvement over the news butcher or platform vendor, eating stops were still too short for the passengers and too long for the railroads. As train speeds increased, pauses for meals became an increasing burden on schedules.

The first attempts at feeding people on a moving train were made in the 1830s with food brought on board from trackside restaurants. The first mobile kitchens appeared on Civil War hospital trains to prepare meals for wounded soldiers. In 1867, George Pullman constructed a hotel car that combined sleeping accommodations with facilities for

A dining car of 1870 features gas lamps and inlaid wood paneling. Otherwise, it is not too different from a modern dining car.

A classic scene in a post–World War II dining car. The china featured the railroad's own custom design. The tablecloths and napkins were linen, and the waiters wore white. China has become one of the most treasured railroad collectibles.

UNION PACIFIC RAILROAD

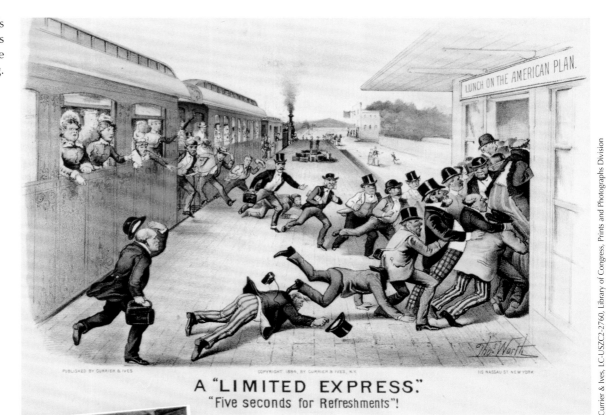

A "LIMITED EXPRESS."
"Five seconds for Refreshments"!

preparing and serving food. Pullman went on to build the restaurant car *Delmonico*, exclusively for preparing and serving food. The Chicago & Alton Railroad operated it. Woe to the railroad that was unwilling to lose money serving superb meals. Passengers would ride another railroad that served better food.

The term "dining car" came into widespread use in the last decades of the nineteenth century, although such cars were limited to railroads' best first-class passenger trains. In the first decades of the twentieth century, food-service cars became ubiquitous, and in 1930 over 1,700 dining cars catered to famished travelers.

As soon as a meal was completed, the dining car was uncoupled from the train. Not only was it a 100-ton anchor on the train's progress but its 10-person crew was

ENJOY Fresh FOODS all the way.. on Union Pacific

Streamliners

"CITY OF LOS ANGELES"
(between Chicago-Los Angeles)

"CITY OF SAN FRANCISCO"
(between Chicago-San Francisco)

"CITY OF PORTLAND"
(between Chicago-Portland-Tacoma-Seattle)

"CITY OF DENVER"
(between Chicago-Denver)

"CITY OF ST. LOUIS"
(between St. Louis-Kansas City-Pacific Coast)

Also between Chicago...and The Pacific Coast
LOS ANGELES LIMITED...SAN FRANCISCO
OVERLAND...and GOLD COAST

In the still of night while you sleep soundly, your train glides gently to a stop. Then into the dining-car kitchen are loaded the fresh meats, poultry, fruits, vegetables and other fine foods you will enjoy the following day.

Stocks of these foods are stored at points along the route, always available for passing trains. When you travel on Union Pacific you're assured of wonderful meals, prepared from fresh foods, all the way!

Ask your ticket or travel agent to route you by Union Pacific through the West.

UNION PACIFIC RAILROAD

The logistics of feeding railroad passengers fresh food was staggering. All necessities had to be on the train—a quick trip to the local super market was out of the question. Menu item preferences were known but food had to be overstocked to account for variations in passenger preferences. It's is no wonder that food services on trains have always lost money and existed to attract passengers to the trains.

being paid. A dining car might be uncoupled after dinner by a westbound train to be picked up before breakfast by an eastbound train. Even so, diners were notoriously underutilized since they only could be used at the convergence of the railroad's train schedule and the passengers' stomach schedule.

On May 1, 1971, Amtrak became the operator of most U.S. passenger trains. Since then, Amtrak food services have run the gamut from great to poor to nonexistent. Congressional mandates have required Amtrak to not lose money on feeding passengers, despite the fact that privately run passenger trains almost always lost money on food service.

Union Pacific served diners in dome cars on the *City of Los Angeles* and *City of Portland*. No other railroad offered dining service in a dome car.

All Voyageur Press collection

www.archivesofadvertising.com

The Illinois Central's *Panama Limited* dinner, breakfast and drink menus had a familial resemblance. The train operated between Chicago and New Orleans, an impressionistic image of which is featured on the drink menu.

Number 1
85¢

Fruit or Fruit Juice

Choice of Cereal or Egg

Toast or Muffin

Milk or Cocoa

With Bacon (2) . . . . 25c extra

Number 2
$1.10

Choice of
Cup of Soup   Fruit Juice
Ready-to-Eat Cereal

Choice of
Poached Egg on Toast
Vegetable and Potato
Hot Fresh Vegetable Plate
Grilled Bacon (3 slices)
Vegetable and Potato

Ice Cream or Fruit

Milk or Cocoa

Left and below: The New York Central die-cut an especially attractive children's menu in the shape of its streamlined locomotives.

Voyageur Press collection

ENGINEER

Our engineer has lots of fun,
He likes to wave at everyone,
But just for boys and girls he saves
His biggest and most friendly waves.

FIREMAN

We think the fireman's job is swell,
He tends the fire, rings the bell,
And blows the whistle merrily
To clear the track for you and me.

CONDUCTOR

Conductors always worry so
Whenever trains are running slow,
But this conductor smiles. Why not?
Our trains are always on the dot.

PORTER

The Pullman porter's work is light,
He used to polish shoes all night.
But on our air-conditioned line
He can't find dust on shoes to shine.

BRAKEMAN

The brakeman with his flags and lights
Is quite the funniest of sights,
For coming up the aisle, you see,
He looks just like a Christmas tree.

WAITER

And meet the waiter, trim and neat,
Who brings delicious food to eat.
And look! He balances each meal
As jaunty as a circus seal.

COOK

Our jolly chef is nice to know,
He cooks the best that farmers grow,
Collecting it from near and far
To serve you in the dining car.

FARMER JONES

Next, farmer Jones, he works all day
Improving crops and pitching hay,
And making quite a lot of fuss
So he can sell his food to us.

SUSIE

And looking mighty happy now
Is Susie, farmer Jones' cow,
For ever since we came that way
She knows her milk must be Grade A.

CUT CUT CUT

"Cut-cut-cut," says every hen,
"Here comes that railroad man again,"
And then they sit and pop their eyes
Producing eggs of giant size.

SPINACH

The spinach plants all celebrate
Whenever we select a crate,
For even spinach tastes much finer
When eaten in an S. P. Diner.

QUEENS and PRESIDENTS

And so you see our food compares
With things prepared for millionaires,
But here it's served at less expense
To future Queens and Presidents.

Voyageur Press collection

Now just before you eat, please look
At all the pictures in this book.
It only takes one little minute
To introduce the people in it.

Left and above: A Southern Pacific children's menu also included job descriptions of the train crew and the virtues of spinach.

FRISCO

In 1876, the bankrupt Atlantic & Pacific Railroad's main line from St. Louis to the Missouri–Oklahoma border was sold to the newly incorporated St. Louis & San Francisco Railway. A&P would continue to exist west of Missouri.

The St. Louis & San Francisco, known as the Frisco, was centered on Springfield, Missouri. Besides its St. Louis route, its tracks would reach Wichita and Kansas City to the northwest, and Memphis, Birmingham, and Florida tidewater at Pensacola to the southeast. Rails would radiate southwest to Tulsa, Oklahoma City, Dallas, and Fort Worth.

Jointly constructed by the Frisco and the Santa Fe Railway, the A&P's line west from Albuquerque was completed in 1883 to a connection with the Southern Pacific at Needles, California. In 1896, the newly reorganized Frisco purchased A&P's lines in Oklahoma while the Santa Fe bought the A&P line from Albuquerque to Needles. The Frisco was merged into the Burlington Northern in 1980.

In 1947, the diesel-powered streamlined *Texas Special* was yet to come and the Frisco, as did all railroads, retained high hopes that passengers would return to the rails after World War II.

Voyageur Press collection

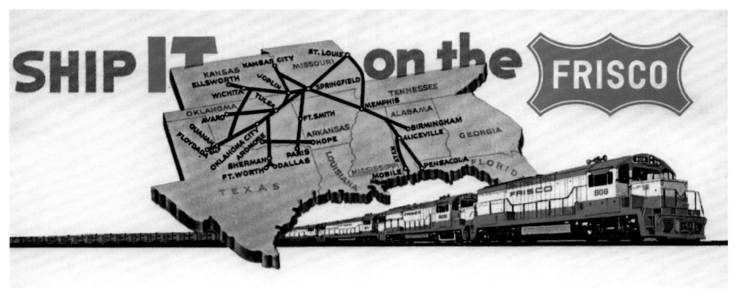

The Frisco's route map appears on a notepad distributed to shippers.

In 1937, a Frisco Atlantic-type locomotive rests in St. Louis. This semi-streamlined look had a skirt below the locomotive's running boards (walkways for maintenance). The skirt's lines were continued in the paint scheme on the tender.

In 1940, the Frisco's all-streamlined, steam-powered *Firefly* enters the outskirts of Kansas City after a run from Tulsa, Oklahoma.

GREAT NORTHERN

"Most men who have really lived have had,
in some shape, their great adventure.
This railway is mine."

—James J. Hill, 1912

James J. Hill began acquiring railroads in 1878. By the end of 1890, the Great Northern was operating over 3,000 miles of Midwestern railroad. The railroad's Pacific Coast extension was begun that year and completed in 1893.

The railroad crossed the Rocky Mountains over the undemanding Marias Pass. It would not be so lucky crossing the Cascade Mountains, where switchbacks were later bypassed by a 2.6 mile-long tunnel; in 1929, a new Cascade Tunnel replaced the old. Trains reached Duluth, Minnesota, and nearby iron mines; Sioux City in Iowa; and Billings in Montana, as well as the copper mines of Butte. Trains would also reach Oregon and California, although extensions into Canada would not last.

In 1901, the Great Northern and Northern Pacific purchased the Burlington to ensure access to Chicago. Regulators refused merger until 1970 when the three railroads and the Spokane, Portland & Seattle became the Burlington Northern.

The Great Northern's postwar streamlined *Empire Builder* shot from Chicago to Seattle in a mere 45 hours. The railroad's advertisements were chock full of adjectives, including *refreshing, spacious, cheerful, gay,* and *charming,* to describe this train.

Voyageur Press collection

A Great Northern 2-10-2 locomotive hisses gently at Portland, Oregon, in the autumn of 1949. It is autumn for all steam locomotives, with only about five years left before steam operations will cease on main-line railroads. Since steam locomotive driving wheels were fastened to a rigid frame, 10-drivered locomotives put great stress on track structures as they rounded curves. A few 12-drivered locomotives were built for use in the United States, but articulated locomotives were more common when more than eight driving wheels were needed. To negotiate curves, an articulated steam locomotive's front set of driving wheels swivels separately from the rigidly attached rear set of driving wheels.

www.cabincreekcds.com

An EMD F7 streamlined locomotive idles at the Seattle roundhouse in February 1970.

A double-headed *Oriental Limited* is about to enter Horseshoe Tunnel in the Cascade Mountains of Washington. James J. Hill understood that the success of his railways depended not only on colonization of the sparsely settled lands along his routes, but also on the prosperity of the settlers who relocated to those lands. Thus, he and his railroads were intimately involved in the development of farming and ranching. He introduced the first threshing machine to Minnesota, advocated crop rotation, and imported purebred cattle. The Great Northern carried the first shipment of Minnesota wheat to market.

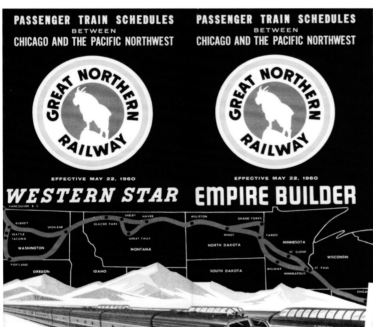

It is 1960 and the clock is ticking on the end of privately run rail passenger service in the United States. The *Western Star* duplicated the route of the *Empire Builder* but stopped at many more towns and thus had a slower schedule from Chicago to the West Coast.

INDUSTRIAL RAILWAYS

An industrial railway carries only the freight and passengers of its owner. As early as the sixteenth century, men were pushing wooden carts on wooden rails in German mines. Modern industrial railways might carry minerals, agricultural harvests, wood products, or manufactured goods: limestone to cement plants, clay to brickworks, and coal to power plants, for example. Although industrial railways frequently have been short in length and narrow in gauge, some were and are monumental enterprises. Before trucks were suitably large and durable, industrial railways were used to construct everything from dams to highways.

Baldwin, Porter, Lima, and other locomotive manufacturers built specialized locomotives for various industrial uses. Geared locomotives were built to haul trains of logs. Fireless steam locomotives were inexpensive to maintain and operate, as they were simply periodically filled with steam from an industrial plant's stationary boilers. Flameproof diesels prevented combustible gases—such as the methane in a coal mine—from igniting. Many industrial railways met their demise because locomotives were easily replaced by conveyor belts, pipelines, or trucks.

Classic industrial railways hauled dirt. Here a steam shovel loads that commodity into dump cars that will be hauled away by a "dinky," a slang term for a very small steam locomotive.

Not all industrial locomotives were small. Here, a huge Indiana Hill & Iron Range 0-8-0 switcher hauls coal from ships on Lake Michigan to an industrial plant in Hammond, Indiana, in 1955. A conveyer would handle the short run today.

KATY

A year after the Union Pacific, Southern Branch (no relation to the Union Pacific) began construction in 1869 from Junction City, Kansas, to New Orleans, the railroad assumed the name Missouri, Kansas & Texas Railway, which would be popularly contracted to "Katy." It later extended to St. Louis, Kansas City, Topeka, and Omaha. It reached Dallas in 1881, Houston in 1893, San Antonio in 1900, and eventually Tulsa, Oklahoma City, Abilene, Galveston, Shreveport, and more.

Perhaps haphazard expansion—almost 4,000 miles by 1915—was responsible for the Katy's financial woes. It was reorganized as the Missouri-Kansas-Texas Railroad in 1923. Prosperity was mirrored in its bright yellow cabooses during World War II.

Galvanized by losses from 1957 to 1971, two new presidents abandoned unprofitable lines, rebuilt profitable ones, and saved enough cash to purchase new equipment. Seventy percent of the railroad's traffic had become bridge shipments of unit trains loaded with grain and coal, and the line was understandably concerned when mergers threatened to reroute these trains off its tracks. The Union Pacific absorbed the Katy in 1988.

Voyageur Press collection

The Missouri-Kansas-Texas Railroad Better Known As The KATY chronicled the history of that railroad in celebration of its centenary.

Voyageur Press collection

This is the cover of a 1950 pocket calendar issued by GM's Electro-Motive Division and featuring the Katy.

The Katy's San Antonio depot was patterned after the string of mission churches in the city. It may have been the most beautiful railroad station in the southern United States. Sadly, the building was not preserved.

Claude Wiatrowski collection

LOGGING

European colonists of North America built log cabins for shelter and burned firewood for warmth, but logging companies replaced do-it-yourself harvest of trees. Early on, trees were cut near a river and dragged to its banks by teams of oxen. Made into rafts, the logs were floated to market. In the 1880s, steam "donkey engines" pulled logs through the woods by cable. As trunk railroads built farther from rivers, loggers found new sources of timber. It was an obvious step to replace oxen with locomotives.

Some early logging railroads made their rails from wood. Grades were steep and curves sharp. Trains were slow and as soon as the nearby timber was harvested, the track was torn up and moved to another stand of trees. Since logging railroads usually did not interchange cars with common-carrier railroads, their gauge was determined by whatever used rolling stock could be purchased, or by the whim of the owner. Either castoff antiques or geared locomotives designed specially for logging service pulled flatcars loaded with logs from the woods.

Three main types of geared steam locomotives were produced: the Shay, the Climax, and the Heisler. Each powered all the wheels on their four-wheel trucks with geared shafts, eliminating the heavy rods and large driving wheels that transmitted power to the rails in conventional locomotives. Geared locomotives were slow but powerful. Without large drive wheels fixed to the frame, they could negotiate the most irregular track. Later, *disconnects* replaced flatcars. These were single, four-wheel trucks and logs were suspended between a pair. The logs themselves became the railroad car so that any length logs could be hauled.

As nearby stands of timber were harvested, new timber required still-longer hauls. Large railroad logging operations developed main-line routes to transport logs from the woods and lumber from sawmills. Locomotive builders responded to the longer routes. Large articulated *Mallet* locomotives capable of pulling 100-car trains were built especially for logging companies.

The last true logging railroad—one that hauled logs from the woods—ceased operation in 1957. After that, logs were loaded onto diesel trucks and driven to the main-line portions of logging railroads.

The first geared locomotive was invented by Ephraim Shay, a northern Michigan logger. Shay locomotives were built by the Lima Locomotive Works in Ohio and were the most popular type of geared locomotives, with close to 3,000 constructed between 1880 and 1945. The vertical cylinders on one side of the boiler drove a crankshaft that was part of a line shaft, which powered every axle of the locomotive. Slip joints and universal joints gave the locomotive's trucks complete freedom of motion. In order to balance the weight of the offset three-cylinder engine, the boiler is mounted to one side, giving Shays a distinct asymmetric appearance. The Shay locomotive in the lead in this photo is followed by a Heisler on the Mt. Rainier Scenic Railroad in Washington.

Claude Wiatrowski photo

Claude Wiatrowski photos

C. L. Wasson, LC-USZ62-56636, Library of Congress, Prints and Photographs Division

Above: A log train is an excuse for an outing in the Cascade Mountains. The well-built wooden trestle indicates this line was intended to last a little longer than the average woods line.

Above right: The first Climax locomotive had a vertical boiler and a gauge of 6 feet with concave wheels for operation on a "pole road" (a railroad using round logs for its rails). A small vertical-cylinder engine and a line shaft were centered on the locomotive. The vertical boilers soon gave way to larger horizontal boilers, and the small vertical-cylinder engine gave way to more conventionally mounted cylinders, parallel to the axis of the boiler but inclined, as shown here on the Mt. Rainier Scenic Railroad. These cylinders drive a cross shaft that is geared to a line shaft under the boiler.

Right: A Heisler geared locomotive has two cylinders arranged in a V that directly power a crankshaft incorporated into a line shaft centrally located underneath the locomotive. The 3-foot-gauge Sumpter Valley Railway included an 80-mile main line west from Baker, Oregon. Two of its locomotives were mammoth articulated types, purchased used from Colorado's Uintah Railway. This wood-burning Heisler carries passengers along a restored portion of the Sumpter Valley.

C. L. Wasson, LC-USZ62-101045, Library of Congress, Prints and Photographs Division

Logging locomotives were frequently antediluvian relics purchased from other railroads. Not only were they inexpensive, they were small and light, perfect for operation on the undulating track of logging lines. At least one source for this photo identifies this single train of logs as having been cut from a single redwood tree.

MILWAUKEE ROAD

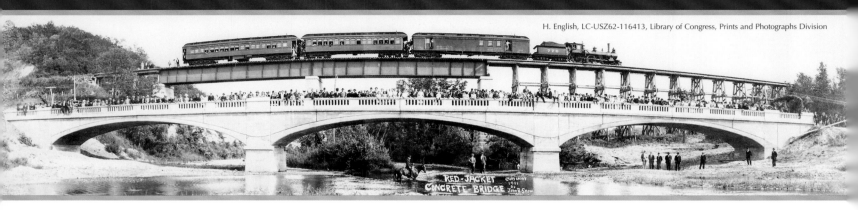

On August 22, 1911, the Red Jacket concrete road bridge was dedicated near Mankato, Minnesota. A Milwaukee Road passenger train that would eventually be replaced by automobiles crossing bridges like this attended the celebration. A classic American-type 4-4-0 locomotive powers this train.

The LaCrosse & Milwaukee Railroad was reorganized as the Milwaukee & St. Paul Railway in 1863. In 1873, it memorialized arrival in Chicago by changing its name to the Chicago, Milwaukee & St. Paul Railway.

By 1901, it had grown to over 6,500 miles, and in 1905 it began construction of its Pacific Extension. Actual construction cost totaled $235 million when completed in three years—an inexcusable quadruple of the original estimate of $60 million! An additional $22 million was spent electrifying two sections of the extension, an expense justifiable only if many trains ran, but the Milwaukee overestimated traffic.

In 1928, the railroad was reorganized as the Chicago, Milwaukee, St. Paul & Pacific. Bankruptcy followed in 1935 and later in 1977. The Pacific Extension was abandoned.

The Milwaukee Road was a railroad in the wrong century. Its Midwestern routes were a maze of agricultural branches, vulnerable to competition from trucks. A single daily freight train rumbled over its expensive Pacific Extension. Only its double-track main line between Chicago and Minneapolis–St. Paul was a modern railroad. Its route map continued to be pruned and in 1986 the Soo Line merged what was left of the once great Milwaukee Road.

An 1851 locomotive struggles across the Wisconsin prairie, a far cry from the EMD-built diesel locomotives that served the railroad's 225-mile Mountain Division from Avery, Idaho, to Othello, Washington, during World War II.

This photo of a construction train in Idaho's Bitter Root Mountains includes two flatcars of workers leaning on their shovels, one car in front of the locomotives and one at the end of the short train.

"ON THE CHICAGO, MILWAUKEE & ST. PAUL RAILWAY"

THE OLYMPIAN ON WEST SLOPE OF THE CASCADE MOUNTAINS, WASH.

CASCADE MTS., WASHINGTON
VERDANT AND BEAUTIFUL ALWAYS

The line through Washington's Cascade Mountains was one of two electrified segments on the Milwaukee Road where passengers sitting on the rear observation platform could stay free from the soot and cinders of a steam locomotive.

Built by General Electric, the Milwaukee Road's Bi-Polar locomotives were huge, powerful monsters generating 4,000 horsepower and measuring 76 feet long. In one publicity stunt, a single Bi-Polar easily won a tug of war with two large steam locomotives. Frequently pulling heavy trains up steep grades at 25 miles per hour, Bi-Polars could run as fast as 70 miles per hour.

"ON THE CHICAGO, MILWAUKEE & ST. PAUL RAILWAY"

MILLING DISTRICT, MINNEAPOLIS, MINN.

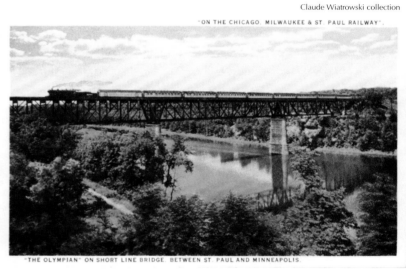

"ON THE CHICAGO, MILWAUKEE & ST. PAUL RAILWAY".

"THE OLYMPIAN" ON SHORT LINE BRIDGE, BETWEEN ST. PAUL AND MINNEAPOLIS.

During the Industrial Revolution, the Minneapolis Milling District was the subject of a postcard in a booklet of sights to be seen along the Milwaukee Road.

A steam-powered *Olympian* crosses between Minneapolis and St. Paul.

A 10-car Milwaukee Road passenger train crosses an unidentified steel bridge in 1914.

In 1935, Milwaukee Road locomotive No. 1 was an Atlantic-type with a 4-4-2 wheel arrangement. Underneath the Otto Kuhler–designed sheet-metal cover, she looked and worked like any steam locomotive. The streamlined covers may have helped sell passenger tickets, but they made maintenance much more difficult.

Voyageur Press collection

This image appeared in an ad quoting the personal attention the train's steward gave to a mother and her infant on a trip from Tacoma, Washington, to Chicago aboard the *Olympian*.

Because the vastly superior view from the classic dome cars was coveted by all passengers, full-length dome cars like that shown on the right followed.

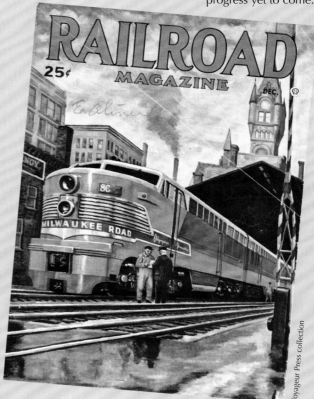

The *Olympian Hiawatha* on this 1947 cover of *Railroad Magazine* is a sign of postwar progress yet to come.

Sex sold in 1948, just as it does today, although in a more subdued way. The Milwaukee Road built Skytop Lounge observation cars that gave the passenger an experience similar to sitting on the open observation platform on the rear car of older passenger trains.

A diesel-powered freight is stopped at a semaphore signal in the shadow of Idaho's Mount Baldy. The white flags designate the train as an unscheduled "extra," likely operated just to take this photograph. The horizontal position of the semaphore blades signals the train to stop.

FADED GLORY   125

MUSIC OF THE RAILS

During their early years, railroads were idolized by the public. Music about them was similarly positive. The 1859 "North Western Railway Polka" praised the corporate officers of the Chicago & North Western, a far cry from today's perception of corporate officers. In the late nineteenth century, songs criticized robber barons and their activities. Corruption, safety, and high transportation rates all were subjects of songs.

Railroad songs began to be recorded in the 1920s, mostly in the categories of *hillbilly* and *race records*, with instruments such as slide guitars, harmonicas, and fiddles used to approximate the sounds of trains. The former evolved into country and western music, while the latter included African-American blues musicians. The blues in particular were a superb vehicle for railroad stories. Songs such as "Dixie Flyer Blues," "Railroad Blues," "Casey Jones Blues," and "John Henry" were recorded. Who can forget the Blues Brothers' 1981 rendition of "She Caught the Katy" written by Taj Mahal and Yank Rachell? It was first recorded by Albert King in 1971.

Hillbilly music's railroad spokesman was Jimmie Rodgers, "The Singing Brakeman." Rodgers dominated the industry from 1927 to 1933 with such hits as "Ben Dewberry's Final Run." Subsequently in the country genre, The Carter Family and Roy Acuff released versions of the "Wabash Cannonball." Johnny Cash sang "Rock Island Line." Steve Goodman's 1970 "City of New Orleans" became a modern classic as it told of the end of passenger rail in America. In 1974, "Choo Choo Ch'Boogie" was Asleep at the Wheel's first hit single. These are just a sampling of the hundreds of "train songs" that populate the annals of American popular music.

Other genres are also represented. Johann Strauss wrote "Eisenbahn-Lust–Walzer" (translated as "Railway Delight Waltz") in 1836. Irving Berlin penned the show tune "When that Midnight Choo Choo leaves for Alabam'," And Glen Miller recorded the 1941 swing classic "Chattanooga Choo Choo," the first gold record of all time with over a million copies sold. Jazz is represented with Duke Ellington's "Happy Go Lucky Local" from 1946 and Buddy Morrow's 1952 recording of "Night Train." Bernie Witkowski's Orchestra recorded "Choo Choo Polka."

Many train songs were written or adapted for children. "Down by the Depot" is a traditional song that this author remembers being sung to him by his mother. "Big Rock Candy Mountain" was first recorded in 1928 by Harry McClintock and later made famous by Burl Ives in 1940. A song about hobos, its words were sanitized even for the first recording in 1928. Cigarette trees were replaced by peppermint trees, streams were running full of lemonade and not alcohol "trickling down the rocks," And twin lakes of gin and whiskey gave way to a single basin of soda pop!

Far left: "I've Been Working on the Railroad" is certainly one of the most famous songs of the rails. This 1936 sheet music includes notation for Hawaiian guitar as well as ukulele and piano.

Left: Irving Berlin's classic, "When That Midnight Choo Choo Leaves for Alabam'," was published in 1912, long before railroad songs were first popularly recorded in the 1920s. It has been recorded countless times since.

Top left: Other than this cover image, this song's only connection with railroads is a father's stated desire to obtain a ticket to Tennessee to see his newborn. The lyrics don't even explicitly mention a *railroad* ticket, for train travel was the logical choice in 1921.

Top right: The 1930 song "Sleepy Town Express" is an analogy between railroad operations and a child being put to bed. Like most songs, this one did not survive as a classic.

Right: Sponsored by the Association of American Railroads, "The Railroad Hour" presented musical comedies to American radio audiences from 1948 to 1954. The show was hosted by singer and actor Gordon MacRae.

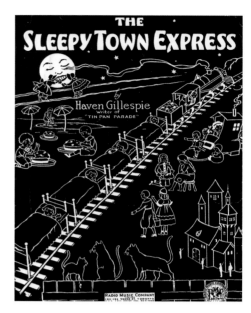

Top left: The Merrill Jay Singers entertain with 15 railroad songs, including "Big Rock Candy Mountain," a hobo's idea of paradise. It was first recorded in 1928 by "Haywire Mac" Harry McClintock. Over the years, the song became a children's classic as the original lyrics, which spoke of cigarette trees and lakes of whiskey, were changed to peppermint trees and soda pop lakes.

Top right: This album of railroad songs includes children's classics such as "Down by the Station" and folksongs such as "John Henry."

Bottom left: Railroads inspired all types of popular music, from country and western to big band jazz. Here, Buddy Morrow's Big Band plays the classic song "Night Train." The track is the only railroad-themed song on the album of the same name.

Bottom right: Railroad themes have long been important to country music and legend Johnny Cash recorded many railroad songs. This album includes "The Wreck of Old 97" and "Rock Island Line," among others.

All Voyageur Press collection, except lower right, courtesy Sun Entertainment Corporation

NORTHERN PACIFIC

The Northern Pacific Railway was the first of the northern U.S. transcontinentals. Its goal was to connect navigation on Lake Superior with that on Puget Sound. Chartered in 1864, it had reached only as far as Bismarck, Dakota Territory, when the financial panic of 1873 halted construction. In 1881, construction resumed under new owner Henry Villard and the last spike was driven at Gold Creek, Montana, in 1883. Trains detoured over the tracks of the Oregon Railway and Navigation Company from Pasco, Washington, to Portland, Oregon, until 1887, when the Northern Pacific opened its own line to Tacoma, Washington, on Puget Sound via temporary switchbacks over Stampede Pass. Stampede Tunnel was completed the following year.

In 1896, reorganization put James J. Hill and banker J. P. Morgan in control of the Northern Pacific. Hill completed the Spokane, Portland & Seattle Railway's line on the north bank of the Columbia River from Pasco to Portland in 1908, again giving his trains access to Portland.

Attempts at merging the Northern Pacific and Spokane, Portland & Seattle with the Great Northern and Burlington were thwarted until 1970 when the Burlington Northern was created from these roads.

The attention to detail on the *North Coast Limited* included color-coordinating train attendants' uniforms with the shades of green on the Vista Dome passenger cars. The red and black symbol, part of Northern Pacific's logo, is a Chinese representation of the duality of nature, of balance between the forces of yin and yang.

A Northern Pacific motorcar with its wind-splitting nose and porthole windows must have been a symbol of modernity in 1910. The photo was probably taken near Roslyn, Washington.

Challenger-type locomotive No. 5133 spouts steam from every pore. These 4-6-6-4 locomotives were built during World War II by Alco and weighed 644,000 pounds in working order and carried 25,000 gallons of water and 27 tons of coal. They were the last steam locomotives built for Northern Pacific.

In 1962, streamlined diesel 6701A waits to leave Seattle.

FADED GLORY   129

PASSENGER TRAINS

Three passenger trains meet a ship at the Flavel, Oregon, terminal of the Great Northern Steamship Company in 1915. The Great Northern formed the company in 1900. Some of its destinations were in Japan.

Early passenger cars resembled stagecoaches, with riders sitting both inside and on top. Now, in addition to rain and snow, hot cinders and soot were hazards for those riding outside. Passenger cars evolved into boxes with undivided interiors and seats arranged on each side of a central aisle. Passengers could walk the length of the car or train, use the toilet, or engage in conversations with strangers, a social interaction common in the United States that would have been scandalous in Europe.

By the 1840s, the first examples of dining cars, parlor cars, sleeping cars, and women-only cars appeared. Darkness was relieved by gas lamps that evolved into electric lights. Coal stoves, which roasted some passengers even as others froze, were replaced with steam heat provided by the locomotive's boiler.

Railroads also began to name their trains. Initially, the name simply described the train's function (e.g., *Mail Train*, *Up Train*, and *Night Express*), the train's performance (e.g., *Cannonball*, *Fast Mail*, and *Midnight Flyer*), and sometimes the destination (e.g., *Boat Train* and *Capitol Limited*). Even individual passenger cars were named, frequently with geographic names (e.g., *Lake Zurich*, *East Youngstown*, and *Durango*). Both cars and trains were named for people (e.g., *General Palmer* and *George Washington*); Commodore Vanderbilt modestly named his private car *Vanderbilt*.

American Express Train. Currier & Ives.

At first, the popular color for passenger cars was yellow. Passenger cars of the Durango & Silverton are still painted yellow, although the official name is "Rio Grande Gold." New York Central's passenger trains were crimson but changed around 1890 to a dark olive green with gold striping. Archrival Pennsylvania Railroad chose "Tuscan Red" to differentiate their trains from the Central's. The name of the Baltimore & Ohio's *Royal Blue* inspired its dark blue finish.

Industrial designers were charged with the task of making trains beautiful. In the 1930s, Henry Dreyfuss redesigned the New York Central's *Twentieth Century Limited* and Raymond Loewy did the same for the Pennsylvania's competing *Broadway Limited*. Appearance was considered so key to attracting passengers that designers styled the insides and outsides of the cars, the locomotives, napkins, dinnerware, and nearly everything the train carried.

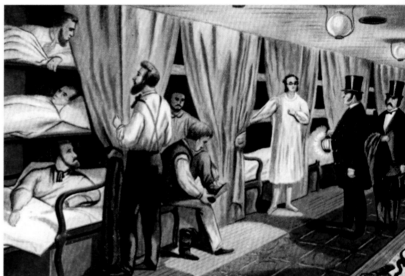

Although bunks were a great improvement over sleeping in a seat, travelers were sometime stacked three high. On some lines, strangers shared the same narrow bunk. An unconfirmed story is that one reason General William Palmer decided to build the Denver & Rio Grande to a narrow gauge is that the uncivilized practice of sharing a bed with a stranger would be impossible in the narrow cars.

Somewhere in the Midwest, train passengers must have thought they had gone to sea in 1907. Steam locomotives could traverse deep flood waters while the traction motors near the wheels of diesel locomotives would short-circuit. A steam locomotive fireman once told the author that oil-fired steam locomotives would run in even deeper torrents, as the oil would float and burn on the surface of the flood water in the firebox of the boiler.

Mixed trains offer the economy of running only one train for both passengers and freight. In 1916, two mixed trains meet at Fox Station along the narrow gauge Tanana Valley Railroad in Alaska. Alternate transportation—sled dogs—rest on the snow in the foreground.

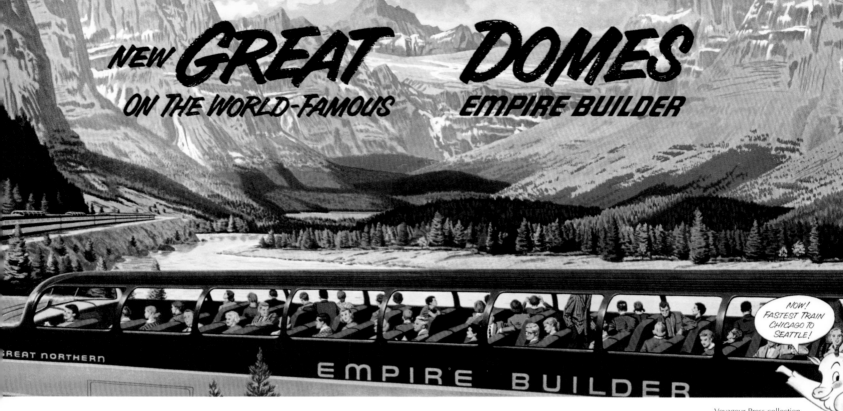

NEW *GREAT* *DOMES*

ON THE WORLD-FAMOUS *EMPIRE BUILDER*

NOW! FASTEST TRAIN CHICAGO TO SEATTLE!

The dome car was conceived in the mountains and this image shows why. Soon, every passenger wanted to sit in dome cars, and full-length domes like this one on the Great Northern's *Empire Builder* began to appear.

The copy on the back of this postcard read, "Cozy Lounge chairs, card tables, a magazine table with current periodicals, radio, bar, speedometer, and all features of the beautiful Observation Lounge Car on North Western's *Twin Cities 400* Streamliner between Chicago and St. Paul–Minneapolis."

The copy on the back of this postcard distributed on the Chicago & North Western's *400* streamliner providing service between Chicago and the Twin Cities stated, "Comfort to the point of luxury! Latest type seats—with plenty of room between. Solex glassware glass, draftless air-conditioning, Stewardess Service, Smoking and Powder Rooms."

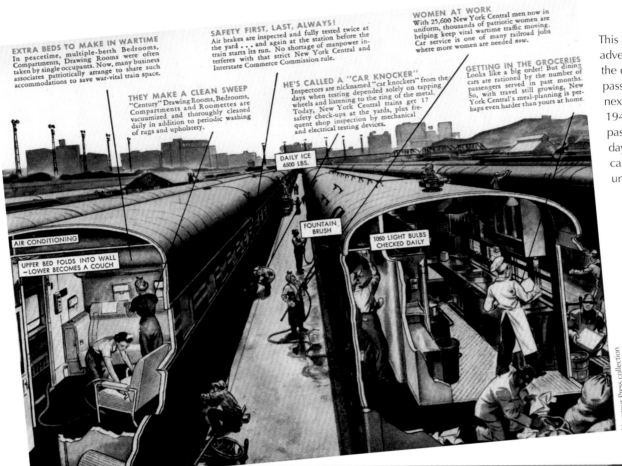

This New York Central advertisement stresses the difficulty of preparing passenger cars for their next assignment. In wartime 1944, 800 New York Central passenger trains ran each day, even with a national campaign to curb unnecessary travel.

Voyageur Press collection

Amtrak's version of the westbound *California Zephyr* arrives at Glenwood Springs, Colorado, in August 1985.

Claude Wiatrowski photo

RAILWAY EXPRESS

Although the U.S. Postal Department had a monopoly on carrying letters, until 1913 it was forbidden to carry packages. Entrepreneurs started express companies to carry packages via railroads and waterways. The railroads themselves also carried packages, but initially shipment was slow, handling rough, and security uncertain.

Large express companies bought small ones. Offices were erected in big cities. Small towns relied on railroad station agents as express company representatives. Fleets of horse-drawn wagons prowled the streets, dropping off and picking up express packages. Where a small trunk was once sufficient, express companies now had their own railroad cars. Since the express companies were the only viable alternatives for the movement of money, jewelry, and other valuables, train robbers most often blasted open the express car first—the primary reason for the holdup.

In 1913, the Postal Department introduced parcel post. Express businesses continued, although wounded by government competition. When the government nationalized the railroads in World War I, it also merged the major express companies—Adams, Southern, American, and Wells Fargo—into American Railway Express. In 1929, the 86 railroads on which express service was conducted purchased this collective express firm, which was renamed the Railway Express Agency.

In 1940, 57,000 Railway Express Agency employees worked in 23,000 offices providing service on 12,000 daily passenger trains that covered 213,000 route miles! Although REA operated water, air, and eventually truck routes, it depended on passenger trains as the central element of its business model. As passenger trains declined after World War II, so did REA. Service was terminated in November 1975. That same year, United Parcel Service began service to every address in the 48 contiguous United States. In an interesting twist, today, UPS trailers are often carried piggyback on railroad flatcars.

All Voyageur Press collection

Not unlike today's express companies, REA provided labels for specialized shipments. Unlike today's advertising, however, ads on ink blotters like the one at left became obsolete with the advent of the ballpoint pen.

Railway Express trucks were familiar sights in most U.S. towns for decades.

Although 23,000 cities were served by Railway Express, this booklet mentions limits on pick-up and delivery services. The cover depicts a traveler arranging for the store at which she shopped to ship her purchase home via Railway Express.

Eventually, Railway Express shipped by every transportation mode. Nevertheless, it was unable to survive the end of the passenger train on which it shipped most packages.

RAILWAY EXPRESS AGENCY

(740)
2-40
Printed in U.S.A.

HATCHING EGGS
HANDLE WITH EXTREME CARE
DO NOT DROP
KEEP FROM EXTREME HEAT AND COLD

Railway Express Agency carts were a familiar sight on depot platforms across America. This scene is recreated at the Colorado Railroad Museum.

TOY TRAINS

History has not recorded the name of the first man to whittle a wooden likeness of a train for his children. Early toy trains were made of wood and cast metal. They were pulled or pushed along the floor or down a track. By 1856, clockwork motors could power tiny trains a few times around a loop of track before their spring ran down. By the 1870s, even steam was powering some tiny locomotives. All these propulsion technologies still exist today. The children of the wealthy played with trains and five common track gauges varied from almost 5 inches (bigger was better) to a mere 1 inch or so (for the poorer of the wealthy). Size was of little consequence in a mansion that sat on an estate, but as toy trains were marketed to the masses, smaller sizes became more common. Size did matter in a small home or apartment.

The idea that exploded the toy train market was electricity. Not only would electric trains run as long as desired, but they were remote-controlled so little tots (or Dad) could pretend to be real engineers. Isolated instances of small electrically powered trains appeared in the 1890s, but Joshua Lionel Cowen is credited with giving birth to the electric train industry. His first product was a simple flatcar that looped around store windows to attract customers who marveled at an animated display. Soon, customers were asking to buy the little cars and track. It was a never-ending market. Cars, locomotives, stations, roundhouses, tunnels, and bridges gave way to animated cars that unloaded milk cans or load tiny plastic cattle, all automatically powered by electricity. Loops of track encircling Christmas trees became elaborate year-round, tabletop layouts.

Other competitors sprang up but, in the end, only Lionel and American Flyer held the American market. Lionel trains ran on O gauge track, 1 1/4 inches in width. American Flyer trains were smaller and ran on S gauge track. Proportions of American Flyer trains were more like the prototype trains they represented, but Lionel's less realistic proportions allowed sharper curves so larger layouts with bigger trains could be built in smaller spaces. Lionel's combination clearly beat American Flyer in sales. Children interested in more accurate replicas of trains would grow into adults who practiced scale-model railroading.

The 1954 Lionel catalog cover stressed the relationship between father and son in constructing and operating a Lionel train layout.

Voyageur Press collection

The 1957 American Flyer catalog stressed the realism of its trains. Besides being more realistic than Lionel trains, American Flyer trains were smaller, allowing more railroad to be built in a smaller space.

The intergenerational relationships promoted by Lionel advertising didn't end with Dad but extended to Grandpa, as well. Like Lionel trains themselves, these relationships mirrored reality, as multiple generations were often employed by the same railroad!

Cardboard trains did not cease to exist in the twentieth century as evidenced by this model of a Santa Fe streamlined locomotive, shown with it's packaging.

TROLLEYS AND INTERURBANS

Before streetcars, city dwellers lived within walking distance of their workplace, a grocery store, and their children's school. Traveling farther than you could easily walk was an inconvenience without renting some form of horse-drawn transportation. With new technology, however, you could shop, work, or attend school anywhere streetcars ran, not just in your own neighborhood. Streetcars ran to amusement parks in the country (frequently built by the streetcar company). They ran to cemeteries, and special cars were even outfitted to conduct funerals. Streetcars radically changed American city life.

To move urbanites down streets ankle-deep in mud, horses pulled small wooden coaches along steel railroad tracks. But horses are high-maintenance. In some cities, underground cables pulled along cable cars, but the length of such lines was limited by the weight of the long cable, and all the cars ran at the same speed. Some cities had steam dummies, small steam locomotives hidden inside wooden coverings that looked like horse cars, a ruse to avoid scaring horses. But steam locomotives were also expensive to maintain and they rained down cinders and soot. The development of electric motors provided the perfect form of propulsion for street railways. Nicknamed *trolleys* after the trolley pole that conducted electricity from an overhead wire, electric cars were quiet, quick, and pollution-free. America's first successful trolley system was energized in Richmond, Virginia, in 1887.

Starting in New York City in 1867, railroad cars were forced onto steel structures elevated above the congested street beneath. These steel supports amplified the noise of the train, shaded the street from what little sunlight was left in the polluted city, and were unsightly. Starting in New York City in 1904, street railroads went underground. Called subways in the United States, underground railways better preserved the quality of life but were much more expensive to construct.

The advent of passenger railways allowed the wealthy to commute from their rural estates to offices in city centers. It wasn't long before electric trolleys were venturing beyond city borders to neighboring cities to provide similar services to the less affluent. Over short distances, the electric cars were competitive—even superior—to the steam cars. These electric interurban railroads came into vogue as the twentieth century began. Some systems grew to hundreds of miles. Cities that now long for high-speed public transportation once were blanketed with speedy

Horse cars were the earliest solution to rail transit on the muddy streets of American cities. The horse hauled the car uphill and then rode the platform as the car coasted back downhill.

Claude Wiatrowski photo

Many cities combine new light-rail systems with historic trolleys, attracting both tourists and locals. One such city is Memphis, Tennessee, where several brightly painted cars provide transportation through downtown and along the Mississippi River. The system is being expanded to serve the medical center and may continue to the airport.

SIGHT SEEING CAR. QUEBEC

CHAR OBSERVATOIRE—QUEBEC

Tiered sight-seeing trolleys were an enjoyable way to see Montreal, Quebec, in Canada's summer months. The 11-mile tour was 1 hour long and the cars ran every 15 minutes. Note the electric lights arranged on the arches above the passengers.

This small four-wheeled streetcar is a rolling billboard of destinations as it travels down New York Avenue in Washington, D.C., circa 1890.

railcars. Most interurban railways traveled on private traffic-free rights-of-way whenever possible. Where not possible, the railcars shared the public streets with automobiles. Longer distances and their own rights-of-way encouraged interurbans to use larger railroad equipment, more like the steam railways than trolleys. Many lines added freight service, sometimes substantial, to increase their revenues. In truth, the distinction among trolley lines, interurbans, and steam railways (which also operated electric propulsion) blurred except in the minds of government regulators.

True or not, one intrepid traveler was storied to have ventured from Maine to Wisconsin using only trolleys and interurbans. The legend does not mention the condition of the traveler after what must have been days of locomotion.

A hand-tinted 1900 photo of a New York City elevated train at 110th Street shows that steam locomotives once hauled these trains. Drip pans prevented grease, oil, and water from soiling unlucky pedestrians under the tracks.

A Chicago, North Shore & Milwaukee *Electroliner* waits at Milwaukee to begin its 80-mile-per-hour run to Chicago in 1962, one year before its last run. An *Electroliner* is preserved at the Illinois Railway Museum.

THE WORLD OF TOMORROW

By the 1939 and 1940 New York World's Fair, the world's economies were mending and 44 million people attended to experience marvels that included television broadcasts. A month before the first season closed, Germany invaded Poland. The tension of another world conflict must have subdued the merriment during the second season.

Nevertheless, excited children witnessed the Pennsylvania Railroad's huge model railroad—a fantastic extension of the little train running around their Christmas trees. Full-size locomotives included the *General* of the Civil War's great locomotive chase. A veteran of Nevada silver mining, locomotive *Genoa* masqueraded as the Central Pacific's *Jupiter*, and the Burlington's No. 35 was altered to look like Union Pacific No. 119. Together, the disguised locomotives reprised the golden spike ceremony that had celebrated completion of the first transcontinental railroad in 1869.

Voyageur Press collection

Twenty-seven eastern railroads jointly sponsored a model railroad layout at the 1939 New York World's Fair. Decades ahead of its time, the railroad was automated and included locomotive sounds. A "performance" began in simulated pre-sunrise darkness and ended at dusk. There were 7,000 individual trees, 1,000 buildings, and 280,000 minuscule railroad spikes that held down 3,500 feet of O gauge railroad track upon which ran 50 locomotives and more than 400 cars. Trackside signals utilized 500 red, amber, and green miniature light bulbs, while the lights on each train were powered by batteries so they would remain illuminated even when the train stopped running. Lakes and rivers contained 7,000 gallons of real water. So much wear was expected on the wheels that they were equipped with ball bearings so they could operate for the duration of the fair.

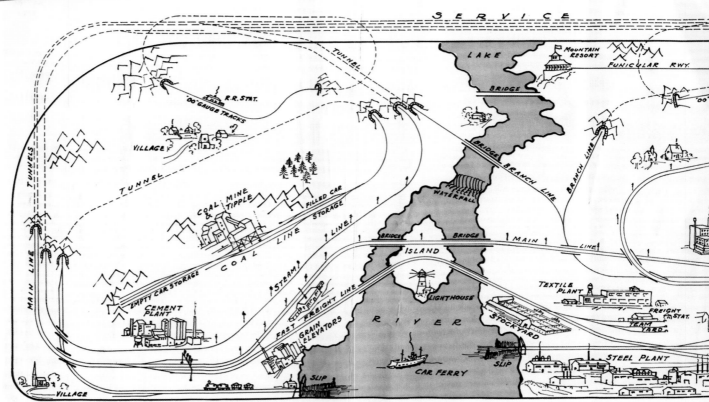

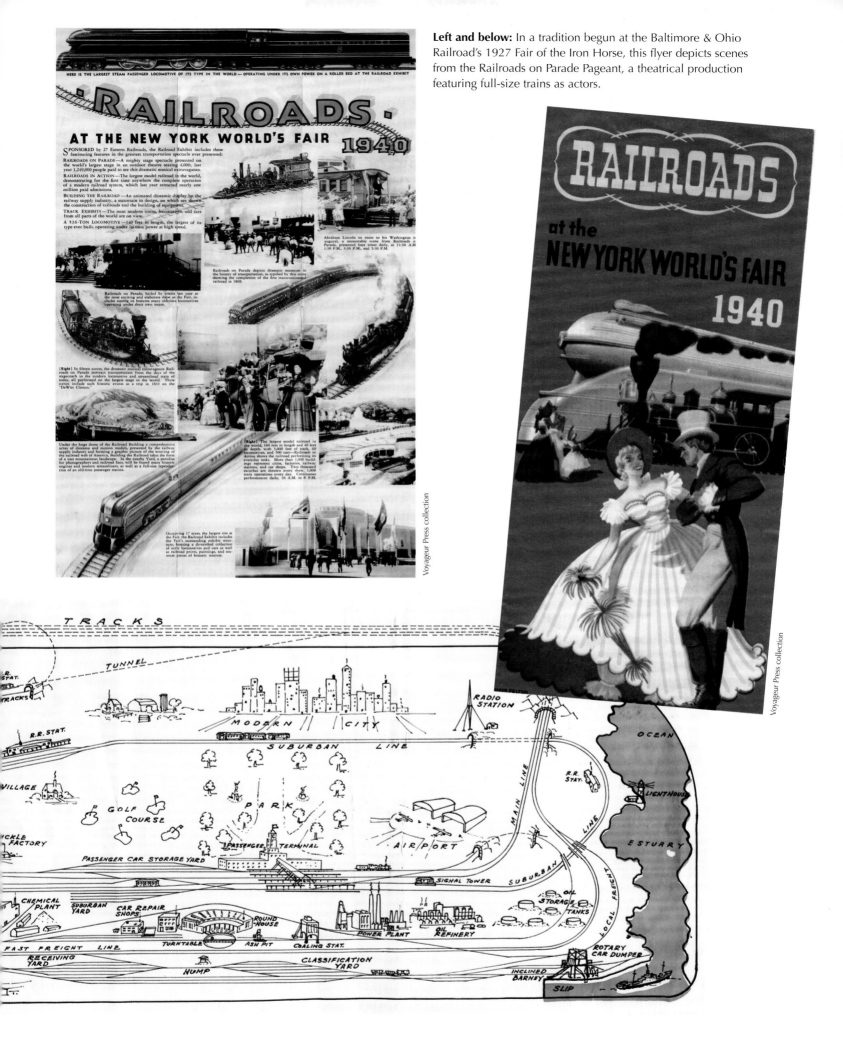

Left and below: In a tradition begun at the Baltimore & Ohio Railroad's 1927 Fair of the Iron Horse, this flyer depicts scenes from the Railroads on Parade Pageant, a theatrical production featuring full-size trains as actors.

CHAPTER FOUR

G. V. "Jerry" Carson photo

The East Tennessee & Western North Carolina had abandoned its narrow gauge operations by 1960, when this photo was taken, but it still ran standard gauge steam locomotives.

OLD PROBLEMS, NEW SOLUTIONS

The nail in the coffin for long-distance passenger trains was the federal government's 1956 decision to build the Interstate Highway System. Slow, dangerous, confusing highways were soon replaced by safe, high-speed, easy-to-follow Interstates.

If automobiles and the Interstate Highway System started the decline of the long-distance passenger train, then surely passenger jet aircraft presided at its final demise. The same technological advances that produced postwar automobiles also produced trucks that were faster and had increased capacity. That same Interstate system gave those trucks the smooth, fast routes on which to operate. Railroads had once thought that trucks would only be short-distance feeders for long-distance freight trains. With impediments removed, trucks competed with railroads and won freight traffic away from them.

The outcome was predictable. With declining revenue, railroad maintenance and service suffered, causing further declines in traffic and revenue. Regulation prevented the usual free-market response. Railroads could not reduce rates or change routes without permission from the tortoise-like Interstate Commerce Commission. A competitive response might require a quotation in days—even hours or minutes—but the ICC could take years to approve a change.

Railroad employment had dropped from 1.4 million workers in 1946 to a mere 700,000 by 1962. Some of this decline can be attributed to the death of steam-powered locomotives and the consequent redundancy of the people that serviced, maintained, and repaired them. However, this steep decline in railroad employment was also a clear sign of ill-health of the industry. With fewer employees, the railroad now had less political power and less influence on everything in America.

It's not that railroads didn't try to solve their problems, but the only avenues open to them were those of reducing costs and, even in these areas, they faced regulatory scrutiny.

THE 100-MILE DAY

Technology had changed in the diesel age, as had the railroads' operating practices. Hard-won early-twentieth-century work rules seemed unreasonable in the mid-twentieth century. Railroads argued that the fireman should be dropped from train crews, since his main function of tending a steam boiler had disappeared with the steam locomotives. The unions argued that he served as a backup engineer, enhancing train safety. Trains no longer crept along at 30 miles per hour and some ran long distances without switching cars in or out. Yet, every train stopped at 100-mile intervals to change crews, with every crew receiving a full day's pay, even if they worked only two or three hours. Some trains still spent considerable time switching cars and work days of eight or more hours were still common, countered the unions. The railroads argued that crew

assignments should be flexible; fewer crewmembers should be assigned to trains that did no switching and those crewmembers should travel farther for their day's pay. Both sides had good points. The solution lay in a formula for just compensation and safe and reasonable working conditions that was compatible with the economic and operational realities of the 1950s and 1960s.

THE URGE TO MERGE

The earliest railroads were often connected end-to-end, forming a longer trunk. But then, railroads began to parallel each other. Why hand over traffic to another railroad when your railroad could build a new track all the way to the final destination and keep all the revenue? Each railroad would, of course, need separate facilities in every city they served. Although passenger terminals were often Union Stations, shared by multiple railroads, other facilities were not shared. Each railroad had its own freight terminal, its own yard tracks, its own engine service facility, and its own repair shop. As railroad traffic dwindled after the war, parallel main-line tracks spent more of their time idle. Yard tracks sat empty. Employees didn't have enough work to make a full day. Nevertheless, railroads still paid property

As World War II was ending in 1945, Union Pacific ran a series of "Your America" ads about the states it served.

taxes on these facilities that produced much less revenue than they once did.

If two parallel railroads merged, only one main-line track would be needed and it would be busier, carrying the combined traffic of both railroads. Only one freight terminal, one set of yard tracks, and one locomotive servicing facility were needed. There could also be a reduction in managers and other employees. The reality was, of course, far more complex. The eastern half of the United States was a spaghetti-like bowl of routes. Some were busy. Some were not. Shortages of facilities existed in some places, surpluses in others.

The most memorable merger was that of the nation's two most legendary railroads: the Pennsylvania and the New York Central. These railroads served the same territory and were heavily laden with surplus facilities and employees. The merger—consummated in 1968—gave birth to Penn Central Railroad. In only two years, Penn Central went bankrupt, the largest bankruptcy in U.S. history up to that time.

Already wary of a sinking railroad industry, the Penn Central bankruptcy sent investors into full retreat. If merger of *these* two railroads caused their downfall, how could other lesser railroads—merged or otherwise—be good investments? Capital dried up and more railroads filed for bankruptcy.

The human toll was incredible. The early 1950s saw reductions in employment as steam locomotives gave way to diesel locomotives. This was quickly followed by a general decline in traffic that made even more employees redundant. Finally, great railroads started going bankrupt and legions of railroaders found themselves out of work. Workers whose fathers—and their fathers—worked for the

This image from a 1947 ad run by the Chesapeake & Ohio almost had it right. It preached modernization to fellow railroads but modernization of their own passenger services would prove to be a dead end.

Voyageur Press collection

railroad found no hope of ever returning to the iron trail. A way of life had disappeared.

The first discussion of nationalizing the railroads, during World War I, was motivated by profitable railroads that were too powerful and allegedly uninterested in the welfare of the nation that created their wealth. The second discussion, in the 1960s, was motivated by bankrupt railroads that had become too weak to assist a nation that needed them. Times had indeed changed.

AMTRAK: THE PASSENGER SOLUTION

Congress created the National Railroad Passenger Corporation—Amtrak—in 1971. Railroads that would normally have had to go through a lengthy and uncertain passenger train abandonment procedure with the ICC were allowed to discontinue all their passenger trains if they allowed Amtrak to run trains over their tracks for a fee. This arrangement was so compelling that all railroads, except for the Denver & Rio Grande and the Southern, agreed to it. Eventually so would the holdouts. The railroads were relieved of the burden of unprofitable passenger trains and Amtrak paid them a fee for rights to use their tracks. Who could resist?

Amtrak began its life with insufficient, dilapidated equipment prone to breakdown. Owning none of its own track, it paid for the privilege of having its passenger trains delayed by host railroads' freight trains. It is no wonder it became a national joke. The importance of railroads being a network, discussed in Chapter 1, came into play. Amtrak had only 200 passenger trains compared to the tens of thousands that roamed the rails at the peak of railroad passenger service. Through the 1950s, this all-inclusive network made railroad passenger service so important to America. It was the lack of this network that limited

Courtesy Milton A. Davis collection

This New York, Ontario & Western steam locomotive was a Consolidation-type with a 2-8-0 wheel arrangement. The railroad was the first major railroad to suffer complete abandonment in the post–World War II era, with its last train operating in 1957.

Amtrak's success. Imagine an Internet that allowed only 200 messages a day, messages that only could be sent at specific times on a route slowed down by other messages. Imagine an Internet with only 500 Web sites (depots). It is a tribute to Amtrak that it does as well as it does, given the limitations it faces.

CONRAIL: THE FREIGHT SOLUTION

In response to the worsening condition of Northeast railroads and their great economic importance to the country, Congress created the Consolidated Rail Corporation—Conrail—in 1974. While technically a private company, most of its stock was owned by the federal government. Conrail owned and operated six bankrupt railroads. Besides the doomed Penn Central, it inherited the Central Railroad of New Jersey, the Erie Lackawanna, the Lehigh & Hudson River, the Lehigh Valley, and the Reading. It began operations in 1976. The federal government provided capital investment to rebuild track and repair locomotives and freight cars. During its formation, the new railroad was allowed to abandon or sell money-losing track, something its bankrupt predecessors would have found difficult to accomplish under the heavy hand of the ICC.

The Staggers Act in 1980 greatly reduced the regulation of all railroads and thus also contributed to the success of Conrail. By 1981, Conrail's revenue had increased to the point where federal monies were no longer required. In fact, in 1987 Conrail held the largest initial public stock offering to that time, repaid its obligations to the federal government from the proceeds of that stock offering, and became a corporation owned by private shareholders.

Congress certainly learned a lesson from this period of railroad history. Once it was forced to own and operate railroads, it began to lift the burden of unreasonable regulation on all railroads. The country learned that railroads, despite being less and less visible, were still vital to the well-being of the economy. Lessons learned about passenger rail service are still unclear and that lack of clarity will continue through the next chapter—and probably beyond.

CANADA: A DIFFERENT STORY

Canada's economy has always been heavily dependent on natural resources, and the expansion of its railroads in the 1950s and 1960s was driven by natural resource industries. While track mileage was declining in the United States, more track was laid in Canada, with the total mileage of Canadian railroads rising to 46,000 miles by 1973 from 41,630 in 1933.

Canadian freight traffic exploded to record levels in the 1960s while passenger traffic plunged. Yet, the Canadian government chose to retain passenger trains for the common good and, with the passage

of the National Transportation Act in 1967, subsidized the railroads for most of their losses on passenger operations.

In 1978, Parliament enacted the Capital Revision Act to relieve Canadian National Railways of most of its debt to the national government, thus reducing the annual interest burden associated with that debt. In return, Canadian National was expected to become profitable and pay dividends to the government. Future capital would be borrowed from commercial markets.

Six years after Amtrak was formed, Canada's passenger train services were consolidated into VIA Rail Canada, a government-owned company.

G. V. "Jerry" Carson photo

Railroad mergers are graphically illustrated in this line of cabooses. All have yet to be painted for their new single owner, the Burlington Northern.

Norfolk Southern Corp.

The federal government formed Conrail from bankrupt railroads of the Northeast, an action taken to prevent the collapse of essential railroad services. Eventually, Norfolk Southern and CSX jointly purchased Conrail.

CANADIAN PACIFIC

Canadian Pacific Railway was Canada's first transcontinental railroad, cresting three mountain passes: Kicking Horse Pass through the Rockies, Rogers Pass through the Selkirk Mountains, and Eagle Pass through the Gold Range. The last spike was driven at Craigellachie, British Columbia, on November 7, 1885.

The railroad's financial condition improved markedly when the government reorganized its debt and provided additional funding in response to its assistance in quelling the 1885 North-West Rebellion in what is now Saskatchewan. The Canadian Pacific reached the Atlantic Ocean at St. John, New Brunswick, in 1889, becoming the first true transcontinental linking the oceans defining the North American continent.

Under a new name, CP Rail acquired full control of the Soo Line in 1990, giving CP Rail access to Chicago. In 1991, CP Rail arrived in New York City by purchasing the Delaware & Hudson from Guilford Transportation Industries, and in 2001 CP Rail was spun off from its holding company and again uses the name Canadian Pacific Railway.

Voyageur Press collection

The Canadian was a luxury diesel-hauled passenger service between Montreal and Vancouver inaugurated on April 24, 1955. In 1978, Canadian Pacific transferred all its passenger services to VIA Rail, a federal government corporation.

Locomotive 2238, a 4-6-2 Pacific, hauled the Canadian Pacific's most glamorous passenger trains after its construction in 1914. Shown here in June 1955, its status had sunk to hauling a one-car freight train through the countryside. The white flags indicate an "extra" unscheduled train, most likely because this one-boxcar train ran only when needed. Thirty-nine Class G1 Pacifics were constructed, with 2238 being the newest. The railroad found the Pacific wheel arrangement very useful and built a total of 498 of them in six classes.

G. V. "Jerry" Carson photo

Switch engine 6968, an 0-8-0, rests with passenger locomotive 1274, a 4-6-2 Pacific, in the Winnipeg, Manitoba, engine-service facility in July 1957.

A happy couple is about to enjoy a meal traveling on a train along Canada's East Coast.

Twenty-two pages of color photos and text emphasize vacation opportunities from the Atlantic to the Pacific. Inside, under the headline "Canadian Pacific Spans the World," a listing of its enterprises includes railways, steamships, airlines, hotels, communications, and express (packages).

CHICAGO RAILROAD FAIR

The Chicago Railroad Fair marked the 100th anniversary of the arrival of Chicago's first railroad, the Galena & Chicago Union. Five and a half million visitors strolled down a mile-long exhibit area. The fair ran for two seasons of three months each in the summers of 1948 and 1949. With this kind of response, it is no wonder that railroads believed they could reclaim long-distance passenger travel.

Exhibits whetted the public's appetite for rail travel. The Chicago & Eastern Illinois Railroad created a strip of Atlantic Ocean coastline, allegedly near Miami, on the shore of Lake Michigan. The Illinois Central built a facsimile of New Orleans' French Quarter. The Rock Island staffed an old western dancehall with instructors in the fine art of country and western dancing. The Burlington, Great Northern, and Northern Pacific staged a rodeo at a dude ranch. The Union Pacific's exhibit showcased sights to be seen in 11 western states. A joint exhibit by nine eastern railroads included a mammoth model railroad and a five-screen theater. The first season, Denver & Rio Grande showed motion pictures in a modern railroad coach; for the second season, the motion pictures were moved inside a replica of Colorado's Moffat Tunnel, probably because the coach could not handle the crowds.

The largest collection of historic steam locomotives ever brought together was displayed on 3 miles of track. Many historic locomotives were operated on the Wheels A-Rolling stage, yet another incarnation of the railroad musical (see Fair of the Iron Horse)!

The cover of the Chicago Railroad Fair guidebook for 1948—the first year of the exhibition—stresses the long history of railroading. A streamlined diesel is paired with a very old wood-burning steam locomotive, the Galena & Chicago Union Railroad's *Pioneer*. The fair commemorates the 100th anniversary of *Pioneer*'s first run into Chicago, the first steam locomotive to enter the city that would become the nation's railroad hub. The Chicago & North Western displayed the *Pioneer* and a historic coach next to a replica of Chicago's first railroad station. *Pioneer* now rests at the Chicago Historical Society museum.

Above: The Milwaukee Road's Chicago Railroad Fair brochure highlighted an aerial view of the fairgrounds on its back cover. The 3 miles of railroad display track are visible at center right in the photograph. Above the display tracks is the 5,000-seat Wheels A-Rolling grandstand facing the shore of Lake Michigan. The pageant was performed as many as four times a day.

Left: As have all railroad pageants since the pioneering 1927 Pageant of Inland Transportation, the Wheels A-Rolling Pageant featured music as an important element of entertainment. This sheet music appears to be signed by its composers.

CHRISTMAS

Railroads have long been associated with Christmas, almost surely because the importance of railroads in daily life was magnified during this holiday. Trains brought Christmas visitors: grandparents, a daughter from college, or a son on leave from the war. Sweethearts reunited and a long-lost uncle showed up at your door. The railroad also brought Christmas presents, and a mailbag dropped from that speeding train was full of Christmas cards.

One gift, in particular, embodied the railroads' importance to Christmas. Train toys appeared soon after the first railroads. Children were thrilled to participate in the technology of the age, even if only through a folded paper likeness. Many a happy child pushed a cast-iron train across the floor. There were train puzzles and paint books. Trains were emblazoned on building blocks and toys of all kinds. Parents read *The Little Engine That Could* to the smallest railroaders. Older children thrilled to reading their own railroad adventures in *Ralph on the Midnight Flyer*. In 1902, electric trains were added to Christmas lists.

Families still lay a circle of track under the Christmas tree, and many preserved railroads operate Christmas trains. Children show up at the depot in their pajamas to board the train. As the old passenger cars ramble through the countryside, someone will read from *The Polar Express*, while the little ones warm themselves with hot cocoa. Perhaps Santa will make an appearance.

A very old train-themed Christmas postcard includes silvered-embossed borders.

Courtesy Kansas City Southern. Photo by Mike Brunner, Ben Weddle & Associates

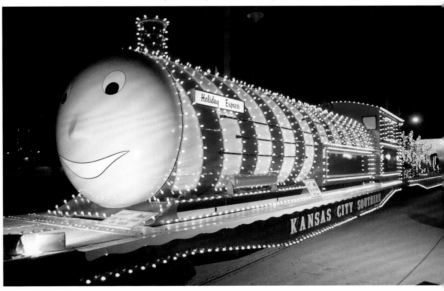

Above: Several railroads run Christmas trains for charitable causes. Decorated with 10,000 lights, Kansas City Southern's *Holiday Express* is a volunteer project of employees, vendors, and friends of the railroad whose purpose is to entertain and provide warm clothing for children in need. Rudy, the pretend steam locomotive, is shown here. In 2005, the train visited 22 towns in eight states. Visitors can tour intricate train displays in three cars of the six-car train and visit with Santa

Left: This 1950 New York Central ad is ahead of its time with an HO scale train under the tree and not Lionel or American Flyer.

COTTON BELT

The St. Louis Southwestern Railway was created in 1891 from the bankrupt St. Louis, Arkansas & Texas. The latter railway was born of the 1886 reorganization and subsequent conversion to standard gauge of the Tyler Tap Railroad whose narrow gauge cars had carried cotton from the fields of Texas to the looms of St. Louis since 1882. Nicknamed the Cotton Belt, its trains also served Dallas, Ft. Worth, Little Rock, and Memphis. In the 1920s, the Cotton Belt was repeatedly sold, first to the Rock Island, then to the Kansas City Southern, and finally to the Southern Pacific. Not only did the Southern Pacific want the Cotton Belt's St. Louis access, it also needed an independent railroad to circumvent a 1923 agreement with the Union Pacific. As a condition of the Southern Pacific's merger of the Central Pacific, it was required to solicit all transcontinental traffic for its Ogden, Utah, connection with the Union Pacific instead of soliciting traffic for its own line across Texas. As an independent railroad, the Cotton Belt could solicit transcontinental traffic to be interchanged with the Texas lines of the Southern Pacific.

After the decision to widen the Cotton Belt's gauge, replacement ties were made long enough to accommodate standard gauge track, standard gauge locomotives and cars were stockpiled, and an outside spike was driven into the longer ties to save time on the day the gauge was to be changed. And it was a day. North of Texas in 1886, 419 miles of 3-foot gauge track were widened to standard gauge in 24 hours. The Texas lines would follow in early 1887.

This beautifully produced booklet was published to commemorate the Cotton Belt's 75th anniversary.

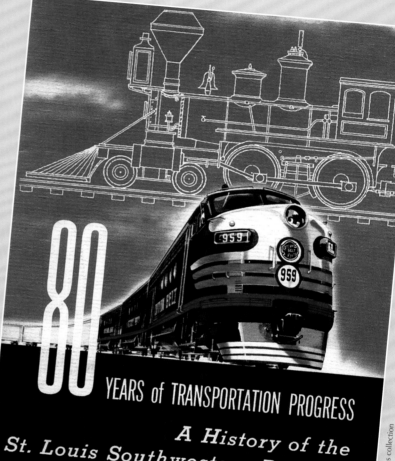

Above and left: Although effectively a part of the Southern Pacific since February 1932, the Cotton Belt retained its corporate identity and in 1957 produced this substantial 98-page booklet on its history, with a cover listing its actual name: the St. Louis Southwestern Railway.

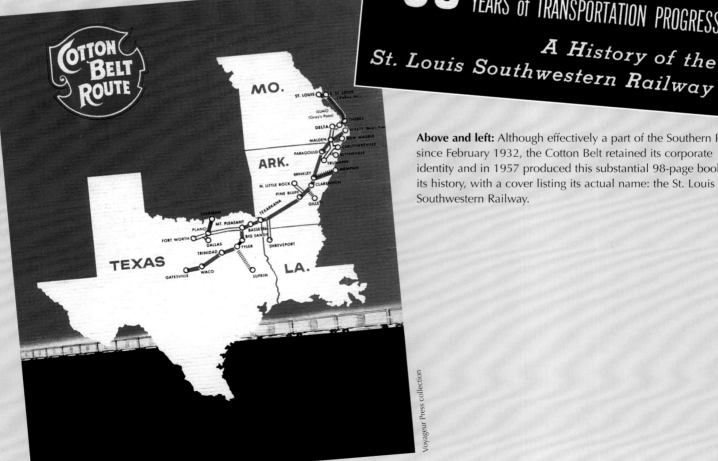

DOWN BY THE DEPOT

Early American railroads were too pressed for funds to build shelters for passengers. Passengers might wait for a train in a nearby store, or better yet a tavern. Railroads weren't even sure what such structures should be called: depots (from a French word) or stations (from civil-engineering practice). Although *station* was used more frequently to describe a large, ornate structure and *depot* to refer to a petite, humble structure, the terms were interchangeable.

Robber baron owners constructed monumental railroad stations after the Civil War. Railroad stations were to America as cathedrals were to Europe. Having an ornate station as the gateway to a community was a source of civic pride that can linger to this day. Many vintage railroad postcards are images of those grand railroad stations. New York City's Grand Central Station was opened in 1871 with a dozen tracks. By 1913, it had exploded to 123 passenger tracks on two levels.

In small, remote towns, the station agent lived in the depot. In fact, in a small town, the station agents handled all the duties required of the railroad. They were ticket agent, baggage handler, and more, but their most important duty was receiving telegraphic orders for trains and passing them on to train crews. Many orders could be "hooped up" without the train stopping. In a breathtaking act of bravery, the agent held out a small hoop on which was stretched a string to which was tied the written train

Down by the station
Early in the morning
See the little pufferbellies
All in a row.

See the station master
Turn the little handle
Puff, puff, toot, toot
Off we go!

order. A crewmember on the locomotive reached out with his arm to snatch the order without stopping. You can imagine the rush of adrenalin that came from standing a few feet from a 200-ton steam locomotive pounding through town at 60 miles per hour. This play was repeated twice for every train since a copy of the order had to be delivered to the conductor in the caboose as well.

Railroad depots, especially small-town depots, were the Internet routers of the day, forwarding messages to their destinations. The railroads provided lines of communication not only by carrying newspapers and letters but also by operating public telegraph lines. Telegraph operators provided instantaneous knowledge of important national and international events. Western Union telegraph operators manned offices in large cities, but it was the station agent who interpreted Western Union's dots and dashes in small-town America.

Besides handling the railroad's affairs and conveying Western Union telegrams, small-town operators handled packages sent though the Railway Express Agency. Before the U.S. Postal Service was allowed to handle packages, rural America relied on express companies to deliver that fancy dress or high-performance plow from the Sears, Roebuck catalog.

Or perhaps today's train brought only a salesman or the new schoolteacher. Friends and relatives arrived and departed. People hung out. Small boys relished in the activity and dreamed of becoming locomotive engineers. Mom and Dad waited for their children to visit from the big city. Grandpa waited for that train that would deliver his new horseless carriage and everyone showed up to watch it pushed

A lone Colorado Midland locomotive waits by the depot at Cardiff, Colorado.

down the ramp from the flatcar on which it arrived from Henry Ford's plant in faraway Detroit.

The activity that once centered on the railroad depot has moved elsewhere. With the exception of a few long-distance passenger trains operated by Amtrak, Americans are most likely to use a railroad station to commute from the suburbs to a job downtown. Many depot buildings are still used by railroads as offices, maintenance centers, or for freight operations. Some are simply derelict with boarded-up windows and graffiti spray-painted on their sides. Still others are reused as museums, private homes, restaurants, gift shops, or municipal offices.

Above: When this foggy photo was taken, this Santa Fe depot had been considerably modified from its original 1940s appearance and was woefully inadequate for Norman, Oklahoma's 1963 population. In 1995, its exterior was restored to its original appearance but the interior was modified into a community center.

Top right: The Denver & Rio Grande's Glenwood Springs depot in Colorado houses a railroad museum maintained by the local chapter of the National Railroad Historical Society and also serves the Amtrak passenger train that follows the route of the original *California Zephyr*.

Right: The Baltimore & Ohio's 1896 Mount Royal Station is now part of the Maryland Institute College of Art and houses an art gallery and related facilities.

EDUCATION

When railroads were the principal mode of transportation, little boys first learned of railroading by standing trackside to watch the arrival of trains, the watering of locomotives, and other railroad activities. It was not unusual for children to be invited into locomotive cabs—sometimes even for a ride. Growing up in Chicago, the author managed a cab ride down the siding that served his aunt's coal yard.

Before the wizardry of Harry Potter inspired young readers, *Ralph of the Roundhouse* mesmerized children with the magic of railroading. This series published in the late 1920s included nine titles, including *Ralph on the Engine*, *Ralph on the Midnight Flyer*, and *Ralph on the Mountain Division*. The other series by the author, Allen Chapman, was *The Radio Boys*. The exciting technologies of the age were clearly radio and railroading.

Today, railroad museums and some preserved railways produce teaching materials about trains and host fieldtrips for school groups. The National Railway Historical Society offers a summer camp for high school students. RailCamp introduces students to railroad history and to current railroad practices. The curriculum runs from the skills needed to restore antique steam locomotives to careers in modern railroading.

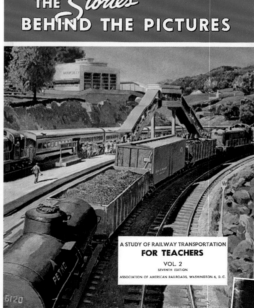
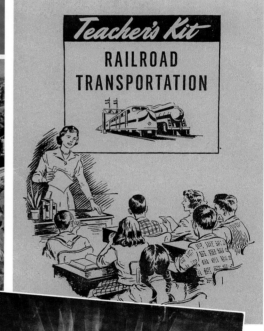

Voyageur Press collection

In 1956 railroads were still visible enough to society that the Association of American Railroads published the seventh edition of this teacher's kit. A great deal of research went into its production and it included:

A book with lesson plans for lower, middle, and upper grades; a chronology of American railroad history; a list of the addresses of 115 principal U.S. railroads and a huge bibliography including reference materials, children's books, children's readers with railroad subjects categorized by grade level, books of railroad poems and rhymes, sheet music and recordings of railroad songs; and sources for motion pictures, maps, and other visual aids.

56 photographs of railroad activities that could be posted on classroom walls.

A book with lengthy explanations of the activities depicted in the 56 photographs.

A copy of the booklet "Railroads at Work" for each student in the class.

The Association of American Railroads still provides educational materials through its website www.railfanclub.org.

www.archivesofadvertising.com

The Association of American Railroads produced this comic book on the role of railroads in the American Civil War.

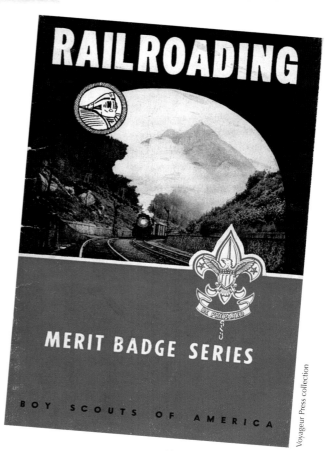

The Boys Scouts of America still offer a merit badge in railroading. It was earned by 163,062 scouts between 1911 and 2004.

If you are small enough, a rail is just the right height for a seat. For many years, a child's only close association with railroads has been a visit to a preserved railroad or museum. The author's son, Kevin, was just two years old when he sat on a rail at the ghost town of Osier along the Cumbres & Toltec Scenic Railroad in 1978.

This coloring book tells the story of Dick and Sue's transcontinental train trip from the East Coast to visit their grandmother in California in 1937.

OLD PROBLEMS, NEW SOLUTIONS   155

FISHY TRAINS

Since the nineteenth century, railroads have transported fish for many purposes. As with many food items, railroads have allowed iced fresh fish to be transported longer distances. Construction of Alaska's Yakutat & Southern Railroad started in 1899. Roughly 10 miles long, it carried salmon from a wharf to a cannery. The railroad ceased operation sometime in the 1960s and some of its equipment, including its locomotives, are on display in the isolated village of Yakutat.

Once, hatcheries could only release fish into nearby waterways since there was no effective way of transporting live fish long distances. The U.S. Fish Commission—which became part of the U.S. Fish & Wildlife Service—first transported live fish by train in 1874. The commission further developed technology to transport live fish and purchased their first railroad car solely for that purpose in 1881. The tenth and last fish car entered service in 1929.

State-run hatcheries used fish cars as well. Unlike the U.S. government's bureaucratic numbering system, the states named their fish cars. Wisconsin's car was the *Badger*, Kansas had the *Angler*, Michigan had the *Attikumain* (whitefish), and Montana the *Thymallus* (a genus within the salmon family).

In 1927, construction of the John G. Shedd Aquarium began in Chicago's Grant Park and included the first saltwater exhibits in an inland aquarium. The problem of transporting live fish from oceans to the shores of Lake Michigan was solved with the construction of the aquarium's own fish car, the *Nautilus*. A new car, *Nautilus II*, remained in service until 1972 when it was replaced by air transport. It is now on display at the Monticello Railway Museum in Monticello, Illinois.

Yakutat & Southern's mightiest locomotive pushes three gondolas of salmon up a steep track behind a cannery.

Fish car *Nautilus II* is displayed at the Monticello Railroad Museum in Illinois.

GULF, MOBILE & OHIO

The Gulf, Mobile & Ohio Railroad was created in 1940 from the Mobile & Ohio and the Gulf, Mobile & Northern. The GM&N connected two gulf ports—Mobile and New Orleans—with Paducah, Kentucky. The M&O had a roughly parallel route except it continued northwest to St. Louis. Close on the heels of World War II, the Alton Railroad was added to the mix, connecting St. Louis with both Chicago and Kansas City. In 1972, the Illinois Central merged with GM&O, creating the Illinois Central Gulf.

The oldest of GM&O's constituent railroads was the Mobile & Ohio, which, in 1850, was sensibly projected to connect the port of Mobile, Alabama, with the confluence of the Ohio and Mississippi Rivers at Cairo, Illinois. One can scarcely imagine more unfortunate timing, since the Civil War began just days after the railroad's completion. Traffic was indeed scarce on a railroad that connected the warring parties!

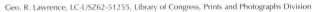

Above: Cavalry pose with a Chicago & Alton locomotive identified as the world's largest in 1907. The Alton would be merged into the Gulf, Mobile & Ohio in 1945.

Left: In 1951, a rubber stamp applied to the front of this timetable indicates the Board of Trade Building was then the highest in Chicago. Passenger services listed inside were somewhat meager.

The attractive colors of the Alton Route show through the grime as a 10-car passenger train leaves St. Louis, Missouri.

MAIL BY RAIL

As early as 1831, the Post Office Department used trains to ship mail to towns along the trains' routes. As railroads established a network, the post office began shipping mail for forwarding on connecting rail lines. Letters bound for the West were forwarded by stagecoach from the railhead at St. Joseph, Missouri. W. A. Davis suggested that westbound mail could be expedited by sorting the mail on the train before it arrived at St. Joseph. The first railroad car for sorting mail made its inaugural run on July 28, 1862.

Two years later, George Armstrong, assistant postmaster in Chicago, suggested widespread adoption of a system for sorting mail in railcars. Armstrong drew up plans for a Railway Post Office (RPO) car and convinced the Chicago & North Western to test his plan between Chicago and Clinton, Iowa. On August 28, 1864, the first official U.S. Railroad Post Office route was established.

George Bangs replaced Armstrong upon his death in 1871. Bangs developed the concept of the "fast mail"—a mail-only train with priority over all other trains—and convinced the New York Central to begin such a service between New York City and Chicago. The Pennsylvania Railroad followed with a high-speed mail-only train between Philadelphia and Chicago.

By 1930, over 10,000 trains were carrying the mail in the United States. Despite "fast mail" trains, railway mail service was largely dependent on the passenger trains in which its RPO cars moved. As passenger service declined after World War II, so vanished the mail service. The last RPO car made its final run between New York City and Washington, D.C., on June 30, 1977.

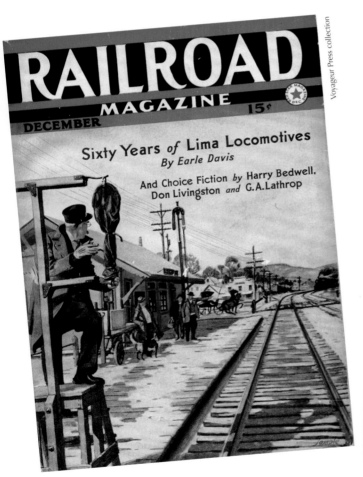

Voyageur Press collection

Stopping and restarting a fast train made it a slower train, so this heart-stopping technology was developed to pick up mail on the fly. This 1939 cover of *Railroad Magazine* depicts a station agent positioning a mail bag on a mail crane. A catcher arm on the side of a Railway Post Office car will snatch the bag as the train passes.

Until 1869, U.S. postage stamps featured the images of America's leaders. In 1869, the Postal Department issued a dozen stamps with other images, one of which was a railroad image. In 1998, a sheet of 20 stamps was issued honoring five of America's famous streamlined trains: the Southern Pacific's *Daylight* trains, the New York Central's *20th Century Limited*, the Santa Fe's *Super Chief*, the Pennsylvania Railroad's *Congressional*, and the Milwaukee Road's *Hiawatha*.

Freight train coming out of the Horseshoe Tunnel near Scenic on the Great Northern R. R., Wash.

448 FREIGHT TRAIN COMING OUT OF THE HORSESHOE TUNNEL, NEAR SCENIC, ON THE GREAT NORTHERN R.R., WASH.

The black-and-white postcard is clearly a photograph while the color postcard is a drawing of that photo, including the man standing on the boxcar roof. Color photography had yet to be invented and this was the only means of producing a color postcard.

"Neither snow, nor rain, nor heat, nor gloom of night stays these couriers from the swift completion of their appointed rounds." Herodotus

Traveling on a POSTAGE STAMP

How 3 billion pieces of wartime mail a year speed over the Water Level Route

No 20th Century Limited passenger ever sets foot here. This car is reserved for wartime travelers of a different kind...tiny V-mail...business letters...registered envelopes packed with war contracts and blueprints...all part of the three billion pieces of mail that speed each year over New York Central.

Hour after hour, as the Century bores through the night, expert postal clerks sort this "preferential mail." Tomorrow, on arrival, it will be ready for immediate forwarding or delivery.

Winter or summer, through any weather, "post offices on wheels"

provide lowest cost transportation for 96% of the nation's vast mail tonnage. A vital war service of American railroads today. A service that will be still more efficient aboard the finer, faster trains of tomorrow.

LAST BAG ABOARD ! Just before the Century pulls out, several bags of last-minute mail are collected from the mail room in the station. Many business firms regularly send messengers to the station with important mail for overnight delivery between New York and Chicago, as well as intermediate points.

MILE-A-MINUTE SORTING
Pouches with mail from all parts of the United States and many foreign countries are dumped on this table for sorting. Here, highly trained clerks work through the night as their car speeds east or west over New York Central's Water Level Route.

WASH ROOM AND LOCKERS

PIGEON HOLES

OVERHEAD PAPER BOXES

CHECKING MAIL BAGS

CINDER SHIELD

DOOR TO BAGGAGE AND EXPRESS COMPARTMENT

TRAVELING MAIL BOX
This letter chute permits passengers to put letters directly aboard the post-office car at stops along the way.

MAGNIFYING V-MAIL
Clerks often read photographically-reduced V-mail addresses under a lens. These tiny envelopes get speed preference, and regularly ride the Century. Soldier mail moves in vast volume, but even more would be welcomed by service men and women far from home.

"PICKER-UPPER"
On most through trains, this Catcher Arm is swung out to snatch mail bags from mail cranes at way stations...providing fast mail service for even small towns.

BUY MORE WAR BONDS

NEW YORK CENTRAL SYSTEM

New York Central
ONE OF AMERICA'S RAILROADS—ALL UNITED FOR VICTORY

During World War II, the New York Central carried 3 billion letters annually. Here, some of that mail is sorted in a Railway Post Office (RPO) car equipped with compartments into which clerks place mail for various destinations. The catcher arm and a mail crane are shown, as well as a mailbox slot. When RPO cars did stop at stations, a slot in the side of the car allowed anyone to deposit mail. Part of this car is a RPO, while part is used to carry the bags of passengers and packages forwarded by Railway Express.

MINE TRAINS

Railroads are especially efficient transporters of commodities wrestled from the earth. Many mines were located in remote, inaccessible, spectacular, and often mountainous locations. Railroads carried miners and their equipment into the wilderness and carried back out the wealth they wrested from the earth.

RAILS TO CARRY IRON

Perhaps no industry had as much synergy with railroads as did the steel industry. The railroads needed steel for rail and for locomotives. In order to make that steel, the mills needed iron ore and coal—all of which were delivered by railroads—requiring yet more rail and locomotives. Steel production exploded from 2,600 tons in 1867 to 930,000 tons in 1879. Although iron mines existed elsewhere, the heaviest concentration was around Lake Superior. The world's heaviest trains discharged their cargo into ships that carted the iron to steel mills also located near the Great Lakes.

RAILS TO CARRY COAL

Coal was once the chief source of all energy, not just the energy source of railroads. Coal-fueled stationary steam engines pumped water. Coal-fueled steamships navigated oceans and rivers. Coal provided warmth. Much of that coal was wrestled out of the Appalachian Mountains and transported by fleets of powerful steam locomotives. Wherever coal was mined, railroads were essential to moving it to market economically.

RAILS TO CARRY COPPER

Edison's 1879 invention of the electric light bulb marked the beginning of the electrical age. In 1895, the first large, alternating current power plant was opened at Niagara Falls, New York. Alternating current made it possible to generate electricity in large, efficient power plants and distribute it through copper wires to customers thousands of miles distant.

Discovery of low-grade copper deposits in the American Southwest was essential to wiring America. Development of these deposits required industrial processes to extract copper metal from low-grade ore and railroads capable of moving the mountains of ore to feed those insatiable processes. Steam train after steam train spiraled up from just one of many open-pit mines, annually

Voyageur Press collection

Locomotive No. 3 of the Duluth & Iron Range Railroad hauled iron ore for 30 years before it was retired to display at Two Harbors, Minnesota. The Lake Country Historical Society still displays this locomotive, along with a huge modern articulated steam locomotive that hauled iron ore for the Duluth, Missabe & Iron Range Railway.

Claude Wiatrowski photo

In June 1979, antique Alco diesel locomotives cross Gordon Creek Bridge with a load of coal from the mines along the Utah Railway.

disgorging 40 million pounds of ore that would be processed into 400,000 pounds of copper metal.

RAILS TO CARRY GOLD AND SILVER

It isn't coal, iron, or copper that quicken the pulse, but the precious metals of gold and silver. No effort was spared driving railroads to the mines that harbored these two precious metals. Colorado is the case study. Thousands of miles of track—both standard and narrow gauge—threaded precipitous snowbound mountain passes, all in the service of precious-metal extraction. Three railroads served 10,000-foot-high Leadville, which first had a gold rush followed by a silver rush. Silverton—at over 9,000 feet—was served by four railroads. One of these lines crested 11,113 feet, served champagne in its dining car, and distributed railroad passes made not of paper but of *gold*—good for free transportation along its 18 miles! The Cripple Creek Mining District included three railroads and two interurban lines connecting the various cities of this 2-mile-high metropolis. The local depot could sell you a ticket to Paris, France, including the steamship coupons!

Trains of the Duluth, Missabe & Iron Range Railway transferred loads of heavy iron ore to ships here at Duluth, from which it was transported to steel mills, including those near Chicago and Detroit.

This photo makes it clear that the Kentucky & Tennessee used the same commodity to power its locomotives as it transported with them.

A pair of locomotives on the preserved Virginia & Truckee passes a tipple where gold ore was once loaded into railroad cars.

Claude Wiatrowski photo

Voyageur Press collection

Left: The March 1946 cover of *Railroad Magazine* showed coal being loaded from a mine into waiting hopper cars.

Below: A Utah Railway locomotive shares the mountain scenery with a leased Union Pacific locomotive in 1979 at the railroad's yard at Martin, Utah. Incorporated in 1912, the Utah Railway, now part of Genesee & Wyoming, hauls 60,000 carloads of coal annually.

Claude Wiatrowski photo

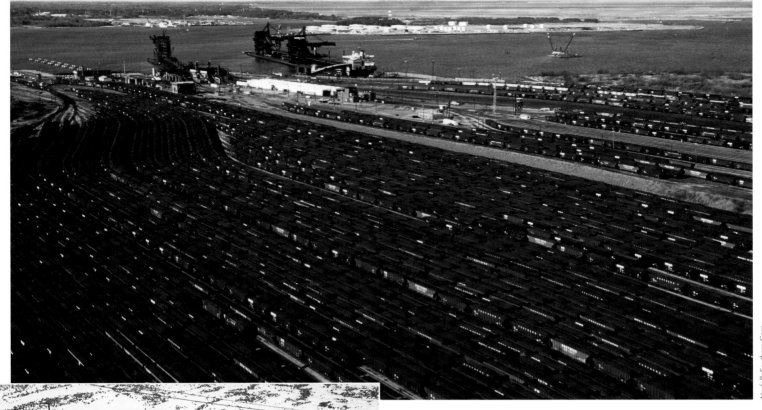

Above: The scope of coal-moving operations is evident in this Norfolk Southern yard full of loaded hopper cars waiting to be emptied into the holds of ships.

Left: Two Nevada Northern diesels switch roles as they continue the cycle of taking empty cars into the mine and returning with cars of copper ore for the mill.

A sampler is a mill that processes batches of ore from many small mines. The Eagle Sampler was in the gold-mining district of Cripple Creek, Colorado. It was served by three railroads, one of which was narrow gauge, as you can see by the three-rail track in the foreground.

MODEL RAILROADS

Electrically powered HO scale trains were introduced to the public at the 1933 Chicago World's Fair as accurate models of railroads in lieu of the caricatures that toy trains represented. HO stands for "Half Oh," or roughly half the size of Lionel O gauge toy trains. With a scant 16.5 millimeters between rails, smaller HO scale layouts, and the locomotives and cars that populated them, could be built to more realistic proportions and still fit in average-size basements and garages.

The practice of building breathtakingly accurate representations of real trains also began in larger scales like O and in smaller scales like N. In North America, HO and N scale model railroads are the most popular. Scale refers to the ratio between dimensions of the full-size train and of the model. HO scale uses a ratio of 1:87 while N scale is 1:160. Scale remains constant but gauge may change with tabletop model trains. HOn3 trains are replicated at the same scale of 1:87 but run on 10.5 millimeter track representing the 3-foot gauge of actual narrow gauge railroads.

Hi Rail is a very popular hybrid of accurate scale of model railroading and Lionel's three-rail track. Less easily derailed wheels and more reliable couplers emphasize ease of operation and construction over absolute adherence to perfect miniaturization. Proportions of locomotives, cars, scenery, and buildings follow the more accurate representation of traditional model railroads.

Model trains need not be confined to your basement. G gauge trains, sometimes called garden railways, usually inhabit an elaborately landscaped area in a yard. With a gauge of 45 millimeters, they are roughly 40 percent larger than O gauge trains, enabling them to cope with flowers, rocks, insects, cats, dogs, and even snow blocking their way down the rails. Unlike tabletop models, G *gauge* remains constant but *scale* changes to model different kinds of trains. A scale of 1:29 is correct to model a standard gauge (4 feet 8 1/2 inches) train on G gauge track, while 1:32 is correct to model a 3-foot gauge prototype train.

Estate railways—also called "live steam" or "grand scales"—are constructed by enthusiasts and are most commonly laid to gauges of 7 1/2 or 15 inches. Locomotives may actually be powered by steam. Gauge is constant and scale varies to match the prototype train being modeled. A model of a 3-foot gauge train built to run on 15-inch gauge track has a scale of 1:2.4. That *model* train would be 41 percent the

The relative sizes of different modeling scales are shown, represented by the same standard gauge prototype locomotive. From left to right are Z, N, HO, S, and O scale locomotives, followed by the largest, a G gauge diesel locomotive.

size of the *real* train and could certainly do useful work hauling ore from a mine! Whatever the scale, actual miles of track sometimes enhance the experience of running such trains. Some hobbyists work in gauges as wide as 24 inches, blurring the line between model and real trains.

Park trains transport people around zoos, carnivals, city parks, and other locations, especially where children congregate for enjoyment. A few still use real steam locomotives—the only choice when park trains first appeared in the nineteenth century—but now most are gasoline-powered. Steam locomotives still operate at Lakeside Amusement Park in Denver, Colorado. They are really not model trains, since their designers stress cost, reliability, capacity, and ease of maintenance over creating an accu-

rate model of a full-size train. Gauges as small as 10 inches were once used, but 15-, 18-, 24-, and even 36-inch gauge trains are more common today. The zoo railways in Omaha, Nebraska, and Portland, Oregon, are particularly impressive, as are the rail systems at Disneyland and Disney World.

MASTER MODEL RAILROADER

Paul Scoles has been modeling railroads since he was a teenager. He has published nearly 70 articles for model railroad magazines and has 23 magazine cover photos to his credit. In 2004, he was awarded the Master Model Railroader certificate by the National Model Railroad Association.

An HO scale Chesapeake & Ohio diesel struggles with an MKT covered hopper. One can guess from their green color that the tractors being delivered to a miniature farm are John Deere products.

Bill Costley collection, Kalmbach Memorial Library

Bill Costley collection, Kalmbach Memorial Library

A Monon streamlined diesel crosses a creek as a couple observes from the rowboat beyond the bridge. The fishermen in the foreground remain intent on their task. Hopefully, the train isn't bothering the fish!

The Pennsylvania Railroad's famous four-track main line is reproduced on Bob Barticek's hi-rail layout. Note the operating signals on the signal bridge, one for each of the four tracks. The track itself is three-rail to accommodate a Lionel-style electrical and wheel system, but there are many more ties in an attempt is made to disguise the center rail, and the profile of the rail itself is more like that of an actual railroad rail.

G gauge (G stands for "Garden") makes larger scales and larger layouts possible. Even landscaping with real miniature trees becomes a component of the garden railroad hobby.

Nick Edwards mans the throttle of his E6 Atlantic on the 7.5-inch gauge Wimberley, Blanco & Southern.

Park trains are not a new development. This photo may have been taken at Dreamland on Coney Island more than a century ago.

Steam locomotive No. 13 is 15-inch gauge and was built by Ken Kukuk. Here it is seen taking on water at the Hillcrest & Wahtoke Railroad in Reedley, California.

Locomotive No. 2 crosses Caliente Bridge, which spans Caliente Inlet, an arm of the Pacific Ocean. The Pelican Bay Railway & Navigation Company fills most of a 22x46-foot basement with 450 feet of Sn3 track. The designation "n3" means that the train is modeled as if it were running on narrow 3-foot gauge track. The "S" stands for the railroad's scale, "S" being a ratio of 1:64. This scale is the province of master builders since little is available from commercial manufacturers and most everything has to be constructed from scratch. Note details such as the rivets holding the bridge together, the cut-stone bridge abutments, and the detailed needles on the trees of the evergreen forest.

Train time at Klamath Station bustles with activity. The passenger train waits at the platform while locomotive No. 9 switches a gondola car on the track beyond. Klamath is named after an actual town in northern California. The mythical Pelican Bay Railway & Navigation Company is set in coastal Northern California to provide an authentic feeling to the modeling.

OLD PROBLEMS, NEW SOLUTIONS

MOVIES AND TELEVISION

The first movie featuring a railroad plot, *The Great Train Robbery*, was filmed by Edison's New Jersey studio. When film production moved to California's sunny climate, railroad scenes were filmed on lines serving Los Angeles. Contemporary steam locomotives were made to look old by changing their headlights and smokestacks, and by dumping firewood on top of their tenders. The studios bought their own trains, rented locomotives and cars, and even rented entire railroads.

The Sierra Railroad was built to carry lumber from Tuolumne in the Sierra Mountains. Close to Los Angeles with varied scenery and railroad equipment of all ages, the line was filmed hundreds of times. It was a Sierra diesel that smashed that DeLorean automobile in *Back to the Future III*.

Shortline Enterprises is headquartered close to the production industry at California's Fillmore & Western Railway and has provided equipment for television, motion pictures, commercials, and more. The 2003 movie *Seabiscuit* was filmed there.

Old equipment and mountain scenery led many film companies to Colorado. Even after the Rio Grande spun off its narrow gauge lines, those railroads continued to host movies. The Cumbres & Toltec Scenic was the setting for the film *Indiana Jones and the Last Crusade*.

Today, many preserved railroads solicit filming to augment meager budgets and the railroad you see in a film may be anywhere in the country.

JOSEPH M. SCHENCK *presents*

BUSTER KEATON

in

"The GENERAL"

UNITED ARTISTS PICTURE

Voyageur Press collection

Legendary comedian Buster Keaton starred in the 1927 silent film named after the locomotive *General* that participated in the daring but unsuccessful Civil War railroad raid.

Claude Wiatrowski photo

This purple coach named *The Jersey Lily* starred, along with Paul Newman, in *The Life and Times of Judge Roy Bean* (1972). This photo was taken on Arizona's White Mountain Scenic Railroad, which ceased to exist decades ago. You can still ride in the car at the Yuma Valley Railway in Yuma, Arizona.

THE GREAT TRAIN ROBBERY

SENSATIONAL AND STARTLING "HOLD UP" OF THE "GOLD EXPRESS" BY FAMOUS WESTERN OUTLAWS

In 1903, the Edison Manufacturing Company produced *The Great Train Robbery*. Some credit this 12-minute movie as the first motion picture with a plot rather than just a collection of interesting scenes

Cecille B. DeMille directed the epic motion picture *Union Pacific* about the building of America's first transcontinental. This image is the movie's recreation of the golden spike ceremony in which rails from the East met those from the West. The movie's 1939 world premier was held in Omaha, the headquarters of the Union Pacific Railroad. It drew 250,000 people and required that the National Guard be called out to keep order. The movie featured purchased or leased Virginia & Truckee Railroad locomotives and cars. This railroad retained a large collection of especially old locomotives and cars that have appeared in many movies.

NICKEL PLATE

To assure highest mileage and utmost safety at high speeds

"Nickel Plate Road" uses U·S·S MULTIPLE-WEAR WROUGHT STEEL WHEELS

U·S·S WROUGHT STEEL WHEELS

One-Wear Freight Car Wheels
Multiple-Wear Freight Car Wheels
Passenger Car Wheels

Diesel Locomotive Wheels
Steam Locomotive Wheels
Electric Locomotive Wheels

Tender Truck Wheels
Electric Transit Wheels
Crane Track Wheels

NICKEL PLATE ROAD

NKP 80097

THIS IS ONE of 2500 70-ton hopper cars, equipped with U·S·S Multiple-Wear Wheels, built for the New York, Chicago & St. Louis Railroad in recent years. Their reputation for dependability in service has made U·S·S Multiple-Wear Wheels the favorites wherever heavy hauling is done.

The New York, Chicago & St. Louis Railway was founded in 1881 to connect Buffalo with Chicago. It was built with cash, perhaps the only major railroad financed by this novel method. The origin of its nickname, The Nickel Plate Road, may be an 1881 newspaper article that referred to the "great New York and St. Louis double track, nickel plated railroad." One wonders why nickel and not gold or silver! Vanderbilt purchased the railroad, most likely to blunt competition with his own New York Central. It was sold to the Van Sweringen brothers—Cleveland real-estate tycoons—in 1916. Acquisitions would extend the Nickel Plate as far southwest as St. Louis and give its trains entrance to additional destinations in Illinois, Indiana, Ohio, and West Virginia. Other mergers were rejected by the Interstate Commerce Commission or shareholders. In 1964, it became part of the Norfolk and Western.

G. V. "Jerry" Carson photo

A Nickel Plate passenger train led by a classic pair of Alco PA1 streamlined diesels races through the Midwestern countryside.

Berkshire No. 754 roars through Hessville, Indiana, with a train of perishables in refrigerator cars. It is December 1957 and photos like this will soon be impossible as steam locomotion is phased out on major railroads.

Nickel Plate's giant 2-8-4 locomotive No. 756 meets another of its species in East Chicago, Indiana, in 1957. This wheel arrangement was nicknamed the Berkshire type locomotive and the Nickel Plate eventually purchased 80 of them. No. 759 was built on the same order as 756 in the mid-1940s and today is preserved at the Steamtown National Historic Site in Scranton, Pennsylvania.

NORFOLK AND WESTERN

The Norfolk and Western Railway was formed from other lines in 1881, though its earliest predecessor was the 1838 City Point Railway. Eastbound N&W trains disgorged coal into ships at Lambert's Point near Norfolk, Virginia. Westbound, its lines pressed into the coal-mining regions of West Virginia and transported "black diamonds" to the Midwest via Cincinnati and Columbus. Its trains called on Hagerstown, Maryland, and on Winston-Salem and Durham in North Carolina.

Although it electrified 56 miles of its coal-lugging main line starting in 1915, its Roanoke shops designed and built exceptional steam locomotives and in the early 1960s, N&W would be the last major railroad to use steam.

In the 1950s, most coal started traveling east to the Atlantic instead of west to the Midwest and in 1959 the N&W merged the Virginian Railway to utilize its easy downhill route to the ocean. In the early 1960s, N&W began to amalgamate railways, including the Nickel Plate and Wabash. The new N&W now included a corridor of lines stretching from Buffalo to Kansas City. In 1982, N&W and the Southern Railway were combined into Norfolk Southern.

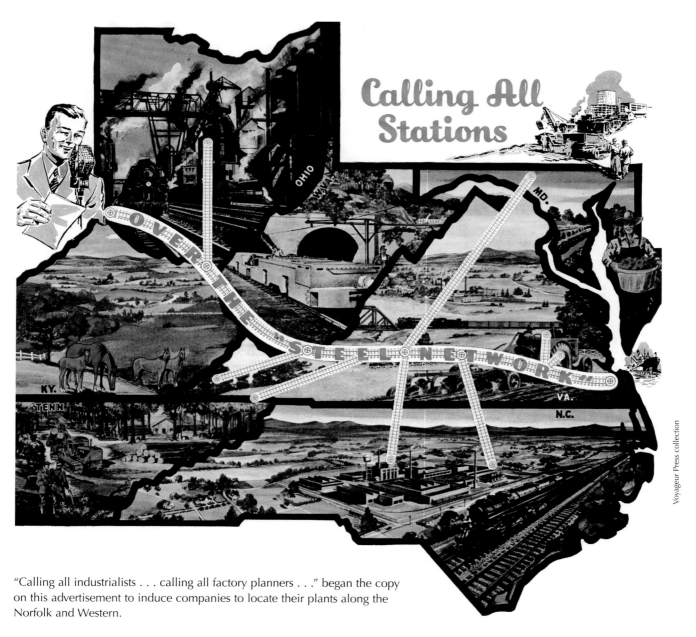

"Calling all industrialists . . . calling all factory planners . . ." began the copy on this advertisement to induce companies to locate their plants along the Norfolk and Western.

Norfolk and Western Class LC1 electric locomotives were permanently coupled pairs, weighed 300 tons, and generated 3,200 horsepower.

Many railroads gave away attractively decorative ink blotters to remind the user to ship by that railroad.

When freight trains have to be broken up, cars sorted, and new trains put together by destination, considerable delays are possible. The Norfolk and Western advertisement above explains that its classification yards are fast. Procedures are well thought out and there are enough tracks and switch engines. Here in Roanoke Yard, switch lists are Teletyped (an antique mechanical device that is a terminal in a primitive data network), and radios allow instant communication.

A postwar ad trumpets Norfolk and Western's crack passenger services, the *Pocahontas* and the *Powhatan Arrow*.

PRESERVED RAILWAYS AND MUSEUMS

"She came at me in sections,
more curves than a scenic railway."

—*Fred Astaire in the movie* The Band Wagon

Although efforts had been made earlier, North America's railway preservation movement began in earnest after World War II, when inexpensive old steamers, an abandoned branch line, and a dedicated group of volunteers could be combined to start a new preserved railroad. Inevitably, private for-profit operators entered the arena. Preserved railroads and museums became entertaining and educational tourist destinations. Ironically, this tourism was booming, thanks to private automobiles. Today, interest in our history has a name, "heritage tourism," and has grown 50 percent from 1995 to 2005.

The first directory of historic railroad sites was published in 1966 with just over 50 listings. The 2005 directory lists over 500 in the United States and Canada, including preserved railways, trips on main-line railways using his-

toric equipment, small railroad museums in old depots, large museum complexes on acres of land, dinner trains, model train layouts, and much more. All have goals of preserving and interpreting railroad history. Visitors experience railroading as it once was and learn why railway history is important.

Keeping antediluvian railroad equipment in good repair is a challenge. If a locomotive is beyond repair, it may have to be completely reconstructed. Sometimes, a very historic artifact is merely stabilized to prevent further deterioration. On rare occasions, replicas are constructed and run so the original artifact may be preserved without further wear. These issues extend not only to locomotives and cars, but also to track, bridges, tunnels, depots, roundhouses, water tanks, coal tipples, and more.

Strasburg Rail Road

Michael Anderson photo, courtesy White Pass & Yukon Route

Above: A White Pass & Yukon passenger train crawls along the shelf at Slippery Rock with the Sawtooth Mountains in the distance. The narrow gauge tourist carrier was completed in 1900 to carry gold seekers to the Yukon for the Klondike gold rush.

Left: The ambiance of the small-town depot can still be experienced at many preserved railways. Here, a Strasburg Rail Road train arrives at Strasburg, Pennsylvania, at dusk.

A self-propelled railcar circles the grounds of the Nevada State Railroad Museum at Carson City in 1992. The structure at left is a gallows turntable, so named for its resemblance to the instrument of execution by hanging. This motorcar has since been returned to its original railroad name and number: Tucson, Cornelia & Gila Bend No. 401 built in 1926. The museum owns about 70 pieces of rolling stock, many from Nevada railroads, including the legendary Virginia & Truckee.

Claude Wiatrowski photo

The Mid-Continent Railway Museum in North Freedom, Wisconsin, offers a turn-of-the-century ambiance. Volunteers are particularly expert at the restoration of wooden passenger cars.

One of the earliest tourist railways in the United States was an accident. In the 1950s, the Denver & Rio Grande continued to carry passengers on its narrow gauge branch-line train from Durango to Silverton, Colorado—initially just a few railfans in the caboose of a freight train. Word spread of this unique experience and soon the railroad had to add a coach, then several coaches, then a separate passenger train, and then several passenger trains! The Rio Grande sold the line to the Durango & Silverton Narrow Gauge Railroad, which continues to operate it.

PULLMAN CARS

George Pullman began building the sleeping car *Pioneer* in 1864. Railroads did not queue up to operate this heavy, oversized car, but after President Lincoln's assassination, Mrs. Lincoln asked that it be part of the funeral train. For 13 somber days, the train proceeded from Washington, D.C., to Springfield, Illinois, with *Pioneer* in the public eye.

Pullman sold all kinds of railroad cars but he provided sleeping cars as a service. Cars were completely furnished, equipped, and staffed by his company. Pullman received a surcharge for each passenger and the cost of operating and maintaining the car. The division that operated cars ultimately was separated from the division that constructed them.

By 1872, more than 500 Pullmans were in operation, more than 2,000 by 1893. At the peak of the business in the 1920s, more than 100,000 tired Americans rested their heads on Pullman pillows each night.

The decline of passenger trains signaled the final years of the operating company, which continued until 1969. In 1987, the manufacturing company was sold to Bombardier, a Canadian manufacturer of aircraft and railroad cars.

PULLMAN TECHNOLOGY

Half of all Pullmans constructed had 12 sections. Sections consisted of two seats facing each other for daytime travel. At night, the seats were folded together to create one bed. A second bed folded down from the ceiling, where bed linens were stored. Heavy curtains provided privacy. Luggage fit under the seats.

Later, private rooms were added. Some cars combined sleeping with other facilities—usually a seating area where drinks and food were served. Combinations of modular components, while still standardized, could be assembled to customize a car for a particular railroad's needs. Procedures manuals instructed employees on everything from folding linen to serving beer.

PULLMAN AND SOCIAL PROGRESS

In 1880, south of Chicago, Pullman began construction of his greatest plant. There, he built homes, churches, libraries, hotels—an entire community named Pullman. He rented homes to his employees, sold them utilities, and even tried to lease the church. Reacting to the financial panic of 1873, he cut wages by 30 percent but failed to cut rents. After rent was deducted from wages, employees returned home with a few pennies for a month's work. The union offered to negotiate but Pullman refused. Even his fellow industrialists were appalled by his behavior. A strike began in 1894 and railroads ground to a halt. The strike was broken by federal troops but Pullman's reputation was ruined.

Pullman sleeping-car attendants enjoyed the best pay and security—and the most adventure—available to African Americans in an era when there was little opportunity for those with a different colored skin.

World War II was barely over when Pullman-Standard began advertising the streamlined cars it was constructing for the Santa Fe's luxurious new passenger services.

No. 3822. "Harney Range."
rseshoe curve on the B. & M. R'y near Custer

A Burlington & Missouri River Railroad passenger train poses for a photo near Custer, South Dakota, in 1891. Here, in the wilds of the Black Hills, the last car is a Pullman sleeping car. This railroad was part of the Chicago, Burlington & Quincy.

Sleeping car accommodations in 1905 were upper and lower berths with curtains providing some privacy. For decades, one of the best careers available to African Americans was Pullman porter.

UPPER   SECTION   BED ROOM   DRAWING ROOM

Using short foldout descriptions, this old Pullman brochure details each type of accommodation available.

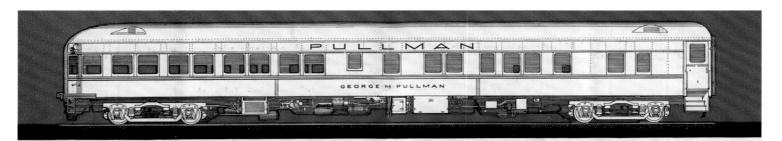

PULLMAN

GEORGE·M·PULLMAN

THE GEORGE M. PULLMAN

America's First All-Aluminum Sleeping Car

BENEATH the dome in the Travel and Transport Building at A Century of Progress stands the first all-aluminum Pullman car. Its name, appropriately, is George M. Pullman.

This latest achievement represents three years of scientific research and design. Engineers, metallurgists, architects, and artists put their ideas into a common melting pot, and construction on

the George M. Pullman was begun.

A steel sleeper weighs 180,000 pounds. The George M. Pullman, with air-conditioning equipment, extra large generator, heavy batteries, and its water supply, tips the scales at 96,980 pounds. Slightly more than half the weight, but with strength equivalent to all-steel construction! The two trucks of the latest steel Pull-

OLD NUMBER 9

man alone weigh 47,500 pounds, or 10,000 pounds more than the entire first Pullman sleeper.

"Contemporary," rather than the much abused and loosely used term of "Modern," defines the striking design and finish of the George M. Pullman. The car has a modified streamline effect, differing in several features from the standard Pullman.

America's First Pullman Sleeping Car

Thermostatic control regulates the air-conditioning of the entire car, cooling it in summer, warming it in winter, and filtering the air at all times so that it is fresh and pure. Each room has its own thermostat.

There are scores of structural improvements throughout the George M. Pullman. Most of them are hidden from view, but all are vital to that supreme travel luxury—Pullman Service.

SLEEPING CAR

This illustration is from a brochure distributed at the 1934 Chicago World's Fair to celebrate Pullman's 75th anniversary.

Voyageur Press collection

The cutaway illustrations in this postwar Pullman ad helped the reader visualize some of the company's various accommodations.

The Pullman division that operated sleeping cars was separate from the division that built them, the latter becoming the Pullman-Standard Car Manufacturing Company in 1930. In much the same way that EMD ran ads encouraging consumers to ride trains drawn by its streamlined diesels, Pullman-Standard ran ads promoting its cars to the traveling public.

www.archivesofadvertising.com

RESORTS AND VACATIONS

Railroad resorts were not limited to the West or to major railroads.

Nestled in the Allegheny Mountains, White Sulphur Springs was attracting visitors to its curative waters before the Civil War. In 1910, the Chesapeake & Ohio purchased the property. West Virginia's elegant Greenbrier Hotel would develop there and include, of course, its own railroad station on the Chesapeake & Ohio.

When Henry Flagler decided to extend his Florida East Coast Railway to the wilderness of southern Florida, he had little choice but to build the hotels that his railroad would serve in Palm Beach and other destinations. His trains reached Key West on a monumental system of bridges now traversed by automobiles.

In 1899, the 30-mile-long Alamogordo and Sacramento Mountain Railroad reached its terminus in the mountains of southern New Mexico. A summer resort community, Cloudcroft was created along with the Lodge at Cloudcroft. The original lodge burned but its 1909 replacement still welcomes visitors who want to try their hand at golf at 9,000 feet above sea level.

Voyageur Press collection

A Chesapeake & Ohio streamliner streaks by the Greenbrier Hotel. The hotel was owned and developed by the C&O, whose trains stopped at a station on its grounds. The world-class luxury hotel, no longer owned by the railroad, gained notoriety when it was discovered that a secret underground bunker had been built there to shelter U.S. government officials in case of nuclear war.

The Lodge- Cloudcroft, New Mexico
Elevation 9000 feet.

The Alamogordo & Sacramento Mountain Railroad connected Alamogordo, New Mexico, with Cloudcroft in the mountains via a particularly convoluted track that included this scenic S curve, a switchback, and incredible 6.4 percent grades. Its destinations were a mountain resort and a connection with logging railroads.

This is the second Lodge at Cloudcroft built in 1911 by the Alamogordo & Sacramento Mountain Railroad after a less ostentatious 1899 lodge burned. Still operated as a lodge, it outlasted the railroad that built it.

Daytrips were popular with both railroads and passengers. Destinations could be amusement parks, sports venues, picnic grounds, or a circus performance. In July 1887, 500 members of the First Methodist Church of Colorado Springs chartered the first wildflower excursion on the Colorado Midland. The excursions became a major source of revenue. Here a 1905 trip poses for a photo at Idlewild in Colorado's mountains.

Left and below: It was not uncommon to send Mom and the kids to the mountains to escape the hot summers. Vacations and daytrips added to the visitors who traveled by train. A Colorado Midland trainload of passengers has just arrived at Green Mountain Falls along a string of resort towns that lined Colorado's Ute Pass from Manitou Springs to Cascade to Green Mountain Falls to Woodland Park. The Ramona Hotel graced the hillside of nearby Cascade.

Travelers started and ended their one- to three-day excursions at the Fred Harvey *La Fonda* hotel in Santa Fe, New Mexico. One trip included the cliff dwellings in Frijoles Canyon, now part of Bandelier National Monument.

The Canadian National had 23,000 miles of track reaching throughout Canada when this advertisement ran between the world wars. The ad assures travelers that "Canada is unique because it offers modern luxury and primeval adventure side by side." This theme of luxury in the wilderness was common in railroad advertising. The Union Pacific emphasized the same experience for travelers to Yosemite National Park.

THE PERFECT VACATIONLAND

Colorado

Burlington Route

THE VACATION ROUTE TO COLORADO

Voyageur Press collection

Left: The Burlington's tracks just skimmed the eastern edge of Colorado's mountains, but the railroad heavily promoted mountain vacations. This 54-page booklet encourages mountain excursions by rented automobiles and makes only brief mention of other railroads' lines into the mountains. It lists hotels, resorts, children's summer camps, dude and guest ranches, national parks, national monuments, and outdoor activities.

Below: With no infrastructure on which to draw, railroads were forced to build hotels that served the great national parks and other attractions they promoted. This 32-page Canadian Pacific booklet lists rates and amenities in numerous railroad-owned resorts. An interior map includes steamship connections to England, Australia, and New Zealand.

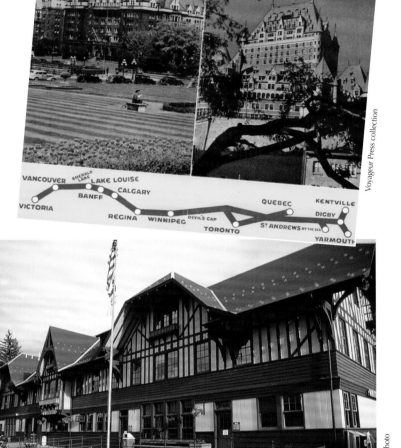

Voyageur Press collection

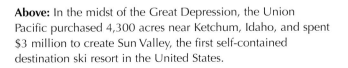

www.archivesofadvertising.com

Above: In the midst of the Great Depression, the Union Pacific purchased 4,300 acres near Ketchum, Idaho, and spent $3 million to create Sun Valley, the first self-contained destination ski resort in the United States.

Right: The Izaak Walton Inn was constructed by the Great Northern Railway on Marias Pass close to Glacier National Park. It is still a flagstop for Amtrak passenger trains.

Claude Wiatrowski photo

OLD PROBLEMS, NEW SOLUTIONS   183

SOUTHERN RAILWAY

LC-USZ62-125528, Library of Congress, Prints and Photographs Division

This remarkable photo of the Southern Railway depot at Charlottesville, Virginia, was taken prior to 1916. Passengers—men in suits and ties, women in long dresses—gaze down the track, hoping for the prompt arrival of their train.

The Southern Railway was chartered in 1894 to consolidate railroads operating 4,400 miles of track, which, themselves, had a rich history of acquisitions. The new railroad's oldest constituent was the South Carolina Canal & Rail Road Company, chartered 66 years earlier. With the acquisition of a line to New Orleans just before World War I, the Southern grew to an 8,000-mile mesh of tracks that covered much of the American South. Anchored in several Atlantic and Gulf Coast ports, its rail stretched to Washington, D.C., Cincinnati, St. Louis, and Memphis.

In 1953, the Southern became the first large U.S. railroad to convert completely to diesel locomotives. It was also one of two railroads that did not initially join Amtrak in 1971 and continued to operate its *Southern Crescent* passenger train from Washington, D.C., to New Orleans until 1979. In 1982, along with the Norfolk and Western, it became part of Norfolk Southern. Their combined routes and trackage rights allow Norfolk Southern trains to prowl a region from Miami to Dallas and from Chicago to Waterville, Maine.

Voyageur Press collection

Left: Green was the color of Southern Railway trains and timetables. In 1960, 14 of its trains were sufficiently important to the railroad to have their own names. The most important was the *Crescent*, which connected Boston and New Orleans. It traveled over Southern Railway tracks between Washington, D.C., and Atlanta, Georgia, while other railroads hauled the train east and west of those cities.

Voyageur Press collection

B-2 Natural Tunnel, in Southwestern Virginia

Voyageur Press collection

76416

The South Atlantic & Ohio built a railroad track through a natural tunnel in southwestern Virginia in 1890, which became part of the Southern Railway in 1906. This postcard (left) shows a steam locomotive emerging from the tunnel and is postmarked 1940. The Southern became part of Norfolk Southern and its locomotive No. 9803 (below) is shown traversing Natural Tunnel. The surrounding area is now Virginia's Natural Tunnel State Park.

Norfolk Southern Corp

OLD PROBLEMS, NEW SOLUTIONS   185

STREAMLINERS

Younger Americans identify the golden age of railroad travel with the streamliner. The mid-twentieth-century competition to attract passengers resulted in many curvaceous tube-like trains of perfectly matched cars and locomotives. Splashy color schemes replaced the dark greens and reds of clunky old passenger cars. Interiors were smooth and modern—the image was of the future, not the past.

The Union Pacific was first when its three-car aluminum streamliner, the M-10000, set sail in February 1934. Powered by a gasoline engine, it shot down the track at 110 miles per hour on a promotional tour. It eventually saw service in Kansas as the *City of Salina*. The Union Pacific would build and operate a fleet of these trains, each named for a city it served.

A mere six weeks after the Union Pacific's streamlined overture, the Burlington's three-car, stainless-steel, diesel-powered, 112-mile-per-hour *Zephyr* arrived. After a 13-hour, 5-minute nonstop sprint from Denver to Chicago, it rolled onto the stage of the railroad pageant at Chicago's 1934 World's Fair! In September, it starred in the motion picture *Silver Streak*, and November saw it in regular service, connecting Lincoln, Nebraska, with Omaha and Kansas City. As the Burlington added more such trains, this first train came to be known as the *Pioneer Zephyr*.

The first M-10000 and the *Zephyr* both served short commercial routes where operational costs of steam trains had already become a burden. The new diesel streamliners—although expensive to purchase—were inexpensive to

Passengers arrive at Alberta's Banff National Park on *The Canadian*. The Canadian Pacific Railway advertised the train's mountain crossing as the world's longest scenic dome ride.

operate, fast, and reliable. Importantly, the public was infatuated with the speedy, smooth-riding, nonstop, flamboyant streamliners, so much so that other railroads—not yet ready or able to abandon steam locomotives—applied the same design principles to steam-powered passenger trains. Steam was not as fast, clean, smooth, or operationally inexpensive, but the trains *looked* like the diesel streamliners.

The Burlington's choice of a diesel engine and stainless-steel car bodies became the standard. To this day, new rail-borne passenger carriages, whether for long-distance service or high-speed commuter lines, follow the streamlined principles first set down by industrial designers of the 1930s.

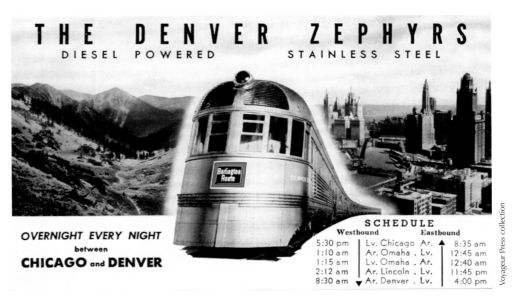

On October 23, 1936, Burlington's *Denver Zephyr* set a new speed record for a long-distance nonstop train by reaching Chicago—1,017 miles distant—in 12 hours and 12 minutes for an average speed of 83.3 miles per hour. Its top speed exceeded 116 miles per hour.

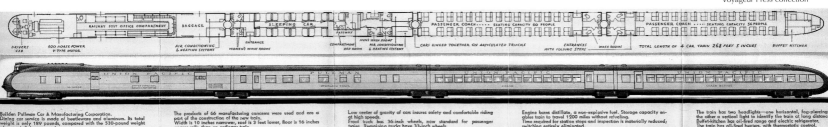

The Union Pacific's M-10000 was an articulated train, meaning that the locomotive and all three cars were permanently coupled, with a single four-wheeled truck sharing the duty of supporting the ends of two cars. This reduced the weight of the train (trucks are heavy), but also eliminated the flexibility of adding and subtracting cars as needed. A Railway Post Office and a baggage compartment were in the power car just behind the cab, and one sleeping car was followed by two coaches. With no dining car, meals were prepared in a small kitchen at the rear of the air-conditioned train and served in airline-style trays at passengers' seats.

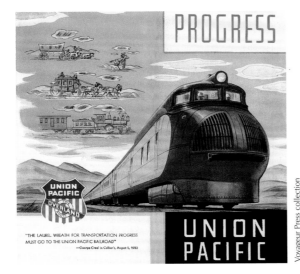

This brochure was distributed to those who toured the Union Pacific's M-10000 streamliner at Chicago's Century of Progress Exhibition in 1934. The aluminum speedster was designed in the manner of airplanes, using wind-tunnel tests. It reached a speed of 111 miles per hour.

The Burlington's *Twin Cities Zephyr* condensed the time between Chicago and Minneapolis to a mere 6 1/2 hours. The articulated train shown here was one of two built by the Budd Company in 1936 and 1937. Conventional coupled cars replaced the articulated trains in 1949 and service ended in 1970.

OLD PROBLEMS, NEW SOLUTIONS   187

A Royal Gorge Route Railroad train emerges from the 1,000-foot-deep gorge of Colorado's Arkansas River. The tourist railroad has since added dome cars to its trains and the food on its dinner train is excellent. A reservation and extra fare will get you a place in the locomotive cab with the engineer.

Claude Wiatrowski photo

THE NEW STREAMLINER "400" — CHICAGO AND NORTH WESTERN LINE

NORTH WESTERN'S NEW "400" STREAMLINER OPERATING DAILY BETWEEN CHICAGO AND ST. PAUL-MINNEAPOLIS VIA MILWAUKEE

The conductor distributed these postcards as a promotional tool. Passengers would address them to friends and the conductor would pick them up and mail them.

THE FAMOUS "400" STREAMLINER FLEET — CHICAGO AND NORTH WESTERN LINE

TAPROOM IN THE TAVERN — LUNCH COUNTER CARS — INSERT. POPULAR LUNCH COUNTER

Voyageur Press collection

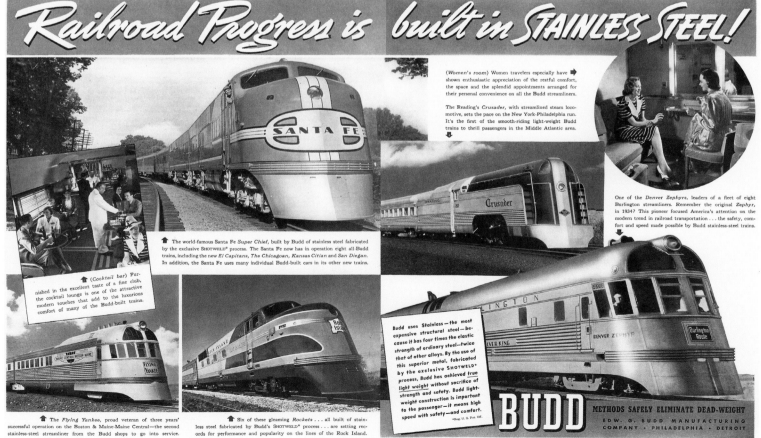

Railroad Progress is built in STAINLESS STEEL!

(*Women's room*) Women travelers especially have shown enthusiastic appreciation of the restful comfort, the space and the splendid appointments arranged for their personal convenience on all the Budd streamliners.

The Reading's *Crusader*, with streamlined steam locomotive, sets the pace on the New York-Philadelphia run. It's the first of the smooth-riding light-weight Budd trains to thrill passengers in the Middle Atlantic area.

One of the *Denver Zephyrs*, leaders of a fleet of eight Burlington streamliners. Remember the original *Zephyr*, in 1934? This pioneer focused America's attention on the modern trend in railroad transportation . . . the safety, comfort and speed made possible by Budd stainless-steel trains.

↑ The world-famous Santa Fe *Super Chief*, built by Budd of stainless steel fabricated by the exclusive SHOTWELD* process. The Santa Fe now has in operation eight all-Budd trains, including the new *El Capitans*, *The Chicagoan*, *Kansas Citian* and *San Diegan*. In addition, the Santa Fe uses many individual Budd-built cars in its other new trains.

(*Cocktail bar*) Furnished in the excellent taste of a fine club, the cocktail lounge is one of the attractive modern touches that add to the luxurious comfort of many of the Budd-built trains.

↑ The *Flying Yankee*, proud veteran of three years' successful operation on the Boston & Maine-Maine Central—the second stainless-steel streamliner from the Budd shops to go into service.

↑ Six of these gleaming *Rockets* . . . all built of stainless steel fabricated by Budd's SHOTWELD* process . . . are setting records for performance and popularity on the lines of the Rock Island.

Budd uses Stainless—the most expensive structural steel—because it has four times the elastic strength of ordinary steel—twice that of other alloys. By the use of this superior metal, fabricated by the exclusive SHOTWELD* process, Budd has achieved true light weight without sacrifice of strength and safety. Budd light-weight construction is important to the passenger—it means high speed with safety—and comfort.

*Reg. U. S. Pat. Off.

BUDD METHODS SAFELY ELIMINATE DEAD-WEIGHT

EDW. G. BUDD MANUFACTURING COMPANY • PHILADELPHIA • DETROIT

www.archivesofadvertising.com

Right: Among the many accommodations celebrated in this ad for Denver & Rio Grande's *California Zephyr* passenger service, the views afforded by the train's Vista Domes are foremost.

Below: The General Motors *Aerotrain* is demonstrated to the Pennsylvania Railroad. The train's light-duty suspension doomed it to failure. The few demonstration units that were built ended up in commuter service on the Rock Island in Chicago. Several times a day, the author would see them streak past the campus of the Illinois Institute of Technology, where he received his undergraduate degree in 1968.

CHAPTER FIVE

A Kansas City Southern trains passes near Clark, Missouri.

Courtesy Kansas City Southern. Photo by Mike Brunner, Ben Weddle & Associates

THE
RIGHT STUFF,
AGAIN

The Staggers Act, passed by Congress in 1980, was a major milestone in the history of railroad transportation in the United States. Although the Interstate Commerce Commission still regulated the process, the act authorized railroads and shippers to negotiate lower rates for volume shippers. Previously, all shippers, regardless of size, would have been quoted the rates in published tariffs for the goods to be transported. This seemingly simple and obvious concept—lower prices for larger customers—was all that it took to not only revitalize the railroad industry but also to change its basic character. Coal, grain, automobiles, and other commodities shipped in enormous quantities filled freight train after freight train. Gone was the once-ubiquitous boxcar carrying many small shipments, which now went by truck.

The Staggers Act did not completely deregulate the railroad industry and the railroads have continued to lobby for more deregulation. On the other hand, shippers have called for more regulation. Mergers have distilled the industry down to seven large freight railroads, decreasing competition. These seven are called Class 1 railroads and are BNSF, Canadian National, Canadian Pacific, CSX, Kansas City Southern, Norfolk Southern, and Union Pacific. Regulators must still approve mergers and often require that a newly merged railroad give trackage rights to its competitors (allow its competitors to use its tracks). Increasingly

important short-line and regional railroads sometimes provide competition to the largest railroads instead of merely augmenting their services. Nevertheless, some shippers will probably always ship via a single track upon which the trains of only one railroad operate. It is these shippers that are likely to continue lobbying for increased regulation of rates.

In 1995, the ICC Termination Act replaced the Interstate Commerce Commission with the Surface Transportation Board. As of early 2007, two primary entities regulate railroads in the United States at the national level. The Surface Transportation Board (STB) regulates economic matters, including rates and service disputes, as well as restructuring issues such as mergers, new railroad construction, and railroad abandonments. The Federal Railroad Administration (FRA) was created by Congress in 1966 and is concerned primarily with safety issues. Its formation also consolidated government support of rail transportation into a single agency.

Before the Staggers Act, railroads were in the business of carrying anything anywhere for anybody. After the Staggers Act, railroads found prosperity in the 1990s by doing what their technology does best: carrying commodities between specific terminals for large shippers. Unit trains move a single commodity from one shipper to one destination. Increasingly, merchandise is carried in standardized containers or in trucks placed directly on railroad flatcars.

In 2003, 44 percent of the tonnage and 21 percent of the revenue of the seven Class 1 freight railroads was derived from the movement of coal alone! Other major commodities carried by railroads include chemicals, agricultural and food products, minerals and ores, petroleum, lumber and wood products, waste and scrap, metals, paper, containers, and motor vehicles including automobiles.

GOODBYE CABOOSE

It wasn't many years ago that the author's children were waving at the crew in the caboose bringing up the rear of every freight train. They always received a friendly wave back. Except in railroad museums, this simple pleasure is now gone. In the 1980s the superfluous caboose was replaced on virtually every train by the end-of-train device. The ETD comprises a strobe light to mark the rear of the train and a radio link to the locomotive's cab. The radio link tells the engineer if the end of the train is moving and the value of the air pressure in the brake line. Hardly as romantic as the caboose, the ETD is much lighter than a caboose and requires much less maintenance.

Norfolk Southern is a large exporter of coal via its Atlantic coastal facility at Lambert's Point in Norfolk, Virginia. It operates close to 22,000 miles of track in the eastern United States and Canada.

Led by five diesel locomotives, a Buffalo & Pittsburgh Railroad train becomes part of the autumn colors. The railroad operates 750 miles of track in Pennsylvania and New York.

Crews on freight trains that run directly from one terminal to another have been reduced down to three or even two. New locomotive cabs are designed to be more comfortable for crewmembers, all of whom now ride there.

SHORT LINES AND REGIONALS

With the Staggers Act, Congress hoped that a more rational process would relieve the railroads of the burden of unprofitable track and that smaller railroads would spring up to profitably operate track that the larger railroads could not.

The railroad system has always included small railroads, collectively termed short lines. Many fell by the wayside or were absorbed into larger railroads. The Staggers Act reversed the direction of that trend and more. Not only were "short" railroad tracks sold to new operators but longer networks of railroad track were sold, leading to a new descriptive term: the regional railroad. According to the definition used by the Association of American Railroads, regional freight railroads are those with at least 350 miles of main line and less than $40 million dollars in annual revenue. In 2007, there are about 30 regional railroads. Railroads smaller than this, as well as switching and terminal railroads, are colloquially called short lines and there are a little more than 500 railroads in this category.

Many industries along regional and short-line tracks could not continue to operate without railroad connections, trucks being either too expensive or technologically incapable of moving certain raw materials or products that are manufactured there.

Entrepreneurs saw advantages of scale to owning multiple short lines and regionals. Holding companies that own multiple railroads, sometimes in many countries, created yet a new type of railroad entity. RailAmerica operates 43 railroads with 8,800 miles of track in the United States and Canada. Pioneer Railcorp operates 16 railroads in eight U.S. states. OmniTRAX has 11 railroads in six U.S. states and three Canadian provinces. Ohio Central has 10 railroads totaling 500 miles in two U.S. states. Gennesee & Wyoming operates 12 railroads in the United States, three in Canada, one in Mexico, three in Australia, and one in Bolivia. Railroad Development Corporation operates the 623-mile regional Iowa Interstate Railroad plus railroads in South America, Central America, Africa, and Europe!

CONRAIL AND AMTRAK

No examination of the current state of railroads can ignore the U.S. government's involvement in Conrail and Amtrak. The Conrail story has been finished. The railroad was sufficiently successful that it was jointly purchased by Norfolk

A calm day enhances the reflection of this Arkansas, Louisiana & Mississippi train between Monroe, Louisiana, and Fordyce, Arkansas.

Southern and CSX Corporation in 1998, a continuation of the trend toward bigger but fewer railroads. Conrail still exists as a switching and terminal railroad that operates for the benefit of its new owners.

Amtrak is another story. After Penn Central collapsed, Amtrak was given the important electrified line from New York City to Washington, D.C., a line once owned by the Pennsylvania Railroad. Its high-speed trains on this route successfully compete with airlines between these two cities. Amtrak has partnered with many states to provide critical and successful railroad service within those states. In 1992, its revenue covered 79 percent of its operating expenses, which was as good as any passenger railroad service in the world. Yet, it is an easy political target for proponents of privatization. The U.S. government has at best been indifferent and at worst hostile to Amtrak. Currently, there is a critical need to repair equipment that is broken beyond the point of usefulness and to purchase new rolling stock. Except for money from the states, there has never been any funding for network expansion, critical to the viability of passenger service. Amtrak's long-term success requires that Congress appropriate money for all these purposes and subsidize operating losses.

FUTURE TECHNOLOGIES

Development of railroad technology continues in North America. The satellite-based Global Positioning System is used to establish the location of trains. Equipment for the essential but difficult and expensive tasks of track maintenance is becoming more and more automated. Concrete replaces wood cross-ties on heavily used track. The Association of American Railroads operates the Transportation Test Center—a facility owned by the FRA—in Pueblo, Colorado. Much new railroad technology originates in the private sector, though. Among the newer developments from the private sector are low-emission diesel locomotives.

MERGERS AND PRIVATIZATION IN CANADA

As a counterpart to the Staggers Act in the United States, the Canadian National Transportation Act of 1987 introduced similar but not as far-reaching reforms. Both Canadian National and Canadian Pacific emphasized their railway roots by selling non-rail businesses and acquiring additional railroad track, much of it by purchasing U.S. railroads. While the major Canadian railways were expanding into the United States, they were selling off unprofitable

Mobile gantry cranes load and unload containers from double-stack cars in a Norfolk Southern train.

Canadian branch lines to new short lines. As in the United States, some Canadian lines would never be profitable, including the Canadian National's narrow gauge tracks in Newfoundland, which were dismantled in the 1980s. As Conrail was privatized in the United States in 1987, Canadian National was also privatized in 1995. In an interesting twist, now-private Canadian National assumed operational control of provincially owned BC Rail in 2004. In some ways, Canadian railroad history has been similar to that of U.S. railroads but delayed in time. Although trends in Canada—as in the United States—have clearly been toward privatization, the Canadian view of its railroads is still different from that of the United States.

SUCCESS AND THE INVISIBLE RAILROAD

In 2003, railroads employed 154,000 people, a mere 8 1/2 percent of their peak employment of 1.8 million in 1920. Yet in 2003, U.S. freight railroads moved four times the amount of freight (but only a fraction of the passengers) they moved in 1920.

While reasonable profits are critical if railroads are to attract new investment capital, freight railroads have become invisible to most Americans. With so many fewer employers, you are unlikely to have a railroader as a neighbor or customer. As rural track is abandoned and disman-

tled, rural America relies more on trucks. New track is still constructed, but for the purpose of increasing capacity along major trunk lines or serving new major traffic sources such as coal mines. Although most of us pay electric bills and purchase automobiles, we don't recognize that we pay less for electricity because railroads are efficient coal-haulers or that we pay less for automobiles because railroads move steel to automobile plants and move finished automobiles across the nation. The manufactured goods with which we most closely identify arrive at our local stores on trucks, but those goods may have traveled part way to their destination on trains

So while railroads are still important to us, they have become invisible to most Americans. The author sometimes wonders how a 10,000-ton coal train can be invisible. A television reporter asked a man if he thought railroads were still important. The man replied that he didn't even know we still had railroads. They were standing next to the railroad track!

Perhaps, it is this invisibility that has sparked our interest in railroad history, with hundreds of preserved railroads and railroad museums in North America. Americans wonder at the romance of the rails and the intimacy we once had with iron monsters on steel track hauling wooden cars to every town.

A Great Western Railway train crosses the highway in the frosty Colorado darkness.

A Canadian National train passes the Chicago skyline. The acquisition of the Illinois Central allowed Canadian National trains to pass through Chicago all the way to the Gulf Coast. Locomotive No. 5748 was built as an EMD SD75 in 1997.

THE RIGHT STUFF, AGAIN   195

ARTISTS

In North America, the earliest railroad paintings showed trains coexisting with idyllic scenery, a way to experience America's natural enormity. When the trains came to the fore, they were often sparkling parodies of reality. Starting in the 1920s, the railroads began to exploit the power of art in their advertising. Today's railroad art is most likely to be purchased by railroads, private collectors, and museums.

There were and are so many great railroad artists, any list is bound to offend someone by omission. Otto Kuhler, Grif Teller, Gil Reid, Leslie Ragan, Bob Jensen, Mike Kotowski, Ted Blaylock, Larry Fisher, John Bromley, Ted Rose, Gil Bennet. One of the most prolific and expert of all railroad painters was Howard Fogg, whose paintings decorate everything from playing cards to book covers. Perhaps he is best known, however, for works reproduced on Christmas cards published by Leanin' Tree. An entire room is devoted to Fogg's original paintings at the Leanin' Tree Museum of Western Art in Boulder, Colorado.

JOHN HUGH COKER

A former steam locomotive engineer on both the Durango & Silverton and Cumbres & Toltec, John Coker has special insight into his subjects. Playing with his Lionel train set primed him to ask his mother to spend an unforgettable day riding the extensive Los Angeles trolley system just before it was abandoned. An excursion on the Southern Pacific's *Sunset Limited* was made more memorable by a porter who let him watch the desert pass from an open Dutch door. School in Denver included a summer job on the Cumbres & Toltec, and long mountain winters gave him the opportunity to hone his artistic skills. He has been a full-time artist since 1995, with a long list of book and magazine cover illustrations and private commissions to his credit. John lives on an 1890 homestead near Durango, Colorado, overlooking the New Mexican plateaus and counts this culturally and visually diverse location as a major inspiration to his work. While his first love is trains, his work has expanded to include landscapes and ghost towns. You can see more of his work at www.rrart.com.

George E. Lawrence photo

John Hugh Coker.

Southern Pacific No. 18 is turned at Laws, California, on September 1, 1952.

The colorful *49er* passes the depot at Echo, Utah, in about 1939.

610 East of Big Spring.

Clinton M. Brown, Jr., collection, original painting by John Winfield

JOHN WINFIELD

In the 1950s, the largest, most modern, last-generation steam locomotives toiled next to the first-generation diesel locos. It is this transition that inspires John Winfield. Not only were technologies intermingled, but mergers had not yet eliminated much of the individuality of American railroading. The lighting techniques that John developed while painting landscapes—starting as a hobby in 1988—became unique elements of his railroad paintings. Many of John's paintings are available as truly exceptional prints, since John is also a professional printer and owns his own commercial printing company. He reproduces his own work with special techniques and, of course, under the direct supervision of the artist! His paintings have been purchased by railroads as well as private collectors. You can view his work in public collections nationwide, on the covers of several books, and at www.WinfieldRailArt.com.

www.WinfieldRailArt.com

John Winfield.

SP SD-45X Locos near Verde, Nevada.

Vern Simpson collection, original painting by John Winfield

Overleaf: *Super C.*

BOOKS AND MAGAZINES

Voyageur Press collection

Railroad unions published their own magazines. Articles in this issue were divided into nine categories: Technical, Industrial, Brotherhood, Cooperation, Safety First, Health, Verse and Fiction, Miscellaneous, and Ladies' Society.

Voyageur Press collection

Railroad Magazine had already changed names twice by the time this January 1939 issue was published. It was formerly *Railroad Stories* and *Railroad Man's Magazine*. It included nonfiction articles on railroad subjects, true stories of railroad adventures, and railroad-themed fiction. Regular columns included book reviews, model railroading features, and pieces about special excursions.

Voyageur Press collection

Trains changed its name briefly in the 1950s to attract riders and join the expected boom in railroad passenger service that never materialized. This spectacular cover shows Norfolk and Western compound articulated 2-8-8-2 helping push a coal train out of a tunnel near Welch, West Virginia.

The October 1954 issue of *Model Railroader* featured Jack Alexander's railroad on its cover. The small amount of standard gauge track on the right exists only to provide an interchange to the majority of the model railroad, which is based on a narrow gauge prototype. A "gallows" turntable is in the foreground, while a water tank can be seen in the background. Inside is an article titled "Narrow Gauge in Buffalo" about a club that operated both standard and narrow gauge railroads in both HO and O scale. *Model Railroader* is the pioneer magazine for modelers and today is read by more model railroaders than any other magazine on the subject.

Voyageur Press collection

Even in 1954, full-color covers were rare on railroad magazines. *Railroad Model Craftsman*'s decision was probably made to allow the back cover to be printed in color as well. The back cover has artwork for an HO scale old-time cafe that could be cut out, pasted to a cardboard substrate, and glued together into a model building.

Voyageur Press collection

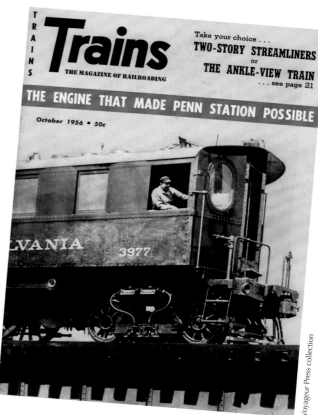

. . . see page 21

Voyageur Press collection

Unlike other magazines, *Trains* appeals to railroad workers, railroad management, railfans, supporters of passenger rail, rail shippers—virtually every constituency related to railroading. The electric locomotive on the cover makes it clear that steam will soon vanish from the rails. Photos of steam locomotives inside the magazine are mostly "where you can still find steam locos running," while diesel and electric locos are presented in articles about modern railroading. Two of the most interesting steam photos are one of the Denver & Rio Grande narrow gauge and the Southern Pacific narrow gauge, documenting the end of two obsolete technologies.

Published by Robinson & Associates, Red Bluff, California, www.grandscales.com

Grand Scales Quarterly is devoted to modeling in gauges of 12 inches and wider.

Narrow Gauge & Short Line Gazette features articles for those who model prototype railroads in the magazine's title. This often involves scratch-building models to the highest standards. This cover is a G gauge, 1:20.3 scale model of a West Side Lumber Company, 3-foot-gauge Shay locomotive.

Bob Poli photo, courtesy Benchmark Publications

CANADIAN NATIONAL

In 1917, the Canadian government consolidated the 16 railroads it operated under one name incorporated as the Canadian National Railway in 1919. By 1923, the Grand Trunk Pacific and Grand Trunk would be added to the puzzle.

In 1995, private investors purchased the railway from the Canadian government, and in 1999 the Illinois Central was merged into Canadian National. The combined railroads' routes would offer a three-pronged attack on major seaports connecting the Atlantic and Pacific Oceans with the Gulf of Mexico.

In 2001, the Wisconsin Central was folded into Canadian National, and Great Lakes Transportation was added in 2004. Great Lakes Transportation included the venerable old railroad names of the Bessemer & Lake Erie Railroad and the Duluth, Missabe & Iron Range Railway, both intimately involved in steel production.

In 2004, CN, the new name of Canadian National, purchased the assets of BC Rail except for its track, which it leased from the province of British Columbia. Originally incorporated as the Pacific Great Eastern Railway in 1912, BC Rail comprises over 1,000 miles now operated by CN through the rugged mountains of British Columbia.

G. V. "Jerry" Carson photo

Mt. Robson towers over a steam-drawn Canadian National passenger train in a 1948 ad. The advertisement lists 10 great holiday trips on passenger trains finally relieved of the duty of moving troops.

Voyageur Press collection

The end of steam is still a decade away in Canada as sister locomotives 6048 and 6049, both Mountain types of a 4-8-2 wheel arrangement, rest between assignments at Winnipeg, Manitoba, in 1955.

Right: By 1958, streamlined diesels had replaced streamlined steamers on Canadian National literature. In a country that needed passenger trains, this timetable totaled a huge 80 pages.

Below: This large fold-out map still features a streamlined steam locomotive on its cover, though it is 1951 and diesels are clearly on the horizon. The map consumes one side of the sheet while the other lists the amenities at Canadian National hotels and the sights to be seen in each Canadian province.

The "SUPER CONTINENTAL" near Jasper, Alta.

Canadian National diesel No. 2450 heads up a freight train near Henry House, Alberta, in the shadow of the Canadian Rockies.

CN photo

COLORADO & SOUTHERN

Claude Wiatrowski pho...

The Colorado & Southern Railway, along with its sister, Fort Worth & Denver Railway encompassed an incredible variety of railroad operations. The railroad ran trains of three different gauges—from the 2-mile-high altitude of Cripple Creek, Colorado, to sea-level at Galveston, Texas—with steam, diesel, and electric locomotion.

C&S was fashioned in 1898 from a number of bankrupt railroads. In 1900, it began to purchase Colorado mountain railroads to serve the mining industry. It bought the Trinity & Brazos Valley in 1905 to gain access to the Gulf of Mexico at Galveston. It purchased or constructed street and interurban railways in Cripple Creek, Fort Collins, Denver, and Boulder.

In 1908, the Burlington purchased C&S. Electric interurbans and narrow gauge mining railroads were discarded and the railroad essentially became part of the Burlington.

C&S was merged into the Burlington Northern in 1981, as was the Fort Worth & Denver a year later. Both are now part of BNSF Railway. Traffic on these rails—beer from Golden, Colorado, and coal from Wyoming—reflects the variety with which they were founded.

The narrow gauge railroad from Denver to Leadville, Colorado, was abandoned except for the portion connecting the molybdenum mine at Climax with Leadville. This track was widened to standard gauge to connect the mine with the Rio Grande's track at Leadville. Though the locomotive is Burlington Northern's, it rests on track far from any other BN-owned rails. Just beyond the locomotive is the roundhouse that once sheltered locomotives of the Denver, South Park & Pacific Railway. The rails to Climax now belong to the Leadville, Colorado & Southern tourist railroad.

H. O. Jones, LC-USZ6-1338, Library of Congress, Prints and Photographs Division

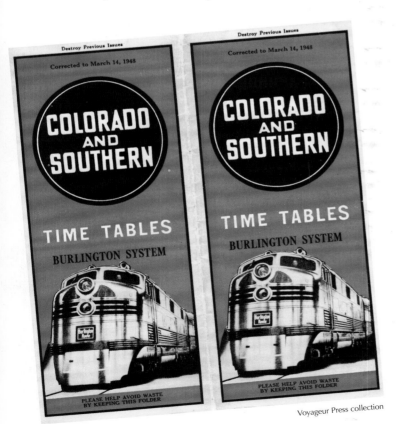

Voyageur Press collection

Above: A judge put together the Colorado & Southern from bankrupt railroads, including several Colorado narrow gauge lines. The severity of running trains at these elevations is evident from the snow almost enveloping the locomotive.

Left: The Colorado & Southern was part of the Burlington system for many years before its 1981 merger into its parent railroad, by then the Burlington Northern. This 1948 passenger timetable lists integrated service with other railroads that were part of this family, including the Fort Worth & Denver City, Burlington, Great Northern, Northern Pacific, and Spokane, Portland & Seattle. All of these railroads would merge into the Burlington Northern.

FANS OF THE IRON HORSE

Railfans probably existed the day of the first railroad trip. The novelty of this new technology was irresistible. When railroads permeated America, railfans blended into the millions that used the railroads daily. In some ways, everyone was a railroad enthusiast as everyone had an interest—either practical or sentimental—in railroads. As railroads began their march toward invisibility in American life, railfans became more obvious. They could be seen standing trackside, collectively clicking the shutters of their cameras as the last steam locomotive of its kind trundled past. They queued up 50 deep to ride the last run of a branch-line passenger train that didn't see 50 passengers in a year!

Railfans are interested in either the technology of railroads, the history of railways, or both. Technology includes locomotives, cars, bridges, tunnels, signals, and anything else that is needed to run trains. Business, engineering, economic, and cultural history are all of interest to many railfans.

For some railfans, collecting is the casual impulsive acquisition of a postcard. Others spend their lives creating museum-quality collections. Collections may be themed by a type of object such as postcards, or they may reflect the collector's interest in a particular railroad. Objects produced and used by the railroad are especially desired. Fans collect dinnerware, timetables, tickets, employee magazines, lanterns, switch keys, station signs, and, most oddly, railroad spikes. With few exceptions, one railroad spike is like another. Yet, fans hike long-abandoned railroad grades to accumulate these rusty reminders of the past, carefully mark them with the location at which they were found, and store them away in 50-pound boxes!

Chasing trains is the railfan activity most likely noticed by the general public and most likely to generate doubts about sanity. Fans race ahead of a train to find a location at which they can photograph it, acquire video of its passage, or record the sounds it makes. As soon as the train passes, the process is repeated.

Riding trains is an activity that is becoming harder and harder to do. In the United States and Canada, riding is limited to commuter trains, a few long-distance trains operated by VIA Rail or Amtrak, and preserved railroads. Some fans own pop cars, small gasoline-powered rail vehicles once used to transport maintenance crews to locations at which they worked. Pop car owners arrange special trips on which they operate their machines.

Several mammoth main-line steam locomotives—owned by railroads, independent operating companies, or

Men predominate in railroad-related hobbies but there are, and always have been, women railfans, as depicted on the cover of this May 1939 issue of *Railroad Magazine*.

Claude Wiatrowski photo

Voyageur Press collection

A "freight train" chugs past photographers on a special trip on the Cumbres & Toltec Scenic Railroad. The fans are actually operators of other preserved railways visiting for a Tourist Railway Association Convention in Denver.

museums—still run occasional excursions over main-line railroads. Since preserved railroads are frequently short and meandering, these main-line trips are the only opportunity to see a 400-ton steam locomotive or antique diesel roar through the countryside at 70 miles per hour.

Most preserved railways were saved and restored to operation by interested railfans. The majority of preserved railroads are operated, in whole or part, by volunteers who run the locomotives, collect the tickets, serve as guides, and clean the restrooms!

FREIGHT TRAINS

F. J. Bandholtz, LC-USZ62-52773 and LC-USZ62-52774, Library of Congress, Prints and Photographs Division

The South Omaha stockyards must have been a busy location, judging by the three switch engines on duty in the substantial yard. There must have been a lull in activity when this photo was taken, as few railroad cars are visible. Most of the holding pens appear empty as well.

Early freight cars were wooden and not specialized. Boxcars were predominant and remained so until the middle of the twentieth century. In 1867, a refrigerator car for meat and fruit was patented. Anheuser-Bush deployed one of the first fleets of refrigerator cars along with trackside facilities to load ice into the cars. Horizontal tank cars made their first appearance in 1868, although the tanks were wood. Cars for hauling coal made the transition from wood to iron before the Civil War.

North American railroads conducted their freight business in the same way for 150 years or so. A locomotive would make a circuit of local industries, picking up loaded railroad cars and dropping off empty cars at many small shippers. Loaded cars were taken to a railroad yard where they were sorted to be taken by main-line trains to various destinations. Freight cars might have to be sorted again in some intermediate railyard to be carried by another main-line train to the railyard closest to their final destination. Here, another locomotive would make a circuit of industries to drop off loaded cars.

The local trains that dropped off and picked up cars were *peddler freights* and the main-line trains were appropriately named *drag freights*, for their speeds were quite slow; the average speed of a freight train was 11 miles per hour in 1921 and rose to a still-not-very-impressive 17 miles per hour by the start of World War II. Scheduling was difficult since numerous high-speed passenger trains shared the rails with low-speed freights.

UNIT TRAINS

Unit trains are loaded with a single commodity, most commonly coal, from a single shipper. An entire train travels to a single destination where it is unloaded. The slow, inefficient, traditional process of assembling trains in classification yards is much more expensive than the operation of a unit train. Railroads would profit from offering lower rates to volume shippers that could load these large efficient trains, but not until federal regulations were repealed that prohibited railroads from offering discount transportation.

www.archivesofadvertising.com

P.F.E.
90225

PACIFIC FRUIT EXPRESS
P.F.E.

Railroads contribute to the variety of food we eat. At one time, perishable fruits and vegetables might have filled a car or two that had been added to a speedy passenger train. Traffic originating in California, Arizona, and Oregon grew quickly, and long trains of nothing but perishable foods became commonplace. Railroads helped promote the products they carried. To deal with the need for specialized refrigerator cars, Southern Pacific and Union Pacific jointly created Pacific Fruit Express to buy and maintain refrigerator cars and the industrial plants along the tracks that supplied ice to cool the interiors of railroad cars. Pacific Fruit Express entered business in 1907. Eventually, ice was replaced by mechanical refrigeration and the sight of large blocks of ice being loaded into rooftop hatches of railroad cars became a memory.

PIGGYBACK

Truck trailers were first carried on railroad flatcars in the 1920s. This service is called TOFC (trailer on flat car) or piggyback. Increased cooperation between railroads and truckers has resurrected a business model that railroads had anticipated decades ago, in which trucks replace railroad branch lines. A similar technology called Road-Railer dispenses with the railroad flatcar entirely and simply mounts the truck's trailer on railroad wheels—reducing weight and improving energy efficiency.

CONTAINERS

Intermodal shipments—containerized shipments moved by railroads, trucks, and ships—have become the most important new business source for railroads. Containers are simply rugged boxes of standard dimensions. They are loaded and sealed by the shipper; transported to their destination by any combination of ship, railroad, and truck; and unloaded by the consignee. The ships, railcars, and trucks that move containers—as well as the equipment that transfers them—can be built to a standardized design. Because containers are loaded and then sealed, shipments are less likely to be damaged or lost as they are transferred from one transportation mode to another. Although containers can be used for almost anything, they were a boon to the movement of manufactured goods. Containers can be stacked two high on specially built flatcars that support them closer to the rails so the two-high formations clear obstructions such as tunnels.

A Pennsylvania Railroad switch engine moves cars around a grain elevator, and a main-line train roars past while a harvester is busy with its task. Railroads and the agricultural industry have had a love-hate relationship. Trains were essential to establishing national markets, but unfair and unequal rates infuriated farmers who lobbied for the first effective regulation of freight rates.

Voyageur Press collection

Claude Wiatrowski photo

The Southern Pacific constructed a boxcar with Plexiglas sides. The *Telavue* car was instrumented to record impact forces and used as an employee training tool to improve loading and shipping methods.

This antique tank car, photographed at the Belton, Grandview and Kansas City Railroad in Belton, Missouri, has since been sold to the Illinois Railway Museum. The line at Belton still exists and carries passengers through the Missouri countryside.

Voyageur Press collection

Left: In 1955, Southern Pacific had the largest fleet of piggyback truck equipment in the United States.

Opposite top: Piggyback trailers on flatcars cast their reflections onto the water of the Colorado River in Glenwood Canyon, Colorado. This Denver & Rio Grande freight was photographed in 1979.

Opposite bottom: Preserved railways frequently assemble freight trains for photographers' specials. This Cumbres & Toltec Scenic Railroad train resembles the Denver & Rio Grande narrow gauge freight trains that passed this way between 1881 and 1968. The water tank was constructed as part of a movie set nicknamed Weed City.

Norfolk Southern Corp.

Trailers are loaded and unloaded in Norfolk Southern's Bayview Yard in Baltimore, Maryland.

THE RIGHT STUFF, AGAIN   213

KANSAS CITY SOUTHERN

A route to carry Midwestern crops to the Gulf of Mexico would be much shorter than existing routes to the Atlantic. With this thought in mind, a railroad was started south from Kansas City along the Missouri-Kansas border. After considering Galveston, Texas, the railroad built its own gulf terminus, named Port Arthur after the railroad's founder, Arthur Stillwell.

Construction had drained the railroad by its completion in 1897. With no source of funds, it was reorganized in 1900 as the Kansas City Southern Railway. In 1901, the first "gusher" of the Spindletop oilfield blasted crude oil high into the air. Refineries were built, as were plants to manufacture plastic, rubber, and other products. KCS ran right through the heart of this industry and prospered.

KCS expanded into Dallas and New Orleans. It added the 1,200-mile Mid South Railroad in 1994. A 1997 purchase of the Great Western Railway added St. Louis. In 2005, it took control of the Texas Mexican Railway with access to Mexico and bought Transportación Ferroviaria Mexicana, a 2,661-mile Mexican railroad.

PANAMA CANAL RAILROAD

What 143-year-old transcontinental railroad connecting the Atlantic and Pacific Oceans is only 48 miles long? The answer is the Panama Canal Railroad, a passenger and freight operation roughly paralleling the Panama Canal. First built in 1855, it was rebuilt in 1909 and again in 2001 by the Kansas City Southern.

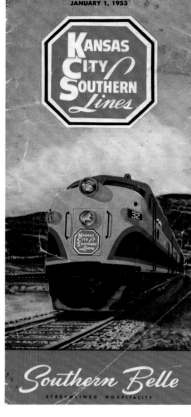

Southern Belle was the Kansas City Southern crack passenger train between Kansas City and New Orleans. Other trains listed in the 1953 timetable (left) were the *Flying Crow* between Kansas City and Shreveport and the *Shreveporter* between St. Louis and Shreveport.

Voyageur Press collection

A northbound Kansas City Southern train crosses the International Bridge at Laredo, Texas.

Courtesy Kansas City Southern. Photo by Mike Brunner, Ben Weddle & Associates

Top and left: Two photos clearly show the evolution of steam locomotives. At left, a huge Kansas City Southern 2-10-4 blasts out of Kansas City in 1937. At top, a tiny 4-4-0 locomotive prepares to depart with a short passenger train.

Below: This three-car passenger train of the Belton, Grandview and Kansas City preserves the attractive color scheme of Kansas City Southern streamliners. The observation car closest to the photographer was a KCS hospitality car.

NATIONAL PARKS

With the completion of transcontinental railways, the American West became a destination as appealing as was Europe. Soon after the Civil War, railroads encouraged elite travelers to experience wonders west of the Missouri River. The newly constructed railways needed both to generate passenger revenue and attract potential investors. As the end of the nineteenth century approached, railroads were already beginning to promote the West's scenery to a mass market. In the early twentieth century, railroads championed the protection of the most unique and spectacular destinations through the establishment of National Parks, both in the United States and Canada.

Yosemite was promoted by the Southern Pacific as an alternative to Switzerland. The Northern Pacific called itself the *Yellowstone Park Line*. Unlike Yosemite, Yellowstone was the epitome of the rough, rugged, and dangerous American West. Utah's Cedar City became the Union Pacific's gateway to the red rocks of Zion and Bryce. The Great Northern lobbied for creation of Glacier National Park, and the Santa Fe built a branch to take its trains to the edge of the Grand Canyon. Burlington's Colorado-bound vacationers could include a side trip to Rocky Mountain National Park, and its trains also traveled to the heart of South Dakota's Black Hills. The Canadian

Pacific pressed for the establishment of Banff National Park, Canada's first. Just north of Banff, Jasper National Park was associated with the Grand Trunk Pacific, a predecessor of Canadian National.

www.archivesofadvertising.com

Union Pacific advertising claimed many of the West's most famous attractions as its own.

Detroit Publishing Co., LC-USZ62-77352, Library of Congress, Prints and Photographs Division

The Northern Pacific station at Gardiner, Montana, was the railroad's gateway to Yellowstone National Park.

Santa Fe Railway tracks entered Grand Canyon National Park on a branch from its main line at Williams, Arizona. That branch is now operated by the Grand Canyon Railway. This ad art touted the route's scenery.

www.archivesofadvertising.com

Above: As did U.S. railways, Canadian railroads promoted the development of national parks along their routes. Jasper National Park was established in 1907 after the Grand Trunk Pacific's rails were driven over Yellowhead Pass. The Grand Trunk Pacific became part of Canadian National.

Below left: The Burlington published this substantial 36-page booklet in 1935 to attract passengers to its Denver trains. You could rent a car to tour Rocky Mountain National Park, or travel with a Burlington escorted tour that provided motor coach transportation into the mountains.

Below: The Great Northern Railway lobbied for the establishment of Montana's Glacier National Park.

NEW HAVEN

Voyageur Press collection

In 1872, the New York, New Haven & Hartford Railroad was formed as a merger of two railroads providing service from Springfield, Massachusetts, via Hartford and New Haven in Connecticut, to New York City. The railroad would eventually control virtually all of Connecticut, Rhode Island, and southeastern Massachusetts.

The line from New Haven to New York City was electrified with locomotives that could operate both on high-voltage alternating current on New Haven tracks and on low-voltage direct current to gain access to New York City via the New York Central. But New Haven's short distances were ripe for the picking by truck lines and after World War II, passengers preferred automobiles. The New Haven was absorbed into Penn Central on the last day of 1968. Though it was unwanted, the Interstate Commerce Commission ordered Penn Central to incorporate it!

What is left of the New Haven is fragmented among freight railroads, commuter railroads, and Amtrak. The New Haven's Boston–to–New York route is part of Amtrak's Northeast Corridor on which both high-speed Acela Express trains and commuter trains run.

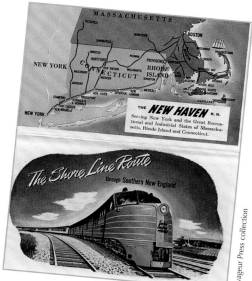

Voyageur Press collection

Above: Although the New Haven served a densely populated region, its short routes made it the ideal target for replacement by highways.

Courtesy Milton A. Davis collection

Left: This New Haven passenger train had as many baggage, express, and mail cars as it had coaches. It graphically illustrates why the end of passenger service was so intertwined with the U.S. mail and package-delivery alternatives to the Railway Express Agency.

By 1953, the New Haven had become the largest purchaser of the Budd Company's self-propelled RDC cars; they were perfect for New Haven's short passenger routes. Even in 1953, half the New Haven's income was from passenger service. Nevertheless, even these RDC cars couldn't compete with automobiles on modern highways.

Just after World War II, the Budd Company advertised an artist's concept of New Haven's train of self-propelled RDC cars with a streamlined nose (opposite top). The rendering became reality, as shown in the photo below of RDC 140 at Davisville, New Jersey, in 1968.

NEW YORK CENTRAL

In 1914, the New York Central & Hudson River Railroad and the Lake Shore & Michigan Southern were combined to create the New York Central. Its main line ran from New York City, paralleling the Hudson River north to Albany, the Erie Canal west to Buffalo, and along the south shore of Lake Erie to Cleveland before proceeding across Indiana to Chicago. Consequently, the New York Central advertised itself as "The Water Level Route" to differentiate its train service from the mountainous route of the Pennsylvania Railroad, its chief competitor.

The Central included about 10,000 miles of railroad track and had several important connections. The Boston & Albany provided access to Boston. The Ohio Central spread south through Ohio to coal mines in West Virginia. Michigan Central provided an alternate route from Buffalo to Chicago—ducking through Canada north of Lake Erie—as well as tracks north through Michigan's lower peninsula. Lease of the Cleveland, Cincinnati, Chicago and St. Louis Railway (nicknamed the Big Four) put the NYC into those cities.

In 1968, a decade of preparation created the Penn Central from the merger of the New York Central with the Pennsylvania. Just two years later, the Penn Central became the nation's largest bankruptcy up to that time.

Record-breaking locomotive No. 999 on the head of the original *Empire State Express* in 1894.

To celebrate the 50th anniversary of its *Empire State Express* in 1941, the New York Central introduced a new streamlined, steam-hauled *Empire* on a New York–Buffalo–Cleveland–Detroit route. On May 20, 1893, 4-4-0 locomotive No. 999 had reached a remarkable 112.5 miles per hour on part of the *Empire*'s run.

New York Central's observation locomotive No. 30, the *Cleveland*, originally was a Lake Shore & Michigan Southern locomotive probably used by executives to inspect the railroad's condition. The New York Central & Hudson River owned an even more unusual but similar observation locomotive called the *Ontario*, which had a rare 2-4-0 wheel arrangement and a four-wheeled tender instead of the customary eight wheels. These two railroads merged in 1914 to create the New York Central.

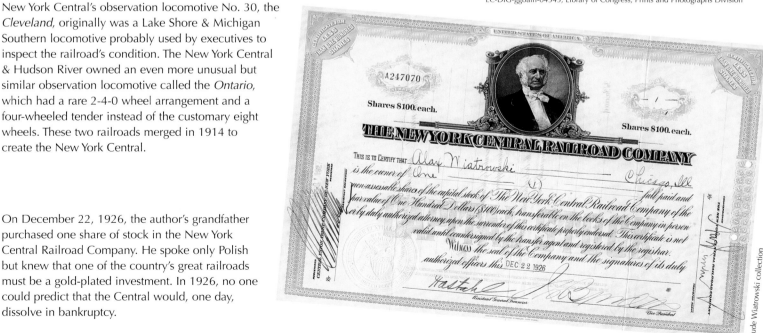

On December 22, 1926, the author's grandfather purchased one share of stock in the New York Central Railroad Company. He spoke only Polish but knew that one of the country's great railroads must be a gold-plated investment. In 1926, no one could predict that the Central would, one day, dissolve in bankruptcy.

THE RIGHT STUFF, AGAIN   221

Above: Smoke abatement laws were the impetus for converting to electric-powered locomotion in many large cities. Electric locomotives replaced steam locomotives before a train entered the city. Here is an example of that process, with a New York Central ES1 locomotive hauling a passenger train through The Bronx in July 1962.

A New York Central ad starring one of Henry Dreyfuss' iconic shrouded Hudsons pulling the *20th Century Limited* promises a sound night's sleep among its many other amenities.

The New York Central's signature locomotive was the Henry Dreyfuss–designed Hudson, with a 4-6-4 wheel arrangement. Streamlined locomotive No. 5450 celebrates Independence Day on July 4, 1941.

G. V. "Jerry" Carson photo

New York Central E7 locomotives leave St. Louis with a streamlined train (save the two older baggage cars directly behind the locomotive). Passing in the opposite direction is a steam-hauled Missouri Pacific passenger train.

ONE MAN'S LOCOMOTIVE

Built in 1875 by the Baldwin Locomotive Works, narrow gauge locomotive *Eureka* ended its career hauling lumber, a dull vestige of its former glory. Sent for scrapping in 1938, the locomotive was purchased in 1940 by Warner Bros. and appeared in numerous motion pictures and television series. It has the distinction of being used in John Wayne's final movie, *The Shootist*. Sold for display in Las Vegas, Nevada, it slowly deteriorated until it was damaged in a fire in 1985. Still buried in the ruins of the fire-ravaged building, *Eureka* was recognized by Dan Markoff for the rare find it was. It was moved to Dan's home where, in the course of six difficult years, it was restored to its original glory. The *Eureka* travels again. It was an invited guest of the California State Railroad Museum for their Railfair '91 and Railfair '99 celebrations.

Today, narrow gauge main lines are scarce in the United States. The two longest 3-foot-gauge passenger railways are in Colorado and New Mexico. Restored *Eureka* has run on both the Durango & Silverton Narrow Gauge Railroad and the Cumbres & Toltec Scenic Railroad.

Claude Wiatrowski photo

Claude Wiatrowski photo

Eureka inches across the High Line above the Animas River. The locomotive is trucked from its home in Las Vegas, Nevada, to run here on the Durango & Silverton Narrow Gauge Railroad.

Eureka was purchased from the Baldwin Locomotive Works in 1875 by the Eureka & Palisade Railroad. She would tramp between the silver and lead mines of Eureka in central Nevada and a connection with the Southern Pacific on the original transcontinental main line at Palisade, Nevada.

Dan Markoff (left) supervises work on *Eureka*, the locomotive he rescued and restored. *Eureka* is one of only three narrow gauge locomotives of the American-type 4-4-0 wheel arrangement left in the United States. The other two reside in the Smithsonian Institution and the California State Railroad Museum.

Eureka crosses the high bridge across the Animas River on the Durango & Silverton. During her restoration she was converted to once again burn wood. Train passengers are asked to help "wood up" the locomotive's tender, a labor-intensive activity.

THE RIGHT STUFF, AGAIN   225

PHOTOGRAPHERS

In the early days of railroading, glacially slow film speeds made photographing a moving train virtually impossible. In an era when chemicals had to be applied to huge glass plates and then developed immediately after exposure, railroad photographers were sometimes given special trains just to carry their laboratories! Sometimes, labs were packed to remote locations on animals and, if no train was visible just then, a facsimile would be drawn into the photo later.

Any list of great train photographers will offend by omission, but some of the most notable are Donald Duke, Richard Steinheimer, David Plowden, and Jim Shaughnessy. Surely, O. Winston Link can be counted as one of the most visionary and unusual railroad photographers. As the technology of steam locomotion waned in the late 1950s, Link made thousands of images of the Norfolk and Western, the last major U.S. railroad to use steam locomotives. Many of his photos were made at night using complex arrays of numerous flash bulbs arranged to illuminate a moving train and its surroundings. Link's works can be viewed at the *O. Winston Link Museum*, located in a restored N&W passenger station in Roanoke, Virginia.

STEVE CRISE

The interest, curiosity, and desire to record the railroad experience has always been inside Steve Crise. In 1968, while aboard the Santa Fe's *El Capitan*, he instinctively knew that it was important to record images of locomotives and stations as they flew past, and so he clicked away with his parents' Brownie. Crise studied photography in college but found that he learned more as an assistant in high-pressure celebrity shoots in Hollywood. Starting his own photography business in 1987, he targeted subjects he enjoyed: railroads and heavy industry. Though his photos are sold commercially through stock photo agencies, he donates his services to nonprofit organizations that preserve and promote railroad history and culture. Crise creates images that evoke the feeling or emotion of railroading, and encourage viewers to fill in the blanks with their own imaginations. He considers some of the best railroad images ever created to be those that have utilized the human element in their composition, an element he tries to include in his own work. You can view some of Crise's work at www.scrise.com.

Nick Russo photo, ninarusso.com

Steve Crise

GORDON OSMUNDSON

With a model railroad in the basement and access to his father's darkroom and cameras, it is no wonder Gordon Osmundson had a predisposition to railroads and photography. He began shooting color slides of trains and dabbling in black-and-white while in the ninth grade. In 1973, inspired by the books of Ansel Adams, he took up large-format photography, which soon developed into a lifelong avocation. Black-and-white landscapes were followed by monochrome close-ups of steam locomotives.

Osmundson's work shows an appreciation for the dynamic forms of, and light reflections from, steam equipment. The quality of his photos is also due to his knowledge of both the technical and subjective aspects of black-and-white photography, something about which he has written expert articles. Beside railroads, he has created photographic series of grain elevators, vintage automobiles, and other subjects. His work has been spotlighted in numerous exhibitions and is part of many permanent public collections. Osmundson passes on his knowledge through workshops, including one that utilizes the Nevada Northern Railway as an exceptional source of railroad images. Learn more about Osmundson's work at www.ihpworkshops.com.

Photographer Steve Crise explains: "Cold weather, damp air, and darkness make for great steam railroad pictures. All three were bestowed upon me on the morning of October 26, 2004. This was the day that the restored steam engine from the old Santa Fe Railway was to leave for a trip from Los Angeles to San Pedro, California, for a public display in that port city. The crew of the Santa Fe 3751 was 10 minutes into their 5 a.m. crew call at the Amtrak locomotive shops near downtown Los Angeles. It had been raining earlier that night and everything was quite wet. I made a few pictures of just the engine's drivers glistening in the darkness. Meanwhile, crewmember Aaron Swain made an early morning inspection of the engine. Unknowingly, Aaron found himself in front of my camera. His presence in the composition seemed to be the missing element that turned an ordinary image into a great one. I asked him to point his flashlight at the drivers and hold as still as he possibly could. I waited for a bit of steam exhaust to bellow from the stack and across the frame before I made the final exposure."

Steve Crise photo

Photographer Steve Crise: "Every now and then I come across a place that has so much character and style of old classic railroading still left in it that it's better to preserve that character by not including a contemporary train in the photo at all. I found Clayburn Junction in beautiful British Columbia to be one such place. I spent hours just wandering around the area documenting as many of the little details that Clayburn Junction interlocking crossing had to offer without caring if a train showed up or not. The lighting on the diamond was so perfectly shaded by the tall trees that surround the area that only the tops of the rails were illuminated by the blue sky above, which added drama to the sharply crossing rails that lead into the bright sunlit fields and mountains in the background. The shaded foreground also helped hide some of the coarse detail of the ballast and ties and made the rail stand out even more so. In addition, all the old locks, semaphores, the weather-beaten shed that housed the levers and phone, and the dwarf signals made for a wonderful afternoon at this magical location."

Photographer Steve Crise: "A great deal of my work depends on a combination of interesting locations and unusual lighting conditions. I found both of these requirements at this location in Riverside, California. The site is situated where the Union Pacific and Burlington Northern Santa Fe join and race past the old Santa Fe station there in town. I tried the same type of shot with a BNSF train, but the orange and green paint scheme didn't have the same impact as the bright-yellow Union Pacific engines. The yellow locomotive against the blue sky, along with the blurred red stripe on the locomotive, really made this image come alive. The palm trees really do lean that way, however an extreme wide-angle 17-mm lens helped distort the image even more, especially on the outer edges. I believe the distortion of the lens really made the shot.

Steve Crise photo

Steve Crise photo

Eccentric Crank, S.P. 4449. Sacramento, California, 1975.

Crosshead, U.P. 8444. Denver, Colorado, 1973.

Rear Driver, AT&SF 3751. Parker, Arizona, 2002.

Gordon Osmundson.

Oiled Rods, S.P. 2467. Golden Gate Railroad Museum, San Francisco, California, 1991.

SEABOARD COAST LINE

The Seaboard Air Line Railroad was formed in 1900 from a number of constituent railways, the oldest chartered in 1832. It connected the state capitals of Richmond, Virginia; Raleigh, North Carolina; Charleston, South Carolina; and Atlanta, Georgia, with Atlantic ports. The words "Air Line" in its corporate title implied that the railroad's route was an absolutely straight line. This approximation was close enough for the marketing department! Further expansion brought the Seaboard Air Line to Alabama's and Florida's capital cities, as well as points on the Atlantic Ocean and Gulf of Mexico. A Miami extension to profit from 1920s Florida land speculation was completed as the land market withered and the Great Depression began. By 1930, the Seaboard Air Line was in receivership and was reorganized in 1946.

The Atlantic Coast Line's history also begins in the 1830s, and the name Atlantic Coast Line Railroad also first appeared in 1900. It served many of the same cities in Virginia and the Carolinas as the Seaboard Air Line and, in some cases, with almost parallel routes. A 1902 purchase of The Plant System gave ACL destinations in Georgia, Alabama, and Florida. Also in 1902, ACL gained control of the Louisville & Nashville. The Atlantic Coast Line was financially sound and boasted of an excellent physical plant; it called itself the "Standard Railroad of the South," a clear comparison to the Pennsylvania Railroad.

Eliminating parallel routes and duplicate facilities, the Seaboard Air Line and Atlantic Coast Line merged in 1967 to form the Seaboard Coast Line Railroad. In 1982, the Seaboard Coast Line merged with the Louisville & Nashville, creating the Seaboard System Railroad. In 1980, the holding company of the Seaboard Coast Line merged with the Chessie System to form CSX Corporation.

The Orange Blossom Special Going Through Orange Groves in Florida

This postcard was mailed in 1953, the last year of operation for the *Orange Blossom Special*. This winter-only train rushed impatient sun-seekers from New York to Florida starting in 1925. A popular country song of the same name was written about this speedster in 1938. Service was suspended during the war years. Resurrected as a diesel-powered streamliner in 1952, the train lasted only until 1953.

WRITING A NEW CHAPTER IN TRANSPORTATION

An EMD ad bragging about the Seaboard's success with its diesel locomotives includes a smaller image of an earlier train with an Adams Express car. Express companies offered fast package delivery, with parcels placed in passenger and not freight trains.

A new era of bygone days was represented by the "American Express Train" of 1855, here pictured by the famous lithographer, Nathaniel Currier. In 1869, that era culminated in the completion of the first transcontinental railroad.

They're **All** Singing the Praises of **SEABOARD'S FLORIDA PACKAGE VACATIONS!**

USING REDUCED ROUND-TRIP COACH FARES, MAY 1 - NOVEMBER 15

FOR AS LITTLE AS **$89⁸¹ FROM NEW YORK**

Plus tax; price based on two persons to hotel room. Slightly higher in July-August.

YOU ENJOY THIS PACKAGE OF FUN...
★ Modern streamliner travel both ways;
★ Your reclining coach seat is reserved for you;
★ 7 wonderful days, 6 glorious nights at your OCEAN-FRONT HOTEL IN FABULOUS MIAMI BEACH;
★ All guest privileges—pool, beach, PLUS hotel entertainment features;
★ Even transfers between station and hotel!

Similarly fine bargain vacations are available at many resorts on both coasts of Florida. Also Circle Tours of ALL Florida!

Pullman Packages, too If you prefer private-room sleeping car accommodations for your Florida vacation trip, you may have them on payment of additional rail fare, and Pullman charge. The hotel rates included in these "packages" are the same regardless of how you travel!

FOR FLORIDA PACKAGE VACATION LITERATURE, SEE YOUR TRAVEL AGENT OR WRITE:
J. R. GETTY
General Passenger Traffic Manager
SEABOARD RAILROAD
Dept. TT
Norfolk 10, Va.
See inside back cover for Package Vacations in the NORTH

SEABOARD RAILROAD

THE ROUTE OF COURTEOUS SERVICE

Above: The Seaboard's 1958 timetable still listed seven named trains and four minor passenger services. Also listed were connecting air services to Havana, Nassau, and Mexico City. Not missing a transportation mode, ship schedules were included to Havana and Nassau. In 1958, you could enjoy a train trip from New York to Miami and six nights in an ocean-front hotel for $89.81, including lodging and train fare.

EMD also ran an advertisement bragging about the Atlantic Coast Line's use of its diesel locomotives. The image of the older train represents the railroad's first deluxe-vestibule Pullman train from New York City to Jacksonville, Florida.

THE RIGHT STUFF, AGAIN   231

SNOW

Canals may freeze in the winter, but railroad tracks are buried under feet of snow. When the rails reached the western mountains, avalanches deposited tons of snow, rocks, and trees on the rails—and sometimes on an unlucky train. The first plows merely pushed aside the snow with the brute force of multiple locomotives galloping along at full speed. Derailments and deaths resulted.

Because such plows were virtually useless in very deep snow, rotary snowplows, much like modern snowblowers, cut through the snow and catapulted the white powder 100 feet to the side of the track. The rocks and trees in avalanches damaged rotaries, so snowsheds—timber structures covering the tracks—protected the rails in areas prone to these cascades of snow and debris.

Claude Wiatrowski collection

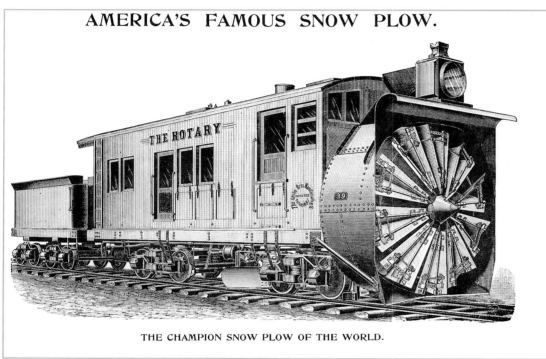

AMERICA'S FAMOUS SNOW PLOW.

THE ROTARY

THE CHAMPION SNOW PLOW OF THE WORLD.

As the nineteenth century drew to a close, several inventors vied to develop an efficient railroad snowplow. The first Leslie Rotary Snow Plow, pictured here, was constructed in March 1885. In January 1890, two of the three leading contenders, the Leslie Rotary and the Jull Excavator, were tested together on the Union Pacific's narrow gauge Alpine Tunnel line. Jull lost the contest. In other tests at about the same time, the final contender, the Cyclone, proved too heavy for the track and the Leslie Rotary Snow Plow became the standard. Several are still in operation, although most are diesel and not steam-powered. Between 1885 and 1950, 139 Leslie Rotary Snow Plows were built. Jull built 11, and only 1 Cyclone was ever built.

Claude Wiatrowski collection

The Cumbres & Toltec Scenic Railroad has run special snowplow trips for photographers. One special plow run was made for a Miller's beer commercial! The author rode the first and second special plow trips. The first featured the railroad's oldest rotary plow; the second, shown here, starred the newest plow. Both narrow gauge plows are steam-operated and pushed by steam locomotives.

There is only one railroad in North America—Colorado's Manitou & Pikes Peak Railway—where you can see a cog rotary snowplow. Here, the old rotary chops through the snow at about 13,000 feet above sea level, pushed by a first-generation General Electric locomotive. This plow has since been replaced by a larger and more powerful self-propelled machine.

This narrow gauge flanger is one of several preserved on the Cumbres & Toltec. A flanger has small blades that are lowered to clear snow and ice from the areas just inside of both rails where the flanges of the train's wheels run.

A Southern Pacific wedge snowplow sits at Dalhart, Texas, awaiting a fierce prairie blizzard. Pushed by a locomotive, it simply drives its wedge-shaped bow through the drifts. Before rotary snowplows, multiple locomotives might have to drive a plow like this into the snow at full speed to make headway. The process was called "bucking snow." If anything derailed, the plow and locomotives became a tangled mess with injuries and death an all too frequent consequence.

THE RIGHT STUFF, AGAIN   233

SOO LINE

The Minneapolis, St. Paul & Sault Ste. Marie Railway was consolidated from older railways in 1888. These railways were constructed to transport flour through a connection with Canadian Pacific at Sault Ste. Marie, Michigan, avoiding exorbitant freight rates to Chicago. The Canadian Pacific soon acquired control of the Minneapolis, St. Paul & Sault Ste. Marie to prevent competitor Grand Trunk Railway from acquiring it as a stepping stone to western Canada. The Minneapolis, St. Paul & Sault Ste. Marie connected with the Canadian Pacific again in both Minnesota and North Dakota. Acquisitions provided new traffic sources in Wisconsin, Michigan's Upper Peninsula, and Chicago.

In 1961, the Minneapolis, St. Paul & Sault Ste. Marie merged with other railroads, creating the Soo Line, a name long used by the railroad. (The French word *Sault* is pronounced *Soo* in English.)

Acquisitions continued. The moribund Milwaukee Road was merged in 1986. Soo trains now ran southeast to Louisville and southwest to Kansas City, but by 1987 they no longer called on Sault Ste. Marie. The Soo vanished in 1992 when Canadian Pacific bought all it did not already own. Contraction continued under Canadian Pacific ownership.

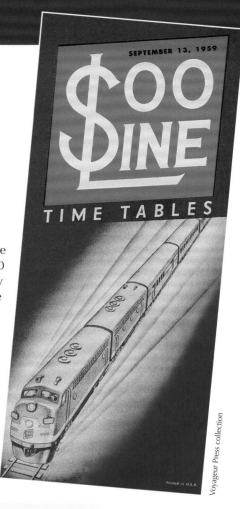

This 1959 Soo Line timetable still lists 20 passenger trains, only two of which are important enough to be named. The *Winnipeger* transports passengers between Winnipeg, Manitoba, and Minneapolis–St. Paul. The *Laker* runs between Chicago and Duluth, Minnesota.

POWER

. . . A Key To Soo Line Progress

From wood burning locomotive to the latest Diesel-electric locomotive, *power and more power* has always been of prime importance on the Soo Line. This policy has helped give the Soo Line its reputation as a top freight carrier to and through the seven state area of the Upper Midwest.

POWER IN 1886 was developed by this typical wood burner. Colorful as they were, these early locomotives had to give way to the Soo Line's insistent quest for more power. A quest that saw in use on the Soo Line the first Mikado type locomotive in the United States . . . and one of the first of the Pacific type locomotives.

POWER IN 1950 on the Soo Line is represented by a fleet of giant Diesel-electric locomotives. Developing 4,500 horse-power per triple engine unit, they are the modern answer to the Soo Line's desire for power. Power to send Soo Line fast freights speeding over 4,200 miles of track.

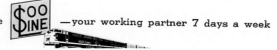

Power that makes the **$OO $INE** —your working partner **7** days a week

SPECIAL PRESERVED RAILWAYS

Of the hundreds of preserved railways in North America, a few stand out because they maintain their original historical character and environment. They remain as if everyone left for lunch in 1925 and never returned. Some preserved railways work diligently to restore this ambiance to their railroads. Others prefer modern amusements added to the experience. A few lucky ones simply inherit an intact historic railroad with all its original equipment.

If you are interested in experiencing railroad history as it once was, there are three railroads you should visit. Prepare yourself for remote and rustic adventures—historical experience does not survive in proximity to golf courses, condos, or fast-food restaurants. The remoteness of these three lines saved them but also makes it difficult for them to attract visitors. All are constantly engaged in funding strategies to restore their rolling stock and infrastructure and to ensure their operation into perpetuity. All three of these railroads use volunteers to restore historic artifacts ranging from buildings to railcars. On some, volunteers help run the trains. On others, they ride along to explain the railroad's history to visitors. You might even decide to join these volunteers from all over the world.

NEVADA NORTHERN
The Nevada Northern Railway was completed in 1906 to serve copper mines. Its 140-mile main line brought supplies to Ely, Nevada, from a connection with the Southern Pacific. Because the Liberty Pit mine was railroad-worked, numerous small steam locomotives spiraled out of the fissure with ore destined for the concentrator at McGill. Trains also carried "blister copper" from the concentrator to be sent east for refining. After mining ended, Kennecott Copper Corporation donated 32 miles of track connecting the mining district at Ruth with the concentrator site at McGill, as well as the

railroad's yards and shops at East Ely, three steam locomotives, a stable of antique diesels, a steam crane, five wooden passenger cars, all the railroad's paper records and buildings, and more to the Nevada Northern Railroad Museum. Today, you can ride a diesel train from East Ely to McGill and a steam train from East Ely to Ruth. Don't miss the interesting tour of the historic shop facilities. Also, visitors are allowed to walk around the substantial railroad yards. The preserved railway purchased its original 140-mile main line in 2006.

CUMBRES & TOLTEC SCENIC RAILROAD
Denver & Rio Grande narrow gauge trains arrived in Chama, New Mexico, on New Year's Eve 1880 as tracks were being built westward to the booming mining district

Nevada is a land of contrasts, proved by snowcapped mountains above the desert valley in which nestles the town of Ely and its historic Nevada Northern Railway, which uses volunteers not only to restore its facilities but also to help run its trains.

Claude Wiatrowski photo

of Silverton, Colorado. Eastbound trains carrying gold and silver would have to cross the steep track up 10,015-foot Cumbres Pass. Substantial railroad facilities were built at Chama to add helper locomotives to those trains. The railroad's 64-mile main line is a charm bracelet from which historic artifacts dangle: water tanks, stations, section houses, telephone booths, telegraph poles, and railyards stretch from one terminus to the other. Standing in the Chama yard, out of sight of the street, it is difficult to tell if it is 1900, 1920, or 1940! The Rio Grande's last major improvements to its narrow gauge system were made in the 1920s. Since it was clear that narrow gauge trains were a dead-end technology, old equipment was made to serve until the railroad closed in 1968. The states of Colorado and New Mexico purchased the 64 miles of track over Cumbres Pass, along with freight cars, snowplows, steam locomotives, and all the historic railroad facilities at Chama and along the line to be preserved as a living history museum. The first tourist trips were made between Antonito, Colorado, and Chama, New Mexico, in 1971.

EAST BROAD TOP RAILROAD

The East Broad Top was completed in 1874 to carry coal from remote mines of south-central Pennsylvania to a connection with the Pennsylvania Railroad at Mt. Union. Its narrow gauge locomotives lugged hopper cars of coal to market until 1956. Its 33 miles of track, 7 steam locomotives, and 200 narrow gauge cars were sold to Kovalchick Salvage but not immediately dismantled. In 1960, Nick Kovalchick began operating passenger trains over 5 miles of track. Since the East Broad Top was the last common-carrier narrow gauge railroad in the East, it maintained its own substantial shop complex at Rockhill Furnace near Orbisonia. It's all still there! Besides rides on the train and tours of the shop complex, there are other reminders of history all along the line, including a museum at the unused southern end of the railroad in the Robertsdale Depot. As a bonus to your visit, the Rockhill Trolley Museum is adjacent to the East Broad Top. Of these three railroads, the East Broad Top is the only one to have a turntable upon which steam locomotives are turned end for end.

Claude Wiatrowski photo

Nevada Northern locomotive No. 93 runs around the caboose of the train to which it will soon couple. The coal tipples and water tank are seen in the distance. The track into downtown Ely is also still in place, terminating in Ely's museum. The railroad sometimes runs shuttles from its yards in East Ely to the museum, in addition to its mine and mill passenger runs.

Sublette, New Mexico, is a beautifully preserved section town on the Cumbres & Toltec Scenic Railroad. Volunteers organized by the Friends of the Cumbres & Toltec Scenic Railroad have donated thousands of hours restoring Sublette and other locations all along the 64-mile railroad. The result is a 64-mile museum representing narrow gauge railroading in its prime.

A Cumbres & Toltec excursion train has just left Chama, New Mexico, to begin its arduous journey over the mountains to Antonito, Colorado.

The East Broad Top ran this coal train in 1993, simulating an image from years past when it was primarily a coal hauler. Photographers still charter such trains.

Philip R. Raynes

Chama stabled helper locomotives for the steep climb eastward over Cumbres Pass. For that reason, all the facilities for servicing steam locomotives were built here. From left to right are a water tank, a coal tipple, and a sand house. At one time, there was so much activity here that the water tank was built with two spouts so a pair of locomotives could take water simultaneously.

Claude Wiatrowski photo

East Broad Top locomotive No. 12 takes a spin on the turntable. The railroad was the last narrow gauge common carrier in the eastern United States and chose to build extensive shop facilities, giving it the capability to build and repair anything it needed. The Friends of the East Broad Top help restore facilities that would otherwise not be needed for current operations.

In late summer 1990, locomotive No. 12 slakes her thirst at Orbisonia on the East Broad Top. The engineer oils around his charge while the fireman keeps on eye on the water in the tender's tank.

THE RIGHT STUFF, AGAIN

WESTERN PACIFIC

The Union Pacific's 1900 purchase of the Southern Pacific siphoned all traffic from the Salt Lake City end of the Jay Gould–owned Denver & Rio Grande. Construction of the Western Pacific—roughly parallel to the Southern Pacific between Salt Lake City and Oakland—began in 1903. The Western Pacific's route through California's spectacular Feather River Canyon was much easier to operate than the Southern Pacific's snow-encrusted route over Donner Pass. Completed in 1909, the Western Pacific was the last link in a chain of Gould family railroads stretching from ocean to ocean. Not particularly successful, the Western Pacific's 1915 bankruptcy funneled the Denver & Rio Grande, which had guaranteed Western Pacific's bonds, into the same hole.

In 1931, the Western Pacific completed a second fork of its California main line north from Keddie to a connection with the Great Northern at Bieber. Together with the Santa's Fe's tracks in Southern California, this formed a route for north-south traffic through the Pacific Coast states. In 1982, the Western Pacific was merged into the Union Pacific.

California Zephyr passengers are treated to a daylight crossing of the Sierra Nevada Mountains from five dome cars.

Western Pacific

5579. Western Pacific Crossing Southern End of the Great Salt Lake. Black Rock at Right, Stansberry Mountains in the Distance.

Voyageur Press collection

Voyageur Press collection

Above: Not only were *California Zephyr* passengers treated to a crossing of the Sierra Mountains, they were also plunged into the depths of California's Feather River Canyon.

Below: The Western Pacific was one of the first major railroads to dieselize. Four 2-8-8-2 articulated locomotives, one shown here, and eight 4-6-6-4 articulateds were delivered in 1938, and the first diesel arrived in 1939. Only six more steam locomotives were purchased amid the war-year desperation of 1943.

Above: The Western Pacific's main line crossed the Great Salt Lake along its southern shore. This postcard states that 30 miles of track is laid on "white, solid salt."

www.cabincreekcds.com

WORKING ON THE RAILROAD

DAWN PATROL

A section gang . . .
None of its members pilots a plane through the early morning sky. Their job is less romantic, less adventurous—even less hazardous. But no less essential.

For they're fighters on the transportation front. They're keeping in top-notch condition New York Central's 24,000 miles of track . . . the famous Water Level Route, now one of America's busiest military supply lines, carrying troops and war materials between the Mississippi and the Atlantic Ocean.

And New York Central passengers and shippers are helping in this vital "war of movement"—as are countless thousands of railroad users throughout the country.

As passengers, they are planning their trips for mid-week. They are travelling light. They are making their reservations and buying their tickets well in advance.

As shippers, they are seeing that freight cars are loaded to capacity, and loaded fast, and unloaded promptly. For every 1% increase in freight car utilization adds 20,000 cars to America's "war of movement."

For the part these people have played already—for their "thumbs up" attitude towards occasional inconveniences—all the employees of New York Central are extremely grateful.

For today the employees of the New York Central, together with the employees of all American railroads, have just one object in view—the complete and crushing defeat of the Axis powers. That is the job to which they have dedicated themselves. And with your help, they'll see it through!

BUY UNITED STATES WAR SAVINGS BONDS AND STAMPS

NEW YORK CENTRAL
THE WATER LEVEL ROUTE

NEW YORK CENTRAL SYSTEM

A Yakutat & Southern track crew poses on a handcar. Alaska had a tradition of Native American women repairing railroad track.

A World War II–era ad compares a New York Central section gang with the "dawn patrol" of fighter planes above them. The New York Central maintained 24,000 miles of track during the war.

This Union Pacific construction train has paused for a portrait near Green River, Wyoming, in 1870. Other than the train itself, mechanization was limited to men, animals, and hand tools.

782. I Helped Build Pike's Peak R. R., Colorado.

Left: When the Manitou & Pikes Peak Railway was constructed to the summit of Pikes Peak, men and mules did most of the work—the steep 25 percent grades of a cog railroad made it impossible to use much machinery.

Below: Workmen finish a cylinder-casting for a small steam locomotive in 1904.

Bottom: Two trains appear to have crashed into each other in what railroaders darkly nicknamed a "cornfield meet." The nickname seems especially appropriate for this Illinois Central wreck at Farmer City, Illinois, in 1909.

THE RIGHT STUFF, AGAIN   243

A rail-mounted crane clears a small mishap on the Southern Pacific in 1962.

G. V. "Jerry" Carson photo

Above: Dynamometer cars were coupled between locomotives and cars to measure performance in actual service.

Right: Moving dirt was and is a common task for railroads. Here, a crawler-equipped shovel, built by the Lima Locomotive Works Shovel & Crane Division, sits on a flatcar while loading dirt into a gondola car.

Voyageur Press collection

A spreader has hydraulically operated "wings" that can extend a considerable distance on either side to clear and contour dirt on the side of railroad tracks. Spreaders are also useful for widening the snow-free area after the rails are plowed.

A tank of water, a diesel pump, and hoses protected not only Southern Pacific snowsheds, but other structures and the forest itself. Fire danger was lessened in the transitions from wood to coal to oil fuel for steam locomotives. Today, older diesel locomotives, overheated wheel bearings—called "hot boxes"—and dragging equipment can all start fires, so fire protection is still an issue with modern railroads, which install automated hot box and dragging equipment detectors to signal problems as trains run past.

RAIL LINES AND TRADE ASSOCIATIONS

American Short Line and Regional Railroad Association	aslrra.org
Association of American Railroads	aar.org
Amtrak	amtrak.com
BNSF Railway	bnsf.com
CN	cn.ca
Canadian Pacific	cpr.ca
CSX	csx.com
Kansas City Southern	kcsouthern.com
Norfolk Southern	www.nscorp.com
Union Pacific	up.com

RAILROADING HISTORICAL SOCIETIES AND RELATED ORGANIZATIONS

Amtrak Historical Society	amtrakhistoricalsociety.com
Anthracite Railroads Historical Society	arhs.railfan.net
Atlantic Coast Line & Seaboard Air Line	aclsal.org
Baltimore & Ohio Railroad Historical Society	borhs.org
Boston & Maine Railroad Historical Society	trainweb.org/bmrrhs
Bridge Line Historical Society (Delaware & Hudson)	bridge-line.org
Burlington Route Historical Society	www.burlingtonroute.com
Chesapeake & Ohio Historical Society	cohs.org
Chessie System Historical Society	chessiesystem.org
Chicago & North Western Historical Society	cnwhs.org
Chicago North Shore and Milwaukee Railroad	northshoreline.com
CN Lines Special Interest Group	cnlines.ca
Electric Railway Historical Association of Southern California	erha.org
Erie Lackawanna Historical Society	erielackhs.org
Friends of the Burlington Northern Railroad	fobnr.org
GM&O Historical Society	gmohs.org
Great Northern Railway Historical Society	gnrhs.org
Illinois Central Historical Society	icrrhistorical.org
Int'l. Society for the Preservation of Women in Railroading	womeninrailroading.com
Kansas City Southern Historical Society	kcshs.org
Katy Railroad Historical Society	katyrailroad.org
Lehigh Valley Railroad Historical Society	lvrrhs.org
Louisville & Nashville Railroad Historical Society	rrhistorical-2.com/lnhs
Milwaukee Road Historical Society	mrha.com
Missouri Pacific Historical Society	mopac.org
National Railway Historical Society	nrhs.com
New Haven Railroad Historical & Technical Association	nhrhta.org
New York Central System Historical Society	nycshs.org
Nickel Plate Road Historical & Technical Society	nkphts.org
Norfolk & Southern Railway Company Historical Society	norfolksouthernhs.org
Norfolk & Western Historical Society	nwhs.org
Northern Pacific Railway Historical Association	nprha.org
Penn Central Railroad Online	pc.smellycat.com
Pennsylvania Railroad Technical & Historical Society	prrths.com
Railroad Station Historical Society	rrshs.org
Railway & Locomotive Historical Society	rlhs.org
Reading Company Technical & Historical Society	readingrailroad.org
Rio Grande Modeling & Historical Society	drgw.org
Rock Island Technical Society	faculty.simpson.edu/RITS/www/
Santa Fe Railway Historical and Modeling Society	atsfrr.com
Shortlines of Chicago Historical Society	dhke.com/schs
Soo Line Historical & Technical Society	sooline.org
South Shore Interurban Historical Society	shore-line.org/
Southern Pacific Historical & Technical Society	sphts.org
Southern Railway Historical Association	srha.net
St. Louis & San Francisco Railroad Company	frisco.org
St. Louis Southwestern Railway	geocities.com/TheTropics/8199
Union Pacific Historical Society	uphs.org

Water Valley Casey Jones Railroad Museum	watervalley.net/users/caseyjones/home.htm
Western Maryland Historical Society	moosevalley.org/wmrhs
Western Mining & Railroad Museum	wmrrm.org
Western Pacific Railroad Historical Society	wprrhs.org

RAILROAD CLUBS, PRESERVATION, AND DATABASES

"470" Railroad Club	470rrclub.org
American Association of Private Railroad Car Owners	aaprco.com
American Railway Caboose Historical Educational Society	arches.org
Association of Railway Museums	railwaymuseums.org
Canadian Pacific Railway Archives	cprheritage.com
Harvey Houses	harveyhouses.net
National Association of Railroad Passengers	narprail.org
RailFanClub	www.railfanclub.org
Railroad Club of Chicago	railcc.org
Railway Preservation News	rypn.org
Rocky Mountain Railroad Club	rockymtnrrclub.org
SteamLocomotive.info	steamlocomotive.info
Surviving Steam Locomotives Database	steamlocomotive.com
Tourist Railway Association	traininc.org
West Side Railway Narrow Gauge Preservation	wsrestoration.com

MODELING AND COLLECTING

The Great Train Expo	gte.ciadvt.com
Key, Lock & Lantern	klnl.org
Lionel Collectors Club of America	lionelcollectors.org
National Model Railroad Association	www.nmra.org
Train Collectors Association	traincollectors.org
Toy Train Operating Society	ttos.org
World's Greatest Hobby on Tour	wghshow.com

NARROW-GAUGE DEADWOOD CENTRAL TRAIN AT CHICAGO RAILROAD FAIR

THE NEW STREAMLINER "400" — CHICAGO AND NORTH WESTERN LINE

15 - "CITY OF SAN FRANCISCO" CROSSING GREAT SALT LAKE ON S. P. LINES IN UTAH

MONTREAL RIVER FALLS, ALGOMA CENTRAL RAILWAY.

APPENDIX B
PRESERVED RAILWAYS, MUSEUMS, AND HISTORIC SITES

This is just a sampling of hundreds of historic railroads and museums in North America. For more detailed information and changes to these listings, see the Web sites listed or telephone.

ALABAMA
Heart of Dixie Railroad Museum
Museum; train ride.
Calera, AL
www.hodrrm.org
(205) 668-3435
(800) 943-4490

ALASKA
White Pass & Yukon Route
Narrow gauge train trip on
    Klondike route to Canada.
Skagway, AK
www.whitepassrailroad.com
(800) 343-7373

Yakutat & Southern Railroad
Exhibits in very remote location.
Yakutat, AK
www.yakutat-southern.org
(907) 784-3482

ARIZONA
Grand Canyon Railway
Railroad trip to Grand Canyon
    National Park; museum.
Williams, AZ
www.thetrain.com
(800) 843-8724

McCormick-Stillman Railroad Park
Miniature, almost half-size, steam
    train trip; museum; model
    railroad.
Scottsdale, AZ
www.therailroadpark.com
(480) 312-2312

Verde Canyon Railroad
Railroad trip through the
    spectacular Verde Canyon.
Clarkdale, AZ
www.verdecanyonrr.com
(800) 320-0718

ARKANSAS
**Eureka Springs & North Arkansas
Railway**
Train ride; exhibits; dinner train.
Eureka Springs, AR
www.esnarailway.com
(479) 253-9623

CALIFORNIA
California State Railroad Museum
Spectacular museum; train ride.
Sacramento, CA

www.csrmf.org
(916) 445-6645 24-hour information
(916) 445-7387 business office
(916) 323-9280 museum front desk

Niles Canyon Railway
Large museum; train ride.
Sunol, CA
www.ncry.org
(925) 862-9063

Pacific Southwest Railway Museum
Large museum; train ride.
Campo, CA
www.psrm.org
(619) 478-9937 Campo Depot
(weekends)
(619) 465-7776 business office
(weekdays)

Railtown
1897 State Historic Park; historic
    roundhouse museum; train ride.
Jamestown, CA
www.csrmf.org/railtown/
(209) 984-3953 business office

Redwood Valley Railway
Miniature, almost half-size, steam
    train trip.
Berkeley, CA
www.redwoodvalleyrailway.com
(510) 548-6100

Roaring Camp Railroads
Narrow and standard gauge train
    rides.
Felton, CA
www.roaringcamp.com
(831) 335-4484

Travel Town Transportation Museum
Large museum.
Los Angeles, CA
www.cityofla.org/rap/grifmet/tt/
(323) 662-5874

COLORADO
Colorado Railroad Museum
Great railway museum; train rides;
    roundhouse.
Golden, CO
www.crrm.org
(303) 279-4591
(800) 365-6263

Cumbres & Toltec Scenic Railroad
Several narrow gauge train rides,

64 miles over mountain pass;
    exhibits.
Antonito, CO and Chama, NM
www.cumbresandtoltec.com
(888) 286-2737

**Durango & Silverton Narrow Gauge
Railroad**
Narrow gauge train ride, 45 miles
    to Silverton mining town;
    roundhouse; depot museums.
Durango, CO
www.durangotrain.com
(877) 872-4607

Georgetown Loop Railroad
Narrow gauge train ride; mine tour.
Georgetown and Silver Plume, CO
www.georgetownlooprr.com
(888) 456-6777

**Leanin' Tree Museum and Sculpture
Garden of Western Art**
Collection of Howard Fogg railroad
    paintings.
Boulder, CO
www.leanintreemuseum.com
(800) 777-8716

Manitou & Pikes Peak Railway
Cog train ride to the summit of
    Pikes Peak, highest railroad in U. S.
Manitou Springs, CO
www.cograilway.com
(719) 685-5401

Rio Grande Scenic Railroad
Train rides over Veta Pass to the
    town of La Veta and rides to
    Antonito, Colorado.
Alamosa, CO
www.alamosatrain.com
(877) 726-7245

Royal Gorge Route Railroad
Streamlined train ride through
    1,000-foot-deep Royal Gorge;
    dinner train.
Canon City, CO
www.royalgorgeroute.com
(888) 724-5748

CONNECTICUT
Essex Steam Train & Riverboat
Combined train and boat ride;
    dinner train.
Essex, CT
www.essexsteamtrain.com
(800) 377-3987

DELAWARE

Wilmington & Western Railroad
  Train rides; exhibits; dinner train.
  Wilmington, DE
  www.wwrr.com
  (302) 998-1930

FLORIDA

Gold Coast Railroad Museum
  Large museum; train ride.
  Miami, FL
  www.goldcoast-railroad.org
  (305) 253-0063

GEORGIA

Roundhouse Railroad Museum
  Museum in historic railroad shops
  and roundhouse.
  Savannah, GA
  www.chsgeorgia.org/roundhouse/
  (912) 651-6823

Southeastern Railway Museum
  Large museum; train ride.
  Duluth, GA
  srmduluth.org
  (770) 476-2013

HAWAII

**Lahaina-Kaanapali and Pacific
Railroad**
  Narrow gauge train ride.
  Lahaina, Maui, HI
  www.sugarcanetrain.com
  (800) 499-2307

ILLINOIS

Illinois Railway Museum
  Large railroad museum; train and
  trolley rides.
  Union, IL
  www.irm.org
  (800) 244-7245

INDIANA

Indiana Transportation Museum
  Several train rides; museum.
  Noblesville, IN
  www.itm.org
  (317) 773-6000

Whitewater Valley Railroad
  Train Ride; museum.
  Connersville, IN
  www.whitewatervalleyrr.org
  (765) 825-2054

IOWA

Boone & Scenic Valley Railroad
  Train ride over high bridge; trolley
  ride; dinner train; museum.
  Boone, IA
  www.scenic-valleyrr.com
  (800) 626-0319

KENTUCKY

Big South Fork Scenic Railway
  Train ride to Blue Heron Mine in
  the Big South Fork National
  River & Recreation Area.
  Stearns, KY
  www.bsfsry.com
  (800) 462-5664

MAINE

**Maine Narrow Gauge Railroad Co. &
Museum**
  Two-foot-gauge train ride; large
  museum.
  Portland, ME
  www.mngrr.org
  (207) 828-0814

Seashore Trolley Museum
  Large museum; trolley rides.
  Kennebunkport, ME
  www.trolleymuseum.org
  (207) 967-2712

**Wiscasset, Waterville & Farmington
Railway Museum**
  Two-foot-gauge train ride;
  museum.
  Alna, ME
  www.wwfry.org
  (207) 882-4193

MARYLAND

Baltimore & Ohio Railroad Museum
  Spectacular museum.
  Baltimore, MD
  www.borail.org
  (410) 752-2490

Western Maryland Scenic Railroad
  Train trip; turntable at Frostburg.
  Cumberland, MD
  www.wmsr.com
  (800) 872-4650

MICHIGAN

**Henry Ford Museum & Greenfield
Village**
  Large museum; train ride.
  Dearborn, MI
  www.hfmgv.org
  (313) 271-1620 24-hour information
  (800) 835-5237

Huckleberry Railroad
  Historic village with narrow gauge
  train ride.
  Flint, MI
  www.geneseecountyparks.org/
  huckleberry_railroad.htm
  (800) 648-7275

MINNESOTA

Lake Superior Railroad Museum
  Large museum; train ride.

Duluth, MN
  www.lsrm.org
  (218) 722-1273
  (800) 423-1273

**Minnesota Transportation Museum
(Jackson Street Roundhouse)**
  Roundhouse museum; trolley rides
  at other sites in area; train ride
  in Wisconsin.
  St. Paul, MN
  www.mtmuseum.org
  (651) 228-0263

North Shore Scenic Railroad
  Train ride; museum adjacent.
  Duluth, MN
  www.northshorescenicrailroad.org
  (800) 423-1273

MISSISSIPPI

Water Valley Railroad Museum
  Museum.
  Water Valley, MS
  www.watervalley.net/users/caseyjones/
  home.htm
  (662) 473-1154

MISSOURI

**Belton, Grandview and Kansas City
Railroad**
  Train ride; museum.
  Belton, MO
  www.beltonrailroad.org
  (816) 331-0630

Museum of Transportation
  Large museum; miniature train ride.
  St. Louis, MO
  www.museumoftransport.org
  (314) 965-7998

MONTANA

Izaak Walton Inn
  Historic Great Northern Railroad
  Hotel.
  Essex, MT
  www.izaakwaltoninn.com
  (406) 888-5700

NEVADA

Nevada Northern Railway Museum
  Large historic railroad yard; two
  train rides.
  Ely, NV
  www.nevadanorthernrailway.net
  (866) 407-8326

Nevada State Railroad Museum
  Museum; train ride; another
  location at Boulder City with
  train ride.
  Carson City, NV
  www.nevadaculture.org
  (775) 687-6953

Virginia & Truckee Railroad

Train ride; major extension in progress.
Virginia City, NV
www.steamtrain.org
(775) 847-0380

NEW HAMPSHIRE
Conway Scenic Railroad

Two train rides; dining car; roundhouse, turntable, and spectacular depot.
North Conway, NH
www.conwayscenic.com
(800) 232-5251

Mount Washington Cog Railway

Cog train trip to summit of Mount Washington; world's first cog railroad.
Bretton Woods, NH
www.thecog.com
(800) 922-8825

NEW MEXICO
Cumbres & Toltec Scenic Railroad

Several narrow gauge train rides, 64 miles over mountain pass; large historic railyard.
Chama, NM and Antonito, CO
www.cumbresandtoltec.com
(888) 286-2737

Santa Fe Southern Railway

Train ride on mixed (freight and passenger) train.
Santa Fe, NM
www.santafesouthernrailway.com
(888) 989-8600

NEW JERSEY
Northlandz

Large model railroad.
Flemington, NJ
www.northlandz.com
(908) 782-4022

NEW YORK
Adirondack Scenic Railroad

Multiple train rides.
Utica, Thendara, and Lake Placid, NY
www.adirondackrr.com
(877) 508-6728

New York Transit Museum

Urban transport museum in historic subway station.
Brooklyn Heights, NY
www.mta.info/mta/museum
(718) 694-1600

NORTH CAROLINA
Great Smoky Mountain Railway

Several train trips; dinner train.

Train orders depended on the correct time, and the regularly checked accuracy of railroad watches was critical. Not surprisingly watchmakers, in this case E. Howard Watch Company, targeted railroaders. This art appeared in an ad in *Harper's Magazine*.

Voyageur Press collection

Bryson City and Dillsboro, NC
www.gsmr.com
(800) 872-4681

North Carolina Transportation Museum (Historic Spencer Shops)

Roundhouse museum; train and turntable rides; shop buildings.
Spencer, NC
www.nctrans.org
(877) 628-6386

OHIO
Cuyahoga Valley Scenic Railroad

Multiple train rides.
Akron, Canton, Independence, and Peninsula, OH
www.cvsr.com
(800) 468-4070

OREGON
Mount Hood Railroad and Dinner Train

Train ride; dinner train.
Hood River, OR
www.mthoodrr.com
(800) 872-4661

Oregon Coast Scenic Railroad

Train ride.
Garibaldi, OR
www.ocsr.net
(503) 842-7972

Sumpter Valley Railway

Narrow gauge train ride.
Sumpter and McEwen, OR
www.svry.com
(866) 894-2268

Willamette Shore Trolley

Trolley ride; museum at Brooks, OR.
Lake Oswego and Portland, OR
www.trainweb.org/oerhs/
(503) 697-7436

PENNSYLVANIA
East Broad Top Railroad

Narrow gauge train ride; large historic railyard and shops; museum at Robertsdale.
Rockhill Furnace, PA
www.ebtrr.com
(814) 447-3011

National Toy Train Museum

Toy train museum; five large train layouts.
Strasburg, PA
www.nttmuseum.org
(717) 687-8976

Middletown & Hummelstown Railroad

Train ride.
Middletown, PA
www.mhrailroad.com
(717) 944-4435

New Hope & Ivyland Railroad
  Train ride.
  New Hope, PA
  www.newhoperailroad.com
  (215) 862-2332

Railroad Museum of Pennsylvania
  Spectacular museum.
  Strasburg, PA
  www.rrmuseumpa.org
  717-687-8628

Rockhill Trolley Museum
  Trolley ride; museum.
  Rockhill Furnace, PA
  www.rockhilltrolley.org
  (814) 447-9576

Steamtown National Historic Site
  Museum; shop tour; train ride.
  Scranton, PA
  www.nps.gov/stea
  (888) 693-9391

Strasburg Rail Road
  Train ride; dining car; exhibits;
    miniature-train ride; pump cars.
  Strasburg, PA
  www.strasburgrailroad.com
  (717) 687-7522

SOUTH DAKOTA
Black Hills Central Railroad
  Train ride; exhibits.
  Hill City and Keystone, SD
  www.1880train.com
  (605) 574-2222

TENNESSEE
Chattanooga Choo-Choo
  Hotel in restored depot; some train-
    car hotel rooms; model railroad.
  Chattanooga, TN
  www.choochoo.com
  (800) 872-2529

Tennessee Valley Railroad Museum
  Multiple train rides; turntable and
    shop tour; exhibits.
  Chattanooga, TN
  www.tvrail.com
  (423) 894-8028

TEXAS
Austin Steam Train Association
  Multiple train rides.
  Cedar Park and Austin, TX
  www.austinsteamtrain.org
  (512) 477-8468

Texas State Railroad State Park
  Train ride, details changing.
  Rusk and Palestine, TX
  www.texasstaterailroad.com
  (800) 442-8951

UTAH
Golden Spike National Historic Site
  Museum; programs; Golden Spike
    ceremony; auto tour.
  Brigham City, UT
  www.nps.gov/gosp
  (435) 471-2209 Ext. 29

Heber Valley Railroad
  Train ride; exhibits.
  Heber City, UT
  www.hebervalleyrr.org
  (435) 654-5601

VIRGINIA
O. Winston Link Museum
  O. Winston Link photograph exhibit
  in restored depot.
  Roanoke, VA
  www.linkmuseum.org
  (540) 982-6956

WASHINGTON
Chelatchie Prairie Railroad
  Train ride; exhibits.
  Yacolt, WA
  www.bycx.org
  (360) 686-3559

Mt. Rainer Scenic Railroad
  Train ride.
  Elbe, WA
  www.mrsr.com
  (888) 783-2611

Northwest Railway Museum
  Train ride; museum.
  Snowqualmie and North Bend, WA
  www.trainmuseum.org
  (425) 888-3030

WEST VIRGINIA
Cass Scenic Railroad State Park
  Train ride on switchback line;
  recreated logging experience.
  Cass, WV
  www.cassrailroad.com
  (800) 225-5982

Durban & Greenbrier Valley Railroad
  Multiple trains rides from
    multiple cities.
  Durbin, WV
  www.mountainrail.com
  (877) 686-7245

Potomac Eagle Scenic Railroad
  Multiple train rides.
  Romney, WV
  www.potomaceagle.info
  (304) 424-0736

WISCONSIN
**Mid-Continent Railway Historical
Society**
  Train ride; museum; authentic
    railyard and station.
  North Freedom, WI
  www.midcontinent.org
  (800) 930-1385

National Railroad Museum
  Large museum; train ride; model
    railroad.
  Green Bay, WI
  www.nationalrrmuseum.org
  (920) 437-7623 Ext. 12

BRITISH COLUMBIA
Kamloops Heritage Railway
  Multiple train trips.
  Kamloops, BC
  www.kamrail.com
  (250) 374-2141

Kettle Valley Steam Railway
  Train ride.
  Summerland, BC
  www.kettlevalleyrail.org
  (877) 494-8424

West Coast Railway Heritage Park
  Museum; miniature train ride;
    Royal Hudson.
  Squamish, BC
  www.wcra.org/heritage/
  (800) 722-1233

ONTARIO
Algoma Central Railway
  Multiple train rides.
  Sault Ste. Marie, ON
  www.algomacentralrailway.com
  (800) 242-9287

South Simcoe Railway
  Train ride.
  Tottenham, ON
  www.steamtrain.com
  (905) 936-5815

QUÉBEC
Exporail: Canadian Railway Museum
  Large museum.
  Saint-Constant, QC
  www.exporail.org
  (450) 632-2410

Hull-Chelsea-Wakefield Steam Train
  Train ride; dinner train.
  Gatineau, QC
  www.steamtrain.ca
  (800) 871-7246

BIBLIOGRAPHY

BOOKS

Abdill, Geo. B. *Civil War Railroads*. New York: Bonanza Books, 1961.

Alexander, Edwin P. *Down at the Depot: American Railroad Stations from 1831 to 1920*. New York: Bramhall House, 1970.

———. *The Pennsylvania Railroad: A Pictorial History*. New York: Bonanaza Books, 1967.

Beebe, Lucius. *Highball: A Pageant of Trains*. New York: Bonanza Books, 1945.

———. *The Central Pacific & The Southern Pacific Railroads*. Berkeley, Calif.: Howell-North Books, 1963.

———. *Trains in Transition*. New York: Bonanza Books, 1941.

Best, Gerald M. *Snowplow: Clearing Mountain Rails*. Berkeley, Calif.: Howell-North Books, 1966.

Fifteen years before bankruptcy, the Rock Island's annual report features an exceptionally interesting cover. The report indicates a profit of $6 million or $2.06 per share. Of that amount, $1.60 was distributed to stockholders as a dividend. The railroad operated 7,533 miles of track with 16,491 employees. The writing was on the wall—earnings per share were dropping while the ratio of operating expenses to operating revenues was rising.

Biancull, Anthony J. *Railroad History on American Postage Stamps*. Mendham, N.J.: The Astragal Pr., 2004.

Botkin, B. A. and Alvin F. Harlow. *A Treasury of Railroad Folklore*. New York: Bonanza Books, 1953.

Chappell, Gordon. *Rails to Carry Copper: A History of the Magma Arizona Railroad*. Boulder, Colo.: Pruett Publishing Co., 1973.

Cohen, Norm. *Long Steel Rail: The Railroad in American Folksong*. Urbana, Ill.: Univ. of Ill. Pr., 1981.

Cook, Richard J. *Super Power Steam Locomotives*. San Marino, Calif.: Golden West Books, 1966.

Cornwell, L. Peter and Jack W. Farrell. *Ride the Sandy River: Visit the past on America's largest two-foot gauge railroad*. Edmonds, Wash.: Pacific Fast Mail, 1973.

Dorin, Patrick C. *The Lake Superior Iron Ore Railroads: The World's Heaviest Trains*. New York: Bonanza Books, 1969.

Farrington, Jr., S. Kip. *Railroads at War*. New York: Coward-McCann, Inc., 1944.

Ferrell, Mallory Hope. *Railways, Sagebrush and Pine: A Garland of Railroad and Logging Days in Oregon's Sumpter Valley*. San Marino, Calif.: Golden West Books, 1967.

Fielder, Mildred. *Railroads of the Black Hills*. New York: Bonanza Books, 1964.

Goldsborough, Robert. *Great Railroad Paintings*. New York: Peacock Press/Bantam Book, 1976.

Goldsack, Bob. *Carnival Trains: A Pictorial History*. Nashua, N.H.: Midway Museum Publications, 1991.

Hanft, Robert M. *Pine Across the Mountain. . . California's McCloud River Railroad*. San Marino, Calif.: Golden West Books, 1970.

The Historical Guide to North American Railroads, 2nd ed. Waukesha, Wis.: Kalmbach Publishing Co., 2000.

Holbrook, Stewart H. *The Story of American Railroads*. New York: American Legacy Pr., 1981.

Hollander, Ron. *All Aboard! The Story of Joshua Lionel Cowen & His Lionel Train Company*. New York: Workman Publishing, 1981.

Huddleston, Eugene L. *Appalachian Conquest*. Lynchburg, Virginia: TLC Publishing, Clifton Forge, Va.: The Chesapeake & Ohio Historical Society, 2002.

Jackson, David. *A Guide to Trains: The World's Greatest Trains, Tracks & Travel*. San Francisco: Fog City Pr., 2002.

Janson, Lone E. *The Copper Spike*. Anchorage, Alaska: Alaska Northwest Publishing Co., 1975.

Jensen, Larry. *The Movie Railroads*. Burbank, Calif.: Darwin Publications, 1981.

Jensen, Oliver. *The American Heritage History of Railroads in America*. New York: Bonanza Books, 1981.

Keilty, Edmund. *Interurbans Without Wires: The Rail Motorcar in the United States*. Glendale, Calif.: Interurbans, 1979.

Kinert, Reed. *Early American Steam Locomotives: 1ˢᵗ Seven Decades·1830–1900*. New York: Bonanza Books, 1962.

Kreig, Allan. *Last of the 3 foot Loggers*. San Marino, Calif.: Golden West Books, 1962.

Labbe, John T. and Vernon Goe. *Railroads in the Woods*. Berkeley, Calif.: Howell-North, 1961.

Lavallée, Omer. *Narrow Gauge Railways of Canada*. Montreal: Railfare Enterprises Ltd., 1972.

Martin, Cy. *Gold Rush Narrow Gauge: The Story of the White Pass and Yukon Route*. Los Angeles: Trans-Anglo Books, 1969.

McKenzie. William H. *Mountain to Mill*. Colorado Springs, Colo.: MAC Publishing Inc., 1982.

———. *Opening the Rail Gateway to the West: Constructing the Rail Gateway to the West*. St. Louis. Mo.: St. Louis Chapter National Railway Historical Society, 2001.

Middleton, William D. *North Shore: America's Fastest Interurban*. San Marino, Calif.: Golden West Books, 1964.

———. *South Shore: The Last Interurban*. San Marino, Calif.: Golden West Books, 1970.

———. *When the Steam Railroads Electrified*. Milwaukee, Wis.: Kalmbach Publishing Co., 1974.

Moody, Linwood W. *The Maine Two-Footers: The story of the two-foot gauge railroads of Maine*. Berkeley, Calif.: Howell-North Press, 1959.

Moore, John F., *The Story of the Railroad "Y"*. New York: Association Pr., 1930.

Myrick, David F. *New Mexico's Railroads: An Historical Survey*. Golden, Colo.: Colorado Railroad Museum, 1970.

———. *Railroads of Nevada and Eastern California*. 2 vols. Berkeley, Calif.: Howell-North Books, 1962.

Neal, Dorothy Jensen. *The Cloud-Climbing Railroad: Highest Point on the Southern Pacific, Centennial ed*. El Paso, Tex.: Texas Western Press, 1998.

Niehoff II, Walter H. *The Reincarnation of the Switch Back Gravity Railroad*. Vestal, N.Y.: Walter H. Niehoff Consultant, 1995.

Nock, O. S., ed. *The Encyclopedia of Railroads*. New York: Galahad Books, 1977.

Parkinson, Tom and Charles Phillip Fox. *The Circus Moves by Rail*. Boulder, Colo.: Pruett Publishing Co., 1978.

Polinghorn, R. S. *Pino Grande: Logging Railroads of the Michigan-California Lumber Co*. Berkeley, Calif.: Howell-North Books, 1966.

Porterfield, James D. *Dining by Rail: The History and Recipes of America's Golden Age of Railroad Cuisine*. New York: St. Martin's Griffin, 1993.

Schafer, Mike and Joe Welsh. *Streamliners: History of a Railroad Icon*. St. Paul, Minn.: MBI Publishing Co., 2003.

Shaughnessy, Jim. *Delaware & Hudson*. Berkeley, Calif.: Howell-North Books, 1967.

Steinheimer, Richard. *The Electric Way across the Mountains: Stories of the Milwaukee Road Electrification*. Tiburon, Calif.: Carbarn Pr., 1980.

Stunkard, Geoff. *Rail Mail: A Century of American Railroading on Picture Postcards*. Milligan College, Tenn.: Quarter Milestones Publishing, 2004.

Sutton, David. *The Comlplete Book of Model Railroading*. New York: Castle Books, 1964.

Tourist Trains 2005: 40ᵗʰ Annual Guide to Tourist Railroads and Museums. Waukesha, Wis.: Kalmbach Publishing Co., 2005.

Wagner, Jr., F. Hol. *The Colorado Road*. Denver, Colo.: The Intermountain Chapter National Railway Historical Society, Inc., 1970.

Westcott, Linn H., *Model Railroader Cyclopedia: Vol. 1: Steam Locomotives*. Waukesha, Wis.: Kalmbach Publishing Co., 1960.

Westing, Fred. *The Locomotives That Baldwin Built*. New York: Bonanza Books, 1965.

Wiatrowski, Claude A. *Railroads of Colorado*. Stillwater, Minn.: Voyageur Pr., 2002.

Wilson, William H. *Railroads in the Clouds: The Alaska Railroad in the Age of Steam, 1914–1945*. Boulder, Colo.: Pruett Publishing Company, 1977.

Withun, William L., ed. *Rails Across America: A History of Railroads in North America*. New York: Smithmark Publishers, Inc., 1993.

PERIODICALS

Garden Railways. Waukesha, Wis.: Kalmbach Publishing Co.

Grand Scale Quarterly Magazine. Red Bluff, Calif.: Robinson & Associates.

Model Railroader. Waukesha, Wis.: Kalmbach Publishing Co.

Narrow Gauge & Short Line Gazette. Los Altos, Calif.: Benchmark Publications Ltd.

O Gauge Railroading Magazine. Poland, Ohio: OGR Publishing, Inc.

Railfan & Railroad. Newton, N.J.: Carstens Publications.

Railroad Model Craftsman. Newton, N.J.: Carstens Publications.

Trains. Waukesha, Wis.: Kalmbach Publishing Co.

About the Author

CLAUDE WIATROWSKI

Like all young boys of the 1950s, Claude Wiatrowski enjoyed toy trains. Scale model trains came next, but three degrees—including a doctorate in electrical engineering—and a career in technology slowed his avocation until his first encounter with Colorado's railroads in 1971. Model trains took a backseat to standing on a mountain pass and watching real, narrow gauge steam trains chug past. He moved to Colorado in 1975, partly to pursue his exploration of Colorado's railroads.

Since then, Dr. Wiatrowski has authored or provided photographs for several books on Colorado and railroad history. He has explored much of Colorado's mountains, searching for remnants of its once huge railroad network. His explorations were the basis for his book, *Railroads of Colorado*. His travels have taken him as far as Wales to see the birthplace of the narrow track gauge, which was an important part of Colorado railroading, and railroad technology of the Industrial Revolution became more compelling to him than the electronic technology of the information revolution. During the 1980s, his hobby gradually became his profession and he now produces DVDs and writes books on historic railroads. His productions have won Telly and Teddy awards and one was selected for the Library of Congress Local Legacies Program.

Dr. Wiatrowski is a member of the Colorado Midland Chapter of the National Railway Historical Society, the Railway & Locomotive Historical Society, The Colorado Railroad Museum, The Friends of the Cumbres & Toltec Scenic Railroad, Friends of the East Broad Top, the Nevada Northern Railway Museum, the Pikes Peak Historical Street Railway Foundation, and the Lexington Group in Transportation History.

INDEX